DEVELOPING CHEVROLET'S PONY CAR

CAMARO CONCEPT CARS

CarTech®

SCOTT KOLECKI

CarTech®

CarTech®, Inc.
6118 Main Street
North Branch, MN 55056
Phone: 651-277-1200 or 800-551-4754
Fax: 651-277-1203
www.cartechbooks.com

Edit by Wes Eisenschenk
Layout by Connie DeFlorin

ISBN 978-1-61325-757-9
Item No. CT690

Library of Congress Cataloging-in-Publication Data Available

Written, edited, and designed in the U.S.A.
Printed in China
10 9 8 7 6 5 4 3 2 1

DISTRIBUTION BY:

Europe
PGUK
63 Hatton Garden
London EC1N 8LE, England
Phone: 020 7061 1980 • Fax: 020 7242 3725
www.pguk.co.uk

Australia
Renniks Publications Ltd.
3/37-39 Green Street
Banksmeadow, NSW 2109, Australia
Phone: 2 9695 7055 • Fax: 2 9695 7355
www.renniks.com

Canada
Login Canada
300 Saulteaux Crescent
Winnipeg, MB, R3J 3T2 Canada
Phone: 800 665 1148 • Fax: 800 665 0103
www.lb.ca

TABLE OF CONTENTS

DEDICATION

This book is dedicated to my son and long-time Camaro aficionado, Kendyll Mayer. Since he was a little boy, Kendyll has shared my passion for fast cars and motorsports. He has been (and continues to be) my constant companion at car shows, on backroad cruises, and at countless race events—from NASCAR to the International Motor Sports Association (IMSA) and Formula 1. As he has grown up, and as I have grown older, our mutual appreciation for fast cars has also grown, and I am forever grateful to share this passion with him—not only as father and son but also as fellow enthusiasts obsessed with satisfying our mutual need for speed.

I love you, son, always.

ACKNOWLEDGMENTS

I would like to thank the following people who helped make this book possible:

- John Kyros and the GM Heritage Center, here we are again. Thank you for working with me on this project and for allowing me/CarTech access to the many incredible photos seen throughout this book. John, I cannot accurately convey to you how much I appreciate the countless hours you spent chasing down obscure images of Camaros, as well as their designers, engineers, etc. I am immensely thankful for your help on this project, and I will be forever grateful for the friendship that has grown between us in the years since we started working together.
- David Newhardt, chief photographer for *Mecum* magazine and author, thank you for allowing me to use your incredible photographs of the Camaro Cherokee. You are a man of many talents (your book on Camaros was a constant companion to me on this journey). I feel very fortunate that I had the opportunity to "meet" you (virtually for now), and I sincerely hope we'll have a chance to talk shop in person one day soon.
- Christine Giovingo, media relations coordinator for Mecum Auctions, thank you for allowing the use of your second-generation Camaro Turbo-Z images.
- A. J. Mueller, photographer, thank you for allowing the use of your images from the sixth-generation Camaro launch.
- Karissa Hosek, photographer, thank you for allowing the use of your images of the Camaro Europo Hurst.
- Kevin Stewart, artist/owner of Evolutionary Studios and my good friend, thank you for being the first to read and edit an early draft of this book. Thanks also for sharing your lifelong passion for F-Body cars (both Camaros and Firebirds alike) with me. I truly hope that you and your boys (Dean, Riley, and Wyatt) enjoy the results.
- Cliff Wanner, my closest friend and neighbor, thank you for the edits you made and the feedback you provided on various sections of this book. As with the *Corvette Concept Cars: Developing America's Favorite Sports Car* book before it, your comments and corrections for continuity were immensely valuable.
- Nicholas Pyka, my friend, recent college graduate (congratulations!) and photographer, thank you for making me look presentable for the back of this book. As someone who has never photographed well, I know it was no easy trick, and the results truly speak to your growing talent behind a camera.
- Joe Kolecki, my brother, thank you for taking time to photograph your 2008 Mustang GT/CS so that I could use its likeness in a book about the Camaro. One of my favorite parts of this experience is being able to share parts of the journey together! I love you, brother.
- Thank you to all of the incredible authors who have written books (or other material) on the Chevy Camaro, especially Michael Lamm (*The Great Camaro*, *Camaro: The Third Generation*), Anthony Young (*Camaro*), David Newhardt (*The Complete Book of Chevrolet Camaro: Every Model since 1967*), Larry Edsall (*Camaro: A Legend Reborn*, *Camaro 2016*), Don Keefe (*Pontiac: Concept & Show Cars*), Gary Witzenburg (*Camaro: An American Icon*), Bob Ackerman, Dick Ruzzin, Jim Hall, Gary Smith (Dean's Garage website), and countless others.
- Nick Dellis, Cameron Martel, Chris Tulumba, and the creative team at A07Online, thank you for your continued

support over the past two years. Your words of encouragement have meant the world to me, and I look forward to sharing this book with all of you.

- To the 1105 Motor Club crew—Jason Cruise and Billy Quinn, as well as Joe, Cliff, Kevin, and Kendyll (previously mentioned)—thank you for your combined support of my first book and your unknowing participation in the creation of this one. Each of you contributed to this narrative in one form or another, and all of you have become an indelible part of my personal automotive experience. I am thankful that I get to share so many amazing adventures with each of you. I hope that never changes.
- Rene (Mom), Joe (Dad), Rose (Mom 2) and Chris, thank you for every word of encouragement over the past two years (with both books). I love you all very much.
- Erika, thank you for always being my biggest cheerleader and the best public-relations person out there! I'll never be able to convey to you just how much your support of these projects means to me. Thank you for always taking the time to promote these books, for sharing every review on social media, and for being an endless source of encouragement. I love you more than words can say.
- Thank you to my entire family: Erika, Kendyll, Sophie, and Ella for giving me the time required to research and write this book. I recognize that these projects have taken up so much of my "spare" time over the past two years, and I want all of you to know how grateful I am to have such a strong support system at all times. I love you all very much, and I always will.
- Finally, thank you to the team at CarTech (especially Wes Eisenschenk) for giving me this second, and equally amazing, opportunity. As with *Corvette Concept Cars: Developing America's Favorite Sports Car*, I am forever grateful that you saw something in me and provided the platform to write and publish this book.

PREFACE

In the fall of 2020, CarTech presented me with the unique opportunity to write a book about the Chevy Corvette told through the lens of the concept cars designed and built by GM's design studios in the second half of the 20th and the early years of the 21st centuries. That book, which was published in May 2022, told the story of Corvette's most famous pioneers (Harley Earl, Zora Arkus-Duntov, Bill Mitchell, and many others) and how their individual contributions to the Corvette shaped America's sports car for generations.

After completing the *Corvette Concept Cars* book project, the question was posed to me: "Could a similar book be written about the Chevy Camaro?" The answer (as evidenced by the book you are currently reading) was yes. I assumed that Chevy's second most iconic sports car would have similar, and equally fascinating, stories about its origin and evolution. I was right.

What I was unprepared for at the start of this project was the lack of available information about the Chevy Camaro, especially from the perspective of its designers and/or concept cars. Where my time spent researching the Corvette's history had frequently resulted in information overload, hunting down information about the Camaro ended up being more like sifting through river sediment as I searched for bits of gold. I spent countless hours combing through books, magazines, message boards, automobile blogs, and websites with the hope of finding enough information to piece together the story of just one of the many incredible concept cars showcased in this book.

The work was more than a little daunting. At the same time, it was also an extremely rewarding experience. I felt (and still feel) incredibly fortunate that I'd been given the opportunity to write this book, and I was both surprised and humbled by how much I learned about the Camaro in the process.

While I think I got most of the history right, I must concede that I may have unintentionally missed some minor details and/or misrepresented certain people, places, events, and situations along the way. If I have, I hope you will forgive every unintended oversight. More than that, I hope you'll take some time to reach out to me (I can be contacted through CarTech) so that I can revise the narrative for future editions of this book.

That said, I do believe that what you are about to read is as factually and historically accurate as I could write it, given the couple of caveats listed above. I am most proud of this book (even more so than *Corvette Concept Cars*) because I feel as though I climbed a mountain to get this book across the finish line.

I sincerely hope you enjoy the results.

— Scott Kolecki, July 2022

INTRODUCTION

Given its long-term success as a popular American performance car, it might be difficult for contemporary Camaro owners/enthusiasts to believe that the original F-Body concept (and the 1967 production model that followed it) was hastily developed in response to the launch of the 1964½ Ford Mustang. Despite the steadily growing demand for an "affordable-but-sporty fun car" by America's Baby Boomer generation, GM leadership failed to see the enormous financial opportunity that producing such a car would have on the company's bottom line—that is, until its biggest competitor did it first.

There's no doubt that Chevrolet's decision to rush the Camaro to production in the summer of 1964 was the correct one, but it should also be noted that Chevrolet's "pony car" (a term created by *Car Life* magazine editor Dennis Shattuck after the launch of the Ford Mustang to describe a sporty, compact car for the masses) might never have existed had it not been for the unprecedented sales numbers of the 1964½ Ford Mustang. To say that the Camaro's creation was the direct by-product of the Ford Mustang is not an overstatement. However, its continued, long-term success through six successive generations is a testament to the talented men and women within General Motors who ensured the Camaro wouldn't just keep up with the Mustang but would surpass it.

In a 2015 article originally published by Chevrolet Media titled "Camaro Design Through the Years," Ed Welburn, GM's former vice president of Global Design, explained how the Camaro became an indelible part of the American automotive landscape: "The Camaro should not have been a design success, as it was based on an existing architecture and admittedly hurried to market to address the personal coupe revolution occurring with Baby Boomer customers. However, the first-generation Camaro delivered a pure, classic proportion that will forever be regarded as one of the best-looking cars of its time. It was very lean and muscular, with comparatively minor embellishments for high-performance models. That was in contrast to some of the brasher competitors during the muscle car era, and it has helped the first-generation Camaro maintain timeless good looks."

It is ironic then that the second-generation Camaro was such a significant departure from its predecessor. Even as Chevrolet moved frantically to build a car that would "level the playing field" with Ford's Mustang, there were those within GM's upper echelon (including GM Vice President of Styling Bill Mitchell) who contended the original Camaro had been "built by committee."

Adamant that the next-generation Camaro would not suffer the same fate, Mitchell assigned Chevrolet Design Chief Henry Haga and Pontiac Studio Chief Bill Porter the task of creating a Camaro that had, in the words of GM's executive director of design for Chevrolet Trucks, "dramatic proportion and lean, muscular form."

As with the Corvette before it, the advancement of the Camaro's "form and function" had become a design statement of GM's styling departments/design studios. Although this same argument can be made (to varying degrees) about every car and truck built since the inception of the automobile, the Camaro's key differentiator was (and still is) that each new generation represented a unique styling expression from the era that inspired it. More than that, the Camaro (along with the Corvette) has inspired generations of designers to stretch their own imaginations and to "create a pure expression."

This book explores the creation and evolution of the Camaro by introducing some of the men and women who helped "breathe life" into Chevrolet's pony car over the past 50-plus years. It looks at the factors, both internal and external, that influenced the evolution of the Camaro through six unique generations, and it pays homage to the designers, engineers, and stylists who advanced its design over the past half century. Lastly, this book is an exploration of the Camaro concept cars, many of which have been lost to history, that helped make the Chevy Camaro one of the most iconic sports cars of all time.

CHAPTER

1 FIRST GENERATION (1967–1969)

"THE PEOPLE IN OUR STUDIO
(DESIGNERS, MODELERS, AND ENGINEERS ALIKE)
WERE ALL ENTHUSIASTS AND PRETTY EXCITED WHEN
THEY FOUND THEY HAD A CHANCE TO DESIGN AN ALL-NEW
FOUR-PLACE SPORTS CAR TO COMPETE DIRECTLY
WITH THE FORD MUSTANG."
— HENRY HAGA, STUDIO DESIGN CHIEF

A full-size clay model (right) of the 1967½ Chevy Camaro (XP-836) is parked next to GM test vehicle 64163 (a 1964½ Ford Mustang hardtop) inside GM's Design Dome in Warren, Michigan. General Motors and Ford had a handshake reciprocity agreement in the 1960s, where each company provided the other with new products for evaluation two to four weeks ahead of their formal public introduction. (Photo Courtesy General Motors LLC)

It is no coincidence that the creation of the pony car (an assortment of affordable, compact, sporty automobiles that were first introduced in the mid-1960s) coincided with the coming of age of the Baby Boomer generation in the late 1950s. An overwhelming majority of these late adolescents and early-20-something consumers were utterly disinterested in the hulking chrome monstrosities that their parents had owned and driven throughout their childhood. They wanted inexpensive transportation that offered excitement behind the wheel and outwardly conveyed their youthful nature to the world.

American automobile manufacturers had virtually nothing available that appealed to this generation of would-be buyers. As a result, the "Boomers" purchased imported automobiles built by European companies. These included Austin, Renault, MG, and Volkswagen. Most of these brands (excluding Volkswagen) proved to be unreliable. They required frequent maintenance, which was both expensive and difficult to have performed given the limited number of American mechanics trained to service these vehicles.

Still, the increase in imported automobile sales on U.S. soil between 1957 and 1959 caused the Big Three manufacturers (General Motors, Ford, and Chrysler) to take notice. Each moved quickly to introduce its own line of compact cars to the automotive marketplace. The 1960 model year saw the arrival of the Ford Falcon, the Chrysler Valiant, and the Chevrolet Corvair. These were followed a year later with the Mercury Comet, the Dodge Lancer, and a slew of automobiles by General Motors, including the Buick Special, the Oldsmobile F85, and the Pontiac Tempest.

The Corvair Monza versus the Ford Falcon

In addition to GM's other models, Chevrolet also introduced a new Corvair (the Monza) at the Chicago Auto Show in February 1960. Officially designated as the 900 series, the Monza was marketed as the Corvair's highest trim package.

While the Monza was little more than a spruced-up version of the 700-series model, it offered consumers two unique features: a sunroof and bucket seats. Both of these options became game changers for the brand. By 1962, the Corvair Monza had become one of the hottest-selling American "sports cars" on the market.

Recognizing Chevy's success with the Monza, Ford introduced the 1963 Ford Falcon with an optional Futura Sprint series package. This package offered consumers bucket seats, upgraded interior and exterior trim, and wire wheel covers. Most importantly, it included a more robust 260-ci V-8 engine that produced 164 hp, which was nearly double the Monza's 84-hp Powerglide 6-cylinder engine. Chevrolet did offer consumers an optional turbo 6-cylinder engine that produced 150 hp but only in the top-of-the-line Monza Spyder Club coupe and convertible models.

Both cars sold exceptionally well. Between 1960 and 1963, Chevrolet sold just under 1.2 million Corvairs. Of these, approximately 50 percent of the cars manufactured were the Monza edition. In 1963 alone, Chevrolet sold a total of 284,680 Corvairs, of which 204,829 were either a Monza coupe, sedan, or convertible.

Similarly, Ford sold more than 1.6 million Falcon automobiles during this same four-year period, with sales totaling 328,339 units in 1963. Of these, the 1963 Falcon Futura Sprint (the one with the "big" V-8) accounted for 15,081 units (10,479 coupes and 4,602 convertibles). The monumental sales numbers set by both mid-size automobiles proved two things.

First, an increasing number of young consumers were looking for sporty cars that delivered a fun and exciting but still practical driving experience. Sure, the Corvair and the Falcon handled well, but both also offered useful amenities, such as a back seat that could be used to transport additional passengers, groceries, or personal property.

Second, these same consumers were looking for practical-but-sporty cars that fit their budget. The challenge

A Ford Falcon (left) and a Chevy Corvair are parked in the courtyard of GM's design studios in Warren, Michigan. (Photo Courtesy General Motors LLC)

To satisfy growing consumer interest in smaller, less-expensive automobiles, Ford introduced the Ford Falcon in 1960. Along with the Chevy Corvair and the Dodge Dart, the success of the Falcon gave rise to the creation of the American pony car. Although they are aesthetically different, Lee Iacocca's 1964½ Mustang was nearly identical mechanically to the 1963½ Ford Falcon Sprint. (Photo Courtesy General Motors LLC)

here was that while both cars offered an enjoyable (even exciting) driving experience, neither the Falcon nor the Corvair exuded that singular, sporty flare that attracted would-be buyers into showrooms. While both models featured a sport package, they were both likewise available as a larger sedan, a station wagon, or even a van (the Corvair Greenbriar and the Ford Falcon Club Wagon).

Some within the industry wondered that if consumers were offered an authentic-yet-affordable sports car, how successful could such an automobile be? Lee Iacocca, Ford's newest vice president and general manager, was the first to answer that question. In so doing, he changed the automotive landscape for decades to come.

"IACOCCA ENVISIONED A YOUTHFUL CAR THAT COULD BE DRIVEN BY CONSUMERS WHO CRAVED FUN AND ADVENTURE ON THE OPEN ROAD."

The restyled, second-generation Corvair Monza debuted in 1965. It featured sleeker lines, better curves, and a sportier, more aggressive stance than its predecessors. If also offered would-be consumers many of the factory amenities they sought in a sporty car, including front bucket seats, door armrests, full wheel covers, and chrome trim. (Photo Courtesy General Motors LLC)

Lee Iacocca and the Ford Mustang

The birth of the pony car began with the promotion of the Ford Motor Company's young "wunderkind" within its managerial hierarchy. Lee Iacocca, who replaced Robert McNamara as Ford's general manager in November 1960, recognized that America's youth was clamoring for something new and sporty. He believed that an automobile ought to be capable of being more than a basic, utilitarian machine. Iacocca envisioned a youthful car that could be driven by consumers who craved fun and adventure on the open road.

Ford had built such a car (the 1955 Thunderbird) a decade earlier as a competitor to the Chevy Corvette. The Thunderbird began life as a small, two-seat roadster that went against everything the traditional American family sedan represented. Despite its limited seating and storage capacities, Ford sold more than 50,000 units during its first three years of production. Unfortunately, Ford's executives intervened and transformed the 1958 Thunderbird into a larger, four-seat model that essentially ended the company's first foray into the sports car market.

Iacocca recounted the early commercial success of the original Thunderbird. He also witnessed the monumental sales

The XP-781

While Lee Iacocca and the Ford Motor Company may have been the first to develop and commercially produce a sports car targeted at America's Baby Boomer generation, it was not the only company to do so. Early in 1962, Chrysler's designers/stylists began developing conceptual art for a car that would evolve into the 1964 Plymouth Barracuda.

Newly appointed Chevrolet Studio Design Chief Irvin Rybicki also began exploring a similar idea in February of that same year. He wanted to create a youthful, four-seat, luxury sports coupe along the same lines as the (at that time unreleased) 1963 Buick Riviera, a car General Motors had developed to compete with the Ford Thunderbird.

In Rybicki's 1982 publication *Evolution of the Camaro*, he commented, "If Buick can sell thousands of cars at that price (original retail $4,333), if we did it smaller, less expensive, we could probably sell 300,000 or 400,000."

Rybicki pondered the idea for some time. As his plans for the concept grew, he began envisioning a car that was smaller than the Riviera and far more affordable to consumers. He achieved the second objective by building the car around the same unibody/front-subframe platform and mechanicals as the 1962 Chevy II. He approached GM Styling Vice President Bill Mitchell with his proposal for a four-passenger sport coupe.

Mitchell saw the potential in Rybicki's ideas. He enthusiastically presented Rybicki's proposal to Chevrolet General Manager Semon E."Bunkie" Knudsen. Knudsen greenlit the XP-781 project on April 30, 1962, as an "A-Body" coupe that would compete against the Ford Thunderbird.

This image features a full-scale clay model of the 1964 Plymouth Barracuda inside of Chrysler's design studios. Although sales of the original Barracuda paled in comparison to the Ford Mustang (Chrysler sold just 23,443 units its first year), the Barracuda's arrival at dealerships predated the Ford Mustang by two weeks. (Photo Courtesy Stellantis Historical Services)

Development of the XP-781 took place in a warehouse across the street from Chevrolet's design studio main campus. Per Rybicki, this location had been selected because Chevrolet's primary studio was "overrun with work." However, it has also been speculated over the years that the XP-781 was developed in secret as a second potential contender for a four-passenger Corvette alongside the XP-796 concept, which was a stretched version of the second-generation Sting Ray being developed by designer Larry Shinoda.

Rybicki assigned a small group of designers, including Phil Garcia (who eventually became chief designer of GM's Advanced Studio One), to begin work on a full-scale clay model of the car. The project, which evolved under the watchful eye of Rybicki and in the secrecy of the warehouse space, took approximately five months to complete. The finished clay-model concept was nearly identical in length, width, and height of the future Ford Mustang. This was especially remarkable given that no one within General Motors had any notion that Ford was developing the Mustang.

The completed concept was built using hardware from the Chevy II, as Rybicki had intended. It featured several design elements that had been directly influenced by the Corvette Sting Ray program, including a similarly styled front grille, fascia, and hood assembly, as well as a sugar-scoop rear-window assembly, the latter of which came into prominence on the Corvette in 1968.

Rybicki contacted Mitchell and invited him to come see the full-size clay model. Mitchell was thrilled and insisted that he and Rybicki show the car to Chevrolet General Manager Bunkie Knudsen. Knudsen visited the studio about a week after

This full-scale clay model of the XP-781 shows the four-passenger sports car concept originally conceived by Irv Rybicki in early 1962. Based on the Chevy II, the model was developed at a secret studio inside one of GM's warehouses across from the street from GM Design. (Photo Courtesy General Motors LLC)

Mitchell. He was also impressed with the clay model and made a point of recognizing the team that designed it. He then turned to the car itself, taking considerable time to evaluate each aspect of the clay model. Surprisingly, he made the following comments: "Damned good-looking car, fellows, but I want to tell you something. The last thing Chevrolet needs right now is another car."

Such was Knudsen's influence that all future development of the XP-781 was halted immediately and the project was abandoned. Had the XP-781 received his approval and been greenlit for production by GM's executive management, it may well have made it to market before the Mustang instead of amounting to nothing more than one of the early footnotes in the development of the Camaro.

An early full-scale tape drawing of the XP-782 was created in GM's design studio prior to project approval by Bill Mitchell and "Bunkie" Knudsen. The overall dimensions of the car in this drawing (and the clay models that followed) were virtually identical to those of the original Ford Mustang. This is doubly significant given that no one (outside of the Ford Motor Company) knew the Mustang was being developed. (Photo Courtesy General Motors LLC)

The four-seat Corvette Sting Ray 2+2 (XP-796) was developed at the direction of Ed Cole, who believed that adding rear seats would make the Corvette more competitive in the marketplace. Built between August 1961 and January 1962, the 2+2 Corvette was poorly received by GM's executives. The project was subsequently canceled, and the single prototype was destroyed. (Photo Courtesy General Motors LLC)

Even though the XP-781 never evolved past the full-size clay-model phase, it contained several styling elements that found their way into the final design of the third-generation Corvette, including the sugar-scoop rear window seen here. (Photo Courtesy General Motors LLC)

Despite being well received by all those involved in its development, the XP-781 project was terminated by Knudsen because he believed that Chevrolet had no space for an additional model in its current lineup. It has also been speculated that the XP-781 program was canceled after Knudsen dismissed the idea of a four-passenger Corvette. (Photo Courtesy General Motors LLC)

This full-scale clay model of Lee Iacocca's Ford Mustang (circa summer of 1962) included many of the styling elements that eventually appeared on the production model, albeit with an alternate bumper and front headlamps. Interestingly, this model included a Cougar emblem in the front grille and "Cougar" badges on its front fenders. Ford used the "Cougar" moniker as a codename during the Mustang's development, and several of the car's designers voted to keep the Cougar name when the car was being officially branded. (Photo Courtesy Ford Motor Company)

numbers achieved by the Ford Falcon despite its utter lack of curb appeal, especially when compared to the aesthetics of the Thunderbird. He wondered how much more successful the Falcon would have been if Ford had invested more money into its outward appearance. He decided he would attempt to answer that question by developing a sporty automobile of his own design. This project quickly became known as "Iacocca's Youth Car."

The Fairlane Committee

Iacocca began by establishing a research group that he dubbed the "Fairlane Committee." Its goal was to develop the parameters around which his Youth Car should be built. Over the course of several sessions, the committee developed the following guideline: the car should have a maximum wheelbase of 108 inches, a total weight of just 2,500 pounds, and a price tag that was no more than "$1 per pound." Additionally, Iacocca's Youth Car would have a back seat.

Development of the Ford Mustang began in early 1962, and by August, the company's design department had created six unique mock-ups. From these, an example created by designer David Ash was selected. Originally dubbed the Cougar, Ash's design evolved (with minimal changes) from a clay concept to a fully realized prototype to an eventual production model. Rebranded as the Mustang, the car was unveiled on April 17, 1964, at the World's Fair in New York City. It was also simultaneously displayed at multiple venues across the country.

The public's response to the Ford Mustang was overwhelming. Dealers were bombarded with orders (reports vary, but somewhere between 22,000 and 26,000 Mustang orders were received across the United States on the day the car was introduced).

Chevrolet Division Manager Bunkie Knudsen initially contested that the Corvair would be sufficient to combat the popularity of the Mustang, but when Ford sold 121,534 units of its new pony car between April and July 1964, GM executives finally took notice. They realized they'd misread the market that Ford had monopolized almost overnight. An order was issued directing Knudsen to begin development of a "personal sporty car" that would not only compete with the Mustang but also outperform it in every way possible. If Chevrolet was going to succeed, its car would have to look better, ride better, and handle better than the Ford Mustang.

XP-836 Panther/F-Body Styling Buck

Although development of the Camaro officially commenced in August 1964 with Knudsen's approval of the XP-836 "F-Body" program, the idea that Chevy might consider

This full-size clay model of the XP-836 Panther was introduced by GM Design in November 1964. While specific details of this design (such as its headlamps, grille, etc.) continued to be refined in the coming months, the car's overall shape was carried forward from this early concept to the production model. (Photo Courtesy General Motors LLC)

One of the earliest XP-836 clay models developed by Bill Mitchell's styling department is shown here. This model, introduced in early August 1964, was developed using styling elements from the second-generation Corvette and proportions/measurements taken from the 1964½ Ford Mustang. (Photo Courtesy General Motors LLC)

This second full-size model of the XP-836, introduced in late August 1964, shows considerable advances over its predecessor toward the final profile/overall shape that the production Camaro would assume in the months ahead. (Photo Courtesy General Motors LLC)

developing its own pony car had started some five months earlier. Knudsen had been present at GM's Milford Proving Grounds on April 6, 1964, for the 2,000-mile break-in test of vehicle number 64163, which was a 6-cylinder 1964½ Mustang hardtop that General Motors had procured from Ford 11 days before its public unveiling.

Now, with the F-Body development program approved, Knudsen leaned on GM Design Vice President Bill Mitchell to advance the project quickly. Fortunately, Mitchell had already commissioned designers Irv Rybicki and Henry Haga to develop scale models of a would-be GM pony car. While these early clay models had more in common with the Chevy Corvette, they nonetheless served as the earliest basis of design from which the XP-836 styling buck evolved.

To accelerate its production, the XP-836 was developed using the underpinnings of Chevrolet's X-car, the Chevy II. Additionally, many of its specific styling cues were drawn from Chevrolet's 1964 Super Nova show car, in much the same way that Ford used the Falcon to develop the Mustang a few years earlier.

According to *Camaro Exposed 1967–1969: Designs, Decisions, and the Inside View* by Paul Zazarine, as Chevrolet's engineers began the transformation of both vehicles into the XP-836 styling buck, the following set of specific baselines were established that dictated the new car's design parameters:

- Distinctively modern aerodynamic styling for a clean, functional appearance
- Small, highly maneuverable size with packaging for four passengers
- A very broad range of available performance capability
- Quick, sharply defined roadability with a firm yet comfortable ride
- Cockpit-type interiors for close driver identification
- An evolutionary, rather than revolutionary, basic design approach to maintain maximum value to the customer
- Wide selection of mechanical and appearance equipment to allow customer tailoring to his needs and desires

Developing the Chassis

To save time and to reduce development and engineering costs, the XP-836's chassis was developed from the Chevy II. Since its introduction in 1962, the Chevy II used unibody

The flared fenders surrounding the front wheel wells was a styling element introduced on the second-generation Corvette and amplified during the evolution of the third-generation model. While this styling element was featured prominently on the early XP-836 models as well, its inclusion on the final design was far more subdued than shown here. (Photo Courtesy General Motors LLC)

Introduced in 1962, the Chevy II Nova convertible was a compact, two-door model that was supposed to be distributed as the Chevy Nova. The Chevy II name was used instead because Chevrolet's management believed the newest car needed a name that began with the letter "C." From 1962 to 1967, the car itself was called the Chevy II and was offered with multiple trim levels: the Chevy II 100, the Chevy II 300, and the top-level Chevy II Nova 400. The top trim-level name was shortened in 1965 to "Chevy II Nova," and finally, in 1969, the car was officially rebranded as the Chevy Nova, which had been the original plan all along. (Photo Courtesy General Motors LLC)

(unitized body) construction, a process by which the chassis, the floor pan, and the frame elements are incorporated to form a single structure. The Chevy II used a subframe assembly from the firewall forward, which was bolted directly to the rear unibody shell. This setup resulted in more body flex, a harsher ride, and a variety of creaks and rattles.

To accommodate this, Chevrolet engineers developed an extended-rail front subframe assembly that would cradle the engine, the steering gearbox, the transmission (via a rear-mounted cross member), and the front suspension. Instead of bolting to the firewall, this assembly attached to the rear unibody assembly via rubber body bushings at four attachment points (two located along the cowl and two beneath the front seats). This unique hybrid chassis design and the inclusion of rubber bushings at the attachment points increased contact area, which helped stabilize the subframe assembly. It also reduced noise and vibration in the cockpit without compromising structural rigidity.

Designing the Body

Development of the F-Body's exterior began in the fall of 1964. Preproduction development mules disguised as Chevy IIs (with incorporated design elements being considered for the XP-836) were driven across the country to field test the prototype chassis that had been predominantly engineered with computer-aided design (CAD) models and simulations. Data accumulated at GM's Desert Proving Grounds in Phoenix and the Milford Proving Grounds in Detroit provided critical engineering data that dictated the design architecture of the car's body.

Designer Henry Haga received the engineering specifications for GM's new F-Car (now codenamed "Panther") at Chevrolet's Studio Two on August 26, 1964. While the data proved to be ideal for the fabrication of a larger/taller two- or four-door automobile, Haga recognized that many of the car's

This full-scale rendering of the XP-836 provided much of the profile for the Camaro's final design. Despite its sweeping body lines and rounded edges, there's little mistaking the similarities between this early styling study and the original Ford Mustang, which served as the basis of the Camaro's initial designs. (Photo Courtesy General Motors LLC)

At the other end of the spectrum, this full-scale drawing depicts a more European design reminiscent of the overseas sports cars that were emerging in the automotive marketplace at that time. It also incorporates the Coke-bottle styling previously introduced by Larry Shinoda on the Corvette. (Photo Courtesy General Motors LLC)

proportions would have to be reworked to meet the design intent of the F-Body coupe. Most notably, the car's cowl would have to be lowered, and the distance between the front wheel and the dashboard would have to be lengthened. Both tasks were accomplished by increasing the windshield rake (the angle of the windshield in relation to the 90-degree vertical plane) and by narrowing the car's A-pillars.

The basic shape of the car was completed by December 1964. To compete with the Mustang, the F-Body maintained most of the same proportions as Ford's pony car. Unlike the Mustang, however, the Camaro featured softer, curved metal surfaces that were strikingly different to the Mustang's straight, chiseled lines. Haga, along with Assistant Studio Chief John Schinella, drew inspiration from the Coke-bottle styling being developed for the third-generation Corvette by Larry Shinoda. They had also incorporated several European styling elements into the F-Body's design.

Recognizing that the Mustang could be purchased as a coupe, a fastback, or a convertible, it was decided from the start that the F-Body would also be offered to consumers in both coupe and convertible versions. Building a convertible would prove to be especially challenging, given the loss of structural rigidity once the car's top was removed.

Chevrolet's engineers discovered that the car would begin to shake violently when driven over roads with even minor imperfections. To counteract these vibrations, spring-mounted iron weights wrapped in a steel cylinder were mounted at each of the car's four corners. Cleverly nicknamed "cocktail shakers," these weighted assemblies dampened the torsional vibrations experienced in the convertibles during normal driving conditions.

GM management decided early on that its new pony car should be offered as both a coupe (shown here) and a convertible (below). As such, most of the conceptual designs for the XP-836 were rendered to include both formats. This September 1964 rendering depicts a strong likeness to what would ultimately become the 1967 Chevy Camaro. (Photo Courtesy General Motors LLC)

Although the Camaro coupe and convertible appeared nearly identical to one another, the latter car required considerably more engineering effort to ensure it had sufficient structural rigidity to handle acceleration and overall drivability once its roofline was removed. (Photo Courtesy General Motors LLC)

Henry Haga

During his tenure as chief designer for Chevrolet Studios Two and Three (1963–1974), Henry "Hank" Haga was heavily involved in the design and development of the second- and third-generation Corvettes, the first- and second-generation Camaros, the Corvair Monza, and the Chevy Vega. (Photo Courtesy General Motors LLC)

Henry C. Haga was born in Milwaukee, Wisconsin, on January 22, 1931. As a young boy, Haga developed a passion for drawing automobiles. It was a passion he continued to pursue throughout his formative years. After graduating high school, he enrolled in college at the University of Wisconsin, but he only studied there for a single year before transferring to the ArtCenter College of Design in Pasadena, California. He graduated from the ArtCenter with a degree in industrial design.

Haga joined General Motors in 1953. He began his career in GM's experimental design studio. Over the next decade, Haga honed his skills as a designer, gaining experience by working in all five of GM's major design studios (Chevrolet, Pontiac, Oldsmobile, Buick, and Cadillac). By the time he returned to Chevrolet in 1962, he'd developed a reputation as being the "master of proportion" among his peers. He was also recognized as one of GM's leading designers.

Bill Mitchell promoted Haga in 1963 to chief designer of Chevrolet Studios Two and Three. One of his first assignments in the new role was to work on the Corvette Sting Ray. According to the National Corvette Museum website, Haga said, "It was a fresh studio (Studio Three) with a new product name, the Sting Ray, and a whole set of new responsibilities for me. The Corvette meant the epitome of design and performance in the GM line."

The following year, Haga's team was tasked with developing the preliminary designs and early clay models for a new pony car that was being developed to compete with the Ford Mustang. Working under Dave Holls, who in turn worked under Chevrolet/Pontiac Executive Design's Charles M. "Chuck" Jordan and Irvin W. Rybicki, it was Haga and his design team at Chevrolet Studio Two that performed much of the early design work on the Camaro.

Haga's group was also responsible for developing the 1965 Corvair as well as for designing the Super Nova show car and the soon-to-be-rebodied 1968 Corvette. Add to that his previous involvement with the split-window Sting Ray, and it's easy to understand how elements from all of these cars found their way into the first-generation Camaro's aesthetic.

By the mid-1960s, GM's design group had adopted a "fluid" design motif. While earlier exterior styling standards resulted in cars with complex architectures, this new approach resulted in more streamlined body panels that resembled canvas stretched over a wire frame. The fluid motif was meant to be very natural looking and free flowing, without the harsh lines so often found in other cars from that era.

Haga's team had used this styling approach with the Camaro's design.

According to *The Great Camaro* book by Mike Lamm, Haga said, "The canvas-stretched-over-wire theme served to give the Camaro its own character and separated it from the Mustang approach, which was much stiffer and more angular. . . . We purposefully avoided any contrived design lines and superfluous detail. Even the execution of the wide, horizontal-loop front end and grille, with its hidden headlamps in the Rally Sport variant, was as pure in content as we could make it."

Ultimately, Haga played a key role in the designs of the Corvette, Camaro, and Corvair Monza as well as several show cars, including the Super Nova, the XP-882, the Reynolds Aluminum Corvette, the 4-Rotor Corvette, and the early Chevy II. In 1974, Haga was promoted to director of design for European passenger cars and transferred to GM's Opel division. He relocated to Russelsheim, West Germany, in this new capacity and remained there for the next six years.

He returned to the United States in 1980 after being promoted to the role of assistant executive designer for the Chevrolet and Pontiac Exterior Design Studio. In 1984, he was named director of the General Motors Advanced Concepts Center in Newbury Park, California. He remained in that role until the time of his passing on August 16, 1988.

Haga (center) reviews a potential side-marker/turnstile assembly that was still under development by his design team. As the director of Chevrolet's Studios Two and Three, he was often tasked with managing the development of multiple automobile designs at the same time. (Photo Courtesy General Motors LLC)

Wind-Tunnel Testing

While many of the finer details of the F-Body's final look were still months from being completed, wind-tunnel testing of the car's aerodynamics began in February 1965. Haga's team had created a quarter-scale clay model of the car based on the Studio Two designs that had been developed over the past several months.

Over the course of 11 days, a total of 76 tests were conducted at the Vought wind tunnel in Dallas, Texas. Remarkably, most of these tests proved that the F-Body's design was aerodynamic and required minimal reworking, which was fortunate given the time constraints that had been placed on this project.

According to the book *Camaro Exposed: 1967–1969* by Paul Zazarine, Camaro Engineer Paul King had this to say about the wind-tunnel tests performed on the car: "To me, wind-tunnel testing was interesting at the time, but we were going to build the car the way it was regardless of what the wind tunnel said. . . . If the wind-tunnel results were positive, that was nice. If they were bad, that was too bad, because we were going to build the car anyway."

The Devil's in the Details

It is important to remember that the most pivital factor behind the evolution of the XP-836 was to get the car to market as quickly as possible. While the basic shape and profile of the car proved itself in the wind tunnels, there was still considerable work to be completed on both the car's exterior and interior.

The XP-836 body styling buck sits next to a Ford Mustang (for design reference) inside the auditorium of GM's Design Center. This styling buck would eventually be wrapped in clay and provide reference for the creation of future models of varying scale, including those used for eventual wind-tunnel testing. (Photo Courtesy General Motors LLC)

Henry Haga's design team worked diligently, refining body panels in the studio and grafting them onto one of several non-running "mules" that had been specifically developed to evaluate the fit and finish of the car's exterior. As the final look of the body took shape, the design team shifted its attention to the car's grille, headlamps, taillamps, and its front and rear bumpers. Elsewhere, references to the Panther moniker began appearing—first with a name badge placed on the front fascia and later with a leaping panther emblem on the car's front fenders.

At the same time Haga's team finalized the look of the Panther's exterior, Interior Designer George Angersbach and his team focused on developing the car's interior. To give the car a greater sports car–like feel, the driver and passenger seats were bolted directly to the floor pan, thereby lowering the occupants'

This is a full-scale clay model of the XP-836 Panther in February 1965. The rapid evolution of the car's exterior aesthetics enabled its designers to begin creating scale models of the car for wind-tunnel testing. Incredibly, this design proved to be sufficiently aerodynamic to be viable without any significant revisions, which was fortunate given the constraints being placed on the design team to prepare the Panther for production. (Photo Courtesy General Motors LLC)

With most of the overall body design complete, Haga's team shifted its focus to refining the details of the XP-836's front and rear ends. This rendering begins to reflect the future face of the 1967 Chevy Camaro. (Photo Courtesy General Motors LLC)

While the Camaro's headlights and front grille layout begin to take shape, the conceptual designs presented for the rear end contain taillight elements similar to those found on the Chevy Corvette. This is not surprising, given that many of Haga's team had recently completed work on the third generation of Chevy's flagship sports car. (Photo Courtesy General Motors LLC)

By March 1965, the front-end styling of the Camaro began to resemble the styling that went to production the following year. Notably absent are the fog lamps mounted next to each of the headlamp assemblies. (Photo Courtesy General Motors LLC)

The evolution of the Camaro's back end took a bit longer to formalize. This model used the same round taillights and a similar split bumper as those found on the 1968 Corvette. (Photo Courtesy General Motors LLC)

By April 1965, the split-bumper concept was abandoned in favor of a longer, single-piece chrome bumper design. However, the round taillights remained. Given that General Motors considered a marketing campaign wherein the Camaro would be advertised as the Corvette's cousin, it's possible that the inclusion of round taillights may have been considered to increase the similarity of the outward appearance of the two cars. (Photo Courtesy General Motors LLC)

George Angersbach's initial clay model of the XP-836's interior (December 1964) included a dashboard with three large gauges and a repurposed steering wheel out of a 1965 Chevy Bel Air. Still, the overall fitment of the cockpit was not dissimilar to the one used in the production model. (Photo Courtesy General Motors LLC)

By the following spring, Angersbach had revised the dashboard to include two primary gauges (a speedometer and a tachometer), along with secondary gauges placed in the center console just below the stereo head. Much of the hardware shown here, including the air ducts, the headlight switch and other toggle controls, and the heater/AC head, were placed in their final configuration. (Photo Courtesy General Motors LLC)

position in the car. The steering column and dashboard were similarly lowered, and the car's instrument panel, heating controls, and stereo controls were slanted down and away from the driver to provide more space in the cabin.

The gauge cluster was comprised of two elliptical instrument pods. The left pod included the speedometer (in mph) as well as "press" (oil pressure) and "water" (engine temperature) gauges. The right pod included the tachometer along with the fuel and volt gauges. The bezels surrounding each pod were finished with a thin chrome trim ring. Similarly, the entire instrument gauge cluster was framed by the car's three-spoke steering wheel, which came stock with chrome spokes and a color-matched rim. An optional wood-grain rim was also offered.

Vinyl seats and door panels were standard on all models. The door panels included integrated armrests, manual window crank handles and recessed door release handles finished in chrome trim, and color-matched carpet panels along the lower portion of the door. Each car also featured door-to-door carpeting.

Beneath the Hood

It was understood from the start that the F-Car would be marketed to a range of varying demographics from college students and recreational operators to executives and high-performance racers. To accommodate this broad range of would-be consumers, Chevrolet elected to offer its pony car with several engine packages when production began in September 1966.

The standard offering would include a 140-hp, 230-ci inline 6-cylinder engine paired to a 3-speed manual gearbox with a column shifter. At the other end of the spectrum (and only offered with the SS package) was a 325-hp, 396-ci, L35 Turbo-Thrust V-8 engine. This engine option was offered to consumers beginning in late November/December 1966. An additional L78 396-ci engine (this one rated at 375 hp) was

Mounting the engine to the F-car's underpinnings required some modification to the original Chevy II chassis. The original Chevy II chassis allowed the engine to sit higher in its cradle given the donor car's greater overall height. (Photo Courtesy General Motors LLC)

Given that the XP-836 Panther was to be offered with an assortment of 6- and 8-cylinder engines of varying sizes, GM engineers and mechanics assembled several prototype vehicles to sort out engine placement and ensure sufficient clearances. (Photo Courtesy General Motors LLC)

When introduced in 1967, the base-model Camaro was equipped with an inline 6-cylinder engine rated at 140 hp. While it lacked the horsepower of the SS/Z28 models, the base Camaro was a popular choice among young consumers looking for a sporty-but-affordable automobile that was equal parts fun and practical. (Photo Courtesy General Motors LLC)

eventually offered to consumers as well as a dealer-installed option.

Between these two extremes were three additional, optional engines selected to satisfy every budget. The first was the 155-hp, 250-ci, L22 inline 6-cylinder Turbo-Thrift. It was paired to the same 3-speed manual as the stock 6-cylinder engine. Second was the 210-hp, 327-ci, L30 Turbo-Fire V-8. This engine was also paired to a 3-speed manual transmission, although this version included a floor-mounted shifter. A 275-hp version of the L30 was introduced as well, as was a pair of optional transmissions: a 4-speed manual or a 2-speed Powerglide automatic.

Lastly, a 295-hp, 350-ci, L48 Turbo-Fire V-8 was offered as an optional powerplant on all variants of the car. Equipped with a Quadrajet 4-barrel carburetor and available with an optional 4.88:1 rear axle, this version of the F-Car had the ability to satisfy even the most discerning sports-car enthusiasts. It boasted a 0-to-60 time of 7.8 seconds and a quarter-mile time of 16.1 seconds at 86.5 mph. Like the L35 (which wouldn't be offered to consumers until November 1966), the L48 was a featured engine with the SS package.

Packaging the F-Body

With most of its engineering and design work completed, Chevrolet product planners began the important task of taking the car to market. It was decided that, in addition to offering various powerplant options to consumers, the new F-Body sports car would be offered in one of three unique packages with each of the latter packages building upon the previous ones with additional options and features.

The first was the standard package, which was referred to as the Style Trim Group. This package included exposed circular headlights; a black, full-width, loop-style plastic grille; inboard-mounted parking lamps; bright (chrome) moldings around the front and rear wheel openings; body-side accent stripes; and bright (chrome) gutter moldings along the edge of the hardtops.

The RS Camaro was essentially a base Camaro with an upgraded appearance package that included hidden headlights, updated taillights, special "RS" badging, and custom exterior "bright" trim. It could be purchased with any model, and many added this option when also purchasing the SS package. (Photo Courtesy General Motors LLC)

The SS Camaro provided consumers with a significant performance upgrade from the other models. SS Camaros came equipped with either a 350- or 396-ci engine. Each was also outfitted with special striping, "SS" badging, and nonfunctional air inlets on its hood. (Photo Courtesy General Motors LLC)

The second package offered was the optional Rally Sport (RS) package. Building on the standard package, all RS cars featured concealed headlamps with special covers that matched the car's black radiator grille when closed. The headlight covers were powered electrically and opened and closed whenever the headlights were turned on or off. The RS package also included factory painted stripes, bright (chrome) moldings, and unique dual taillamp assemblies. "RS" emblems were added to each of the front fenders. A special "RS" badge was also installed in the center of the front grille.

The third package was the aforementioned Super Sport (SS) package. Marketed as the "performance model" of the brand, the Super Sport included a more prominent "SS" moniker in the center of the front grille. Its hood featured a raised center section with a pair of simulated louvers. The front fenders also bore "SS" badges framed by a black bumblebee stripe/band that wrapped around the nose of the car behind the front grille opening. Special engine badges were installed on the lower front fenders behind the wheel openings. These badges identified which engine (the 350 or the 396) was installed beneath the car's hood. In the rear, the car's fuel filler cap bore the "SS" moniker as well, as did the horn button in the center of the steering wheel.

The Panther Becomes the Camaro

By late spring 1966, production of the F-Body pilot cars was ready to begin. Chevy's "Mustang killer" was imminent, and the automotive media was abuzz with rumors of the car's pending arrival. At the same time, Chevrolet was dealing with a considerable amount of bad press, due in large part to the recent publication of the book *Unsafe at Any Speed* by Ralph Nader. Published in November 1965, Nader's book heavily criticized the Chevy Corvair as being poorly engineered and inherently dangerous to operate.

Had it not been for Nader's book and the critical response it received, the XP-836 may have gone to market as the Chevy Panther. As it was, the name "Panther" (and the images it drummed up in consumers' imaginations) was deemed to be too aggressive by GM marketing and merchandising departments.

GM Vice President Ed Rollet and Chevrolet Merchandising Manager Bob Lund set about identifying a new name for the XP-836. Countless names were considered, many lifted from old foreign language dictionaries, until the pair stumbled across the word "camaro" (slang) in the 1936 edition of "Heath's French-to-English Dictionary" by James Boïelle and de V. Payen-Payne. Camaro, which meant "friend," "pal," or "comrade," seemed a perfect description of the relationship future owners were expected to have with Chevrolet's newest automobile.

The factory "Camaro by Chevrolet" front fascia emblem from a 1968 Camaro replaced the 1967 emblem (not pictured), which featured a large, scripted "Chevrolet" accompanied by a much smaller and separate rectangular "Camaro" emblem directly beneath it. The 1967 badging was probably reversed for the Camaro's inaugural year because Chevrolet was still debating what to call its new pony car as it neared production. (Photo Courtesy Scott Kolecki)

According to the book *Camaro: A Legend Reborn* by Larry Edsall, when the car was introduced to more than 200 members of the automotive press on June 29, 1966, Chevrolet General Manager Elliot "Pete" Estes stated: "Chevrolet has chosen a name which is lithe, graceful, and in keeping with our other names beginning with 'C'. It suggests the comradeship of good friends . . . as a personal car should be to its owners."

The closest reference to the word *Camaro* in contemporary French to English dictionaries is the word *camarade*, which means "camrade" or "friend" in English.

1965 Camaro Nomad

The original 1953 Nomad concept was more than a decade old when Chevrolet's design department began reimagining it as a Camaro. Rumors had begun circulating that Ford was developing a station-wagon version of the Mustang. To avoid falling behind again should Ford take its Mustang station wagon to market, GM management ordered Mitchell's styling department to design a Camaro station-wagon concept.

Several clay models of a Nomad-badged, two-door Camaro station wagon were produced in 1965. These models borrowed design elements from the original production Nomad, which Chevrolet had manufactured from 1955 to 1957. The front two-thirds of each car was essentially the XP-836 concept body. The rear third featured forward-leaning B-pillars; an extended roofline; a sloping, lift-open rear hatch; and a revised rear end with smaller taillights and a less-pronounced chrome bumper.

Although the notion of advancing the Camaro Nomad concept beyond the design phase was considered repeatedly throughout the development of the 1967 Camaro, Chevrolet ultimately elected to abandon the concept, especially after learning that Ford would not be taking the Mustang station wagon to market.

1966 Fastback Proposal

Henry Haga's styling department developed the 1966 Camaro fastback proposal as a full-scale clay mock-up, despite Chevrolet's executive order that the Camaro was to be limited to two bodystyles: a coupe and a convertible.

While its design shared the same chassis, dimensions, and much of the same overall shape/styling as the production-model coupe, the fastback featured completely reimagined C-pillars and a pseudo-Kammback treatment. Together, these elements transformed the car's rear glass and decklid assembly into a

The creation of the 1966 Camaro fastback proposal was little more than a "Hail Mary" play by Henry Haga and his design team. Haga hoped that by showcasing a full-scale model of a fastback Camaro, he might convince Chevrolet management to produce the car as a competitor to the Ford Mustang 2+2. (Photo Courtesy General Motors LLC)

Development of the 1965 Camaro Nomad began well after the coupe and convertible prototypes were well underway. The car borrowed several elements from the original Chevy Nomad, including its roofline and its forward-swept B- and C-pillars. Chevrolet seriously considered a Camaro-based sports wagon, but it never evolved past the concept phase. (Photo Courtesy General Motors LLC)

The 1966 fastback Camaro is on display in the outdoor courtyard of the GM Design Center. Although this concept was ultimately shot down by Chevrolet management, the fastback styling eventually found new life in the 1970 Camaro Z28 model. (Photo Courtesy General Motors LLC)

One of the more interesting features of the 1966 fastback Camaro concept was its unique rear hatch. When opened, the entire assembly was intended to rise up, allowing vehicle occupants easy access to the rear luggage compartment. (Photo Courtesy General Motors LLC)

One of the most dramatic features on the fastback concept was its swept-back C-pillars and Kammback treatment of the rear end. Given the incredible success of both the 1966–1970 GT500 Mustang and the 1968–1970 Dodge Charger models, Chevrolet's lack of interest in developing the fastback Camaro seems like another missed opportunity for the company. (Photo Courtesy General Motors LLC)

single-piece hatch that could be opened to allow access into a rear luggage/storage compartment.

Recognizing the longshot for what it was, Haga still elected to have his team create a full-scale model of the Camaro fastback design proposal. He hoped it might sway Chevrolet's executives to reconsider a fastback version of the Camaro as a direct competitor to Ford's Mustang 2+2 fastback, the AMC Marlin, and even the Dodge's Charger and Barracuda models, all of which also featured a fastback configuration. The model was unveiled in Haga's design studio on July 8, 1966. Unfortunately, Chevrolet management was still not convinced, and the fastback Camaro program was immediately—and permanently—canceled.

A Tough Act to Follow

Given the overwhelming commercial success of the Camaro (a total of 220,906 units were sold its freshman year), it came as no surprise when Chevrolet executives began ordering the development of conceptual "study cars" based on the production model. Throughout much of 1967 and 1968, several relatively inexpensive concepts were developed that showcased the versatility of the Camaro platform.

While some of these concept Camaros offered little more than embellishments to the car's outward appearance, concepts such as the Cherokee presented consumers with an exciting glimpse of things to come. The 1968 Caribe concept even proposed to take the Camaro platform in an entirely different direction by asking a simple question: sports car or sports truck?

The 1967 Camaro Aero Coupe

Positive consumer response to the 1967½ Camaro, combined with the undeniable commercial success of the Ford Mustang, triggered both companies to begin developing increasingly powerful versions of their pony-car models. At the same time, many of GM's competitors, including Ford, Mercury, Dodge, and Plymouth, started developing specially built, track-purposed versions of their sportier models. Commonly referred to as "Aero Cars" or "Aero Coupes" today, these extremely limited production models featured exceptional aerodynamic surfaces that enabled them to run faster at the racetrack.

General Motors wasted no time trying to capitalize on this latest trend. It had already started development of a Pontiac GTO aero coupe (also known as the Aero Coupe II), which was earmarked to compete in the 1969 NASCAR circuit. Upon witnessing its overnight and overwhelming commercial success, Chevrolet's executives decided they should also develop a Camaro Aero Coupe.

Badged as a Berlinetta model, the Camaro Aero Coupe concept featured a removable roof panel and a sugar-scoop rear window (like those found on the early third-generation Corvettes). The Aero Coupe's body had smoother, sleeker lines, and appeared to be more aerodynamic than other variants of the Camaro, which likely led to its name. (Photo Courtesy General Motors LLC)

Sadly, there is surprisingly little information readily available about the development of the 1967 Camaro Aero Coupe concept. It is known that Chevrolet advanced the Aero Coupe's design as far as a full-scale tape drawing and a full-size clay model. A drivable prototype was built in late 1967, although this version was fabricated using a production Camaro, and its outward appearance varied significantly from the clay model.

Presumably developed in Chevrolet's Studio Three, both the clay and production prototype versions of the Aero Coupe concept shared the same wheelbase as the production Camaro. The full-size clay introduced a more streamlined version of the 1967 Camaro's body lines. Its rear fenders lacked the prominent Coke-bottle curves of the production model. Instead, the car had broader B-pillars that cascaded down and back toward the rear of the car from the roofline and blended into the fenders at the car's beltline. The pillars framed a convex rear window and collectively formed a sugar-scoop feature at the back half of the car, much like the rear glass and B-pillar assembly found on the 1968 Corvette.

The Aero Coupe also included a removable targa top that was nearly identical to the one originally introduced on Pontiac's Aero Coupe II concept (although the top of the Pontiac version allegedly retracted into the rear roofline). The targa opening started just behind the intersection of the A-pillar and the windshield frame and terminated along the leading edge of the B-pillars just behind the front seat headrests. With the roof panel removed, the opening provided vehicle occupants an unobstructed view of the sky. While a targa top was not planned for track-purposed versions of the Camaro Aero Coupe, the car's designers knew that the larger B-pillars provided enough structural rigidity for a targa-top feature on production versions of the car.

The 1967 Aero Coupe concept is one of the more interesting Camaro concept vehicles in that it was seriously considered for production at one point in the brand's history, yet there is very little information available about the car today. The Aero Coupe was based on the same design profile as the 1966 Camaro Nomad. (Photo Courtesy General Motors LLC)

Chevrolet executives considered building the Aero Coupe as a production vehicle. The car was even rebadged as a Camaro Berlinetta, and a fully functional prototype was assembled using a production 1967 Camaro as the donor car. While the production prototype lacked the reimagined body lines of its clay model predecessor, it allowed engineers to test and evaluate the improved aerodynamics of the Aero Coupe's reimagined upper half.

Unfortunately, there is no evidence that the concept ever advanced beyond this single prototype. While only speculation, it is likely that the excessive cost of retooling required to mass produce an Aero Coupe Camaro brought the program to a quick and final end.

Neither the 1967 Camaro Aero Coupe nor the 1969 GTO Aero Coupe II evolved beyond their conceptual design phase. Because of this, General Motors lacked a viable entrant to compete in the infamous "aero wars" of the 1969 and 1970 NASCAR seasons. Ford, Mercury, Dodge, and Plymouth had the dominant (and most aerodynamic) racers during those seasons, and their individual successes gave rise to some of the most iconic muscle cars of all time: the 1968 Mercury Cyclone Spoiler II, the 1969 Ford Torino Talladega, the 1969 Dodge Charger Daytona, and the 1970 Plymouth Superbird.

1967 Waikiki Woodie Concept

The Waikiki Woodie concept was one of the earliest design-study Camaros developed by Chevrolet after the launch of the production model. From a conceptual standpoint, the Waikiki Woodie was uncharacteristically inexpensive to build when compared to the budgets normally allocated for GM's conceptual vehicles. Then again, it was less a concept car and more a stylized production model designed to showcase the versatility of Chevy's newest sports car.

Even Chevrolet's public relations department acknowledged that the Waikiki Woodie "concept" was anything but. According to a GM press release circa 1967, "Already riding high on a wave of popularity, Chevrolet's sporty Camaro is sure to make another big splash with a new auto show version. The 'idea car' is a remodeled version of a Camaro SS 350 convertible and was designed specially to demonstrate the car's versatility as a sports-type vehicle. Called the Camaro Waikiki, it is 'tailored' for specific use by the sun and surf set."

> "CALLED THE CAMARO WAIKIKI, IT IS 'TAILORED' FOR SPECIFIC USE BY THE SUN AND SURF SET."

The Waikiki contained several unique features that separated it from its production-model counterparts. Out front, the car was equipped with a custom, teak-wood grille and a pair of rectangular Cibie headlights. Elongated side-marker lights were mounted along the leading edge of the front fenders. These preceded simulated-wood-panel trim that ran most the length of the car just below the car's beltline and several

Chevrolet's marketing images for the 1967 Waikiki Woodie were taken on Belle Isle in the Detroit River. Portions of downtown Detroit can readily be spotted behind the models. (Photo Courtesy General Motors LLC)

The 1967 Waikiki Woodie concept started life as a convertible SS350. It was specifically modified to showcase how the Camaro could be adapted to complement the glamorous surf lifestyles of those on the West Coast of the United States and Hawaii. (Photo Courtesy General Motors LLC)

inches above its body base line. This paneling terminated at the rear side-marker lights mounted along the trailing edge of the quarter panels.

Excluding the front and rear side markers, all the paneling was framed in with custom chrome trim that followed the car's body lines. Custom "Waikiki" badging was mounted on each fender. The car also came equipped with both driver- and passenger-side rearview mirrors.

Besides its wood paneling, the two most notable features of the Waikiki Woodie concept were its removable/stowable surfboard carrier and its unique extended taillamps assemblies. The taillamps were developed to communicate what the driver was doing while operating the vehicle. When the driver's foot was on the accelerator (gas) pedal, the taillamp illuminated green. When the driver removed his or her foot from the gas pedal, the lamps changed from green to yellow. When the brake pedal was depressed, the taillights illuminated red.

The car's exterior was painted bright yellow, and its interior was finished in shades of tan and okra. While most of the interior was unchanged (other than color) from its production counterpart, the Waikiki Woodie came fitted with okra-colored shag carpet dyed to match the center console and dashboard trim. The car rode on custom wire wheels wrapped in 15-inch G-70 tires.

The 1967 Waikiki Woodie concept made its debut in April 1967 alongside the Camaro Cherokee concept at the 11th-annual International Auto Show in New York City. The car continued to tour the 1967 car show circuit, and it also made an appearance at the Detroit Autorama. Despite being a popular attraction at these venues, the car never evolved beyond the concept phase and was, presumably, destroyed at the conclusion of its auto show circuit tour.

Although its unique teak wood paneling never found a home on any Camaro after its brief stint on the Waikiki Woodie, this type of styling became mainstream on other more-conventional automobiles, including the Chevette, the Blazer, the El Camino Estate, and even the Suburban. (Photo Courtesy General Motors LLC)

1967 Camaro Cherokee

Arguably one of the most notable examples of all the early Camaro concepts, the 1967 Cherokee began life as a production-model SS/RS convertible with vehicle identification number (VIN) 124677N233228. Built at GM's Norwood, Ohio, assembly plant, the car originally came equipped with a preproduction 396-ci, 375-hp, Mark IV L78 engine paired to a Turbo Hydra-matic 400 transmission. Bill Mitchell was given specific instructions by GM management to have his styling department transform the convertible into a show car for the express purpose of promoting the Camaro brand during the 1967 auto show season.

The 1967 Camaro Cherokee began life as an SS 396 Camaro convertible prior to its transformation at the hands of Mitchell's team. Mitchell had his styling department install a handcrafted fiberglass hood with a Firebird-style exterior tachometer and a Corvette-style hood scoop. (Photo Courtesy David Newhardt/Mecum Auctions)

Having just invested a considerable amount of his time and resources into the development of the third-generation Corvette, Mitchell incorporated many of the same styling elements and technological advancements into the Cherokee. Mitchell knew the Camaro would tour the show circuit well before the 1968 Corvette's unveiling, and he saw the Cherokee as his chance to give the automotive world a "sneak peek" of things to come. General Motors likewise saw it as an opportunity to introduce the Camaro as a "cousin" to the immensely popular Corvette, which it believed would give the Camaro brand the added credibility it needed to compete against the Ford Mustang.

The Cherokee's Corvette-inspired alterations included split front and rear bumpers made from brass; a fully integrated ducktail-style rear spoiler; special driving lamps; a hood-mounted tachometer; a customized, hand-formed domed hood with a clear Lexan window, specially designed to display the car's custom big-block engine; a road-race-style gas cap; and 15x6-inch turbine-style wheels like those featured on the second-generation Stingray. The wheels came wrapped in Firestone red-stripe tires.

Although its exterior was originally painted white, Mitchell had the car repainted with a base coat of Aztec Gold Metallic and a topcoat of Candy Apple Metalflake Red. The combination of these lacquer paints gave the car a deep, rich-looking finish. Gold pinstriping adorned the hood (including a gold "frame" around the Lexan window in the hood's center), fenders, doors, quarter panels, fender wells, and the rear ducktail spoiler.

Mitchell recruited Chevrolet performance expert Vince Piggins to finesse the car's powertrain and underpinnings. The car's original 396-ci big-block engine was upgraded by Piggins to include a set of four Weber down-draft carburetors mounted to a Moon intake manifold. The addition of the Weber/Moon induction system increased engine output by at least 50 hp (although, many claim this to be a conservative estimate). Piggins elected to keep the original automatic transmission and 12-bolt Positraction axle. Power steering, power disc brakes, and Koni shocks out front and AC Delco air shocks in the rear were all added during the build.

Mitchell's team upgraded the car's stock interior with several elements that were immensely popular at the time. The car

The Camaro Cherokee, likely still under development in Chevrolet's design studio, includes a front license-plate insert that identifies the donor car as a "1967 Chevrolet Camaro SS 396 Convertible." (Photo Courtesy General Motors LLC)

The transparent hood panel is one of the most notable features on the Camaro Cherokee. It was designed to showcase GM's new Mark IV 396-ci big-block engine. A Pontiac-derived, hood-mounted tachometer was installed next to the transparent engine window. (Photo Courtesy David Newhardt/Mecum Auctions)

The white striping on the Cherokee's front end was a carryover from the donor 1967 Camaro SS used in its creation. Although the "SS" badging was left in place, the white striping was removed shortly after the show car was completed. (Photo Courtesy General Motors LLC)

was given power windows, an AM/FM stereo, fold-down rear seats, a custom T-handle floor shifter, and a tilt steering column fitted with a Corvette steering wheel adorned with a crossed flag emblem. Although the car started life with red seats and carpeting, Mitchell's team refinished all the interior surfaces in black, except for gray/white accent striping along the seat bolsters and on the interior door skins.

The Camaro Cherokee made its debut at the 11th-annual International Auto Show in New York City's Coliseum on April 1, 1967. It was showcased as one of several special Camaros (including the Waikiki) in an exhibit specifically targeted at a teenage/20-something audience. Interestingly, the car was originally marketed as the "Camaro Carnival" in some of the early press published prior to the show's opening, which at least suggests that the "Cherokee" moniker came late in the car's development.

Following a stint on the 1967 auto show circuit, the Camaro Cherokee served as the official pace car for the first round of the 1967 Canadian American Challenge Cup (Can-Am) at Road America on September 3, 1967. It was driven by British Formula One racing driver Sir Stirling Moss.

In attendance at that race was Augie Pabst, a beer baron and noted racing driver. Pabst had been so impressed with the car after watching its parade lap around the road course that he decided to purchase the Cherokee from Chevy. He allegedly worked out a deal with Bill Mitchell, who was a friend of Pabst. It has also

Bill Mitchell was responsible for the introduction of the transparent roof panel on the Cherokee, as well as the car's unique ducktail spoiler and rear decklid assembly, its split front and rear bumpers, and its unique Candy Apple Metalflake Red over stock Aztec Gold paint. (Photo Courtesy General Motors LLC)

The rear end of the Camaro featured a tall ducktail spoiler that had been specially crafted by the artisans at GM's Design Center. A quick-release gas cap was installed below the spoiler and between the car's taillight assemblies. It was deemed an absolute necessity that all performance cars from this era, including show cars such as the Cherokee, be fitted with this type of gas cap. (Photo Courtesy General Motors LLC)

The 1967 Camaro Cherokee was specifically developed by Bill Mitchell to showcase Chevrolet's preproduction L78 engine. The 396-ci engine was fitted with four Weber down-draft carburetors on a Moon Can-Am intake manifold. The carburetors' tall velocity stacks, visible through the Plexiglas window on the hood, became a focal point of the car. (Photo Courtesy David Newhardt/Mecum Auctions)

When it was first assembled, the Camaro Cherokee donor car included a red interior. To provide greater contrast between its interior and the showy Aztec Gold exterior, (the car has since been repainted) the car's carpeting, upholstery, and dashboard panels were all replaced with black interior components. Additionally, a new steering-wheel assembly and rear fold-down seats were also installed. (Photo Courtesy David Newhardt/ Mecum Auctions)

been alleged that Mitchell gave the car to Pabst. After owning and driving the car for a few years, Pabst traded it in at Vilter Chevrolet in Milwaukee, Wisconsin. Vilter Chevrolet sold the Cherokee in 1971 to Dan Frank, owner of the Custom Top company, for just $3,600.

The car traded hands again in 1979 when Frank sold the car to Edward Maurer of Brookfield, Wisconsin. While in Maurer's possession, the car came to the attention of muscle car enthusiast Terry Lietzau. Upon learning more about the Cherokee's unique history, Lietzau entered into negotiations with the Maurers with the intent of purchasing the car. Their negotiations lasted several years and culminated in a bidding war with several other interested parties. Although the sell price has not been disclosed, it has been reported that Lietzau paid over $20,000 more than the next-highest bidder. The Cherokee had 21,000 miles on it at the time of purchase.

Lietzau invested a significant amount of money into the

restoration of the Cherokee. The car no longer had its original L78 engine, so Lietzau had Luedeke's Automotive of Oshkosh, Wisconsin, build a non-serialized L78 engine to replace the 427-ci engine that had been previously swapped into the car. He also sourced the correct Weber carburetors and Moon intake manifold to replace the original units, both of which had disappeared off the car decades earlier.

The car was sold again in 2011 at the Russo and Steele auction in Scottsdale, Arizona. At the time of its appearance at that auction, the Cherokee received a full mechanical restoration but was still wearing its original paint. It was also missing its Corvette-style turbine wheels. Nonetheless, the car sold for an incredible $357,500 to a pair of private collectors known only as "the Brothers." The car became part of the Brothers Collection, which is comprised of many unique and one-of-a-kind automobiles.

Since purchasing the Camaro Cherokee in 2011, the Brothers have had the entire car professionally restored to its original show condition, including its turbine wheels, by Charley Hutton's Color Studio in Nampa, Idaho. The Cherokee has since been showcased at a select number of automotive events, including at the Muscle Car and Corvette Nationals (MCACN) in Rosemont, Illinois.

The car remains a part of the Brothers Collection at the time of this printing.

1968 Camaro Caribe

The 1968 XP-14 Camaro Caribe Sportsman concept was expressly developed by Chevrolet to gauge public interest in a potential "sportsman's 'dream pickup' in Super Sports form," according to a GM press release circa 1968. The one-of-a-kind show car blended the front half of a production Camaro with a back half that shared a passing resemblance to Chevy's struggling El Camino platform. The Camaro Caribe made its public debut during the Rod and Custom Show, which was at the Toledo Sports Arena from March 7 to 9, 1968.

Although it had been advertised as an entirely new concept, the XP-14 Caribe Sportsman concept may well have been intended as a potential successor to the El Camino, which had been developed by Chevrolet as a competitor to the 1959 Ford Ranchero.

The original El Camino, which was manufactured from 1959 to 1960, was based on the 1959 Chevy Brookwood station wagon. A total of only 36,409 first-generation El Caminos

The Chevrolet Caribe was developed to satiate Chevrolet management's ongoing belief that a hybrid car/pickup truck automobile would succeed in the marketplace. Although the Chevelle ended up serving double duty as the front half of the El Camino, many within General Motors believed that the Camaro's aesthetic would attract consumers to the showroom floor. (Photo Courtesy General Motors LLC)

The second-generation El Camino was based on the popular Chevy II/Chevelle platform from the mid-1960s. This example, a 1964 El Camino, featured the same front-end styling, wheelbase (115 inches), and overall width (74.6 inches) as a 1964 Chevelle, but it was 4.5 inches longer with its truck bed rear end (198.3 inches versus 193.9 inches). (Photo Courtesy General Motors LLC)

This composited set of images taken by General Motors provides a detailed look at the Caribe's open-air cockpit and rear truck bed. The Caribe lacked a roof panel but featured an aerodynamic roll bar behind the driver and passenger seats, which offered some protection in the unlikely event of a rollover. Also worth noting is the unique teakwood flooring in the rear of the vehicle. (Photo Courtesy General Motors LLC)

was sold during its short two-year production run. A reimagined El Camino, this time based on the popular Chevelle platform, made its debut in 1964.

As with its predecessor, the second-generation model performed poorly, selling just 137,221 units between 1964 and 1967. Given the Chevelle's incredible success during that same period (which accounted for the sale of more than 1.6 million units), Chevrolet's executives had once more started looking for alternate platforms upon which to base their unique hybrid car/pickup truck. The successful launch of the Camaro, combined with its newness in the marketplace, led many to believe it might be the perfect car for the job.

Both the exterior and interior of the Caribe concept featured several unique styling elements that separated it from its production Camaro model counterpart. The most notable of these was the Caribe's 5-foot-long pickup box, with its palomino vinyl sidewalls, four concealed storage wells, and teakwood flooring. Additional features included a "between the seats" console extension that contained a hot beverage dispenser and cup storage and an aerodynamic roll bar mounted directly behind the seats designed to help control airflow and reduce wind buffeting inside the cockpit.

Beyond these details, information on the Caribe's cockpit is somewhat limited. It is known that the interior was wrapped in both Palomino- and Ivory-colored vinyl with rich wood trim/accents and charcoal black carpeting, all of which could be found on production Camaros from that same year. Unlike the production convertibles, the Caribe came equipped with a header-less windshield supported by narrow A-pillars, both features that were unique to the concept model.

Out front, the Caribe's grille was believed to include a unique recessed air intake reminiscent of the air scoops found on military aircraft from that era. The intake, framed

This Chevrolet press photo of the Caribe's interior focused on marketing the car to both men and women. The center console contained a hot beverage dispenser, cup storage, and a pair of cup holders, all of which were intended to show the versatility of the Caribe as a more practical automobile to would-be consumers. (Photo Courtesy General Motors LLC)

Much like the Cherokee, it is believed that the Caribe started life as a 1968 Camaro SS. The Caribe features the same Super Sport louvers on its hood, and it has been documented that the car had a 396-ci engine, which was consistent with the powerplant used in the SS Camaro platform. (Photo Courtesy General Motors LLC)

with a chrome accent ring, was alleged to house a set of small high-intensity lamps. Unfortunately, there is only limited photographic evidence to support this claim. There has since been considerable speculation that the Caribe's unique grille was being developed for inclusion on the 1969 Camaro, which might explain why General Motors was careful not to release images of the grille to the public.

The Caribe's front fenders featured the same side-marker lights as those found on the 1968 Camaro. Similarly, the Caribe's hood included the same Super Sport louvers as the production model. At the heart of the Caribe was a 396-ci V-8 engine mated to a fully synchronized 4-speed manual transmission and a Positraction rear end—the same powerplant pairing that was first introduced in the Camaro Super Sport. The many similarities between the front end of both cars strongly suggests that the Camaro Caribe concept began life as a production 1968 Camaro SS model.

The Caribe rode on a set of specially designed, 15-inch aluminum wheels with brushed aluminum inserts. All four wheels were wrapped with specially marked Goodyear Wide Oval tires. Although its rear end framed the back of the pickup-style bed, the sheet metal and chrome bumpers looked remarkably like a stock Camaro from behind. Its taillight assemblies also appeared nearly identical to the production version until they were activated, at which point the brake lights would begin to flash at a high rate of speed.

While more commonplace on modern vehicles, the original flashing brake lights commanded the attention of anyone who saw them and created an "unusually arresting stop signal," according to a Camaro Caribe press release circa 1968.

It is unclear whether Chevrolet ever considered the advancement of the Camaro Caribe beyond its conceptual design phase. Public opinion garnered at Toledo's Rod and Custom Show was varied, although several disparaging remarks about the car were received by people attending the show. Moreover, past poor sales performance of the El Camino combined with the added costs of another retool made the production of the Caribe prohibitively expensive.

Since its introduction in 1968, there has been some debate as to the accuracy of the Caribe's original alphanumeric XP-14 designation. While not all GM experimental prototype (XP) numbers were assigned in ascending numerical order, it seems likely that the assignment of an XP number to another experimental Camaro would have followed the original F-Body styling buck's XP-836 number from a year earlier. In the article "A Camaro Parts Hauler: The Camaro Caribe" by Randy Bolig and published at Chevy Hardcore.com, Bolig attested that a "contact" he had spoken with at General Motors was "unable to locate an official number designation for the Caribe, but (stated that) during the time frame of this car's study, the designations would have been somewhere in the 700 or 800 number range."

CHAPTER 2

SECOND GENERATION (1970–1981)

"THE FIRST-GENERATION CAMARO ENDED UP BEING DESIGNED BY COMMITTEE, WHILE THE SECOND BECAME A DESIGNER'S DESIGN."
— BILL MITCHELL

Chevrolet's marketing team introduced the second-generation Camaro as the Super Hugger, presumably to convey its ability to "hold the road" in any driving condition, even when traversing tight corners or winding roads. Although the Super Hugger title was a bit "too groovy" for serious enthusiasts, the second-generation Camaro was a huge success, selling more than 117,000 units its freshman year. (Photo Courtesy General Motors LLC)

The commercial success of Chevrolet's first-generation Camaro was undeniable. In just three years, the company had sold nearly 700,000 examples of its original pony car (220,906 units in 1967; 235,247 units in 1968; and 243,085 units in 1969). Yet, as prosperous as it had been, the original Camaro's design had never been intended to be a long-term production vehicle. It had been developed as a quick fix with the sole purpose to pull market share away from the equally popular Ford Mustang.

The Camaro Gets a New Look

Bill Mitchell hated the look of the original Camaro. He frequently referred to it as a committee car, an opinion based on his belief that the first-generation production model had been full of corporate and engineering compromises, most of which had detracted significantly from the XP-836's original aesthetic.

Mitchell was adamant that the second-generation Camaro would not suffer the same fate. He insisted that the new model should mirror the more exotic styling of sports cars being manufactured in Europe. It would look sleek, sporty, and expensive. So, in the days following the launch of the 1967 Camaro, Bill Mitchell and his design staffs set to work on the look of the next-generation model.

In the book *The Great Camaro* by Michael Lamm, former GM Vice President Irv Rybicki explained how its design evolved.

This is Hank Haga's early styling for the second-generation Camaro built upon design motifs introduced in the first-generation model. Although its body lines were softer than the 1967–1969 Camaro, there's no denying that Haga's early efforts were more of a design evolution instead of the design revolution that Bill Mitchell was looking for. (Photo Courtesy General Motors LLC)

GM Designer Dave Holls was involved with several of Chevrolet's key sports-car and muscle-car programs, including the 1963 and 1968 Corvettes, the 1970 Monte Carlo, and the 1970½ Camaro. During his tenure with General Motors, he served as the company's head of Advanced Design and was later named director of Corporate Design. (Photo Courtesy General Motors LLC)

Haga felt that the recessed-loop grille should be repurposed from the first-generation model as a means of showing continuity between the two generations. Bill Mitchell rejected this styling element almost immediately, disparaging its look as being too simple for the next-generation Camaro. (Photo Courtesy General Motors LLC)

"We started planning the second-generation Camaro and Firebird immediately after the first project ended," Rybicki said. "That second car, as I remember, wasn't developed in the studios per se. We initially sat down in what we call the body development room, where we package our vehicles, and we worked very closely with Jack Humbert and Dave Holls. We were in there with Vince Kaptur (a body engineer), and we worked every day to get the seat placed just right, the rockers where we wanted them, [and] the cowl at a certain point, always with the mental picture of the silhouette we were after.

"The key to the appearance of a car is in its structure, in its anatomy (where you place the seats, how high, how wide, its length, the correct tumblehome) [and] the proper relationship of the wheels to the sheet metal. If you have those elements, you're going to get an automobile that's very appealing to the eye, and that's the way this one was."

Henry Haga and Bill Porter

Bill Mitchell, along with design executives Chuck Jordan, Dave Holls, and Irv Rybicki (Rybicki wouldn't become vice president of General Motors until August 1977) dictated what the next-generation Camaro would look like. However, it was Chevrolet's Studio Three, under the direction of Henry Haga and the Pontiac design studio (under the direction of Studio Head Bill Porter), who collectively developed the new F-Body's final look.

This was another early rendering of the second-generation Camaro that was completed just a few months after the previous image. It incorporated motifs introduced on the first-generation model. It also continues to include design elements previously introduced on the Corvette. A Kamm rear end was introduced and became an integral part of the next-generation Camaro's final look. (Photo Courtesy General Motors LLC)

At Bill Mitchell's direction, the Chevy Three's early renderings/models of the new Camaro featured more exotic proportions, including a longer front end. Given that Haga's team was responsible for developing all of Chevrolet's small and sporty car designs, it's not surprising that aspects of the third-generation Corvette found their way into the second-generation Camaro's early styling efforts. (Photo Courtesy General Motors LLC)

Rear quarter-panel windows were featured in many of the early second-generation designs between late 1966 and early 1967. When it was discovered that the elimination of these windows (and their roll-up/down assemblies) would save $18 per car, it was decided they should be eliminated and that the money should be allocated elsewhere. (Photo Courtesy General Motors LLC)

In July 1967, the evolving profile of the second-generation Camaro began to reflect elements of the production model. The quarter-panel windows were replaced by a more pronounced B-pillar, and the longer front end (though exaggerated on this model) allowed for a more steeply raked front windshield. (Photo Courtesy General Motors LLC)

In addition to its profile, Chevrolet designers reimagined the car's front end, moving the grille to the center of the car's fascia and widening its maw, which was a feature that found its way onto the 1970½ Camaro when it went to production nearly three years later. (Photo Courtesy General Motors LLC)

Fortunately for Haga's design team, most of the second-generation Camaro's underpinnings remained unchanged from the first-generation model. It used the same subframe assembly, the same unitized main section, the same 11-inch front disc-brake system (which was now a standard feature on the Camaro), and the same 9.5-inch rear drum brakes.

Most of the second-generation engine offerings also remained the same as the original Camaro. Put simply, this meant that Haga's work on the new body shape could progress without the interruptions and redesigns that frequently occurred when developing a new vehicle chassis.

That's not to say that the union between the second-generation Camaro's body and chassis was seamless. Chevrolet engineers reached an impasse when trying to package the car's air-conditioning and heater head unit, radio, glove compartment, and instrumentation into the dashboard. Haga's design had lowered the height of the cowl (the front section of the automobile's frame that supports the rear of the hood, windshield, dashboard, pedals, and instrument panel). Haga insisted that the lowered cowl was vital to the car's sports-car aesthetic. The engineering group insisted that there simply wasn't enough space to make everything fit.

Bill Mitchell was called to address the issue. He sided with his design team and stated unequivocally that the cowl would not be raised "even a fraction of an inch." With that, the matter was settled. The engineering department quite literally went "back to the drawing board" and, after considerable effort, devised a way to make everything fit. Such was Mitchell's influence in those days.

It took Haga approximately 18 months and countless permutations before he finally achieved the desired silhouette for the second-generation Camaro. But once the profile met with Bill Mitchell's approval, the rest of the exterior design came together quickly, taking less than six weeks to complete.

What's fascinating is exactly how it all came together.

The Camaro Is Not a Firebird, Right?

Although Henry Haga (and staff) was chiefly responsible for developing the exterior of the second-generation Camaro, it is worth noting that Chevy Studio Three was also engaged in several other key design projects, including the third-generation Corvette and the soon-to-be Chevy Vega. The group was also responsible for completing styling updates to the Corvair and Nova models. While it was fortunate that most of the development work on the Corvette had been completed by the time the second-generation Camaro program was fully underway, the remaining projects (especially the 1971 Vega) forced Haga's design team to split time and resources between the two cars.

Although it would not appear on a production model until 1975, designers began exploring the idea of using wraparound rear glass on the Camaro in late 1966. This full-scale rendering of a Camaro K-coupe from November 1969 began to accurately depict the final profile of the production-model Camaro and Firebird models. Although, many of its styling elements, including its side glass and its front and rear ends, were still under development. (Photo Courtesy General Motors LLC)

This full-scale clay model of the 1970 Camaro depicts an accurate front fascia but features two different A-pillar/roofline assemblies. Models of this sort were often used to evaluate alternative styling elements throughout the preproduction development of a car. This model also appears to include a removable roof panel on the passenger's side, a feature that was considered for the 1970 model year but later abandoned. Removable roof panels (T-tops) became a factory option starting in 1978. (Photo Courtesy General Motors LLC)

The 1970½ Camaro (so-named because the 1969 Camaro continued production well into the 1970 model year) was arguably one of the most beautiful Camaros ever built. It was the American interpretation of classic Italian sports cars. Bill Mitchell directed the Chevy design studios to study the third-generation Corvette and the Pininfarina-designed Ferrari GT models before developing the exterior architecture of the second-generation Camaro. (Photo Courtesy General Motors LLC)

Several design-related questions also plagued the completion of the Camaro's design: Should the Camaro have a rear quarter window? How long should the doors be? Determining the answer to each of these items (as well as numerous others not referenced here) took time, which encroached on the Camaro's planned completion deadlines. For the record, the rear quarter windows were eliminated as a cost-savings measure. The money saved there was used to pay for better underbody insulation, extra carpeting, and longer doors. The introduction of longer doors was significant because their inclusion provided would-be passengers greater ease of access to the Camaro's back seats.

One of the more interesting questions posed by designers was, "Should the Camaro's rear end be lifted to give it a more aggressive look?" Designers and enthusiasts fervently agreed that it should. Corporate leadership did not. According to Henry Haga, from the book *The Great Camaro* by Michael Lamm, the latter group (the one that held the most influence over the decision) insisted that the Camaro's back end "should terminate in a very slim horizontal loop."

This decision led to one of the first notable design disparities between the second-generation Chevy Camaro and Pontiac Firebird models. The Camaro used a single-wall rear panel that created a concave feature below the rear decklid, and upon which the car's four round taillights were mounted. On the Firebird, a more expensive double rear panel was installed, which created a flat surface upon which a pair of more sophisticated-looking, trapezium-shaped taillights were installed.

Conversely, pieces of the Camaro grew out of the Firebird camp. One of the more significant examples was the car's upper section (everything above the beltline). Haga's group developed a wraparound windshield with narrow, dark, nearly vertical A-pillars that framed the trailing edge of the windshield glass and were positioned just behind the front cut lines for the doors.

Porter's team at Pontiac designed a U-shaped windshield framed by stemware-shaped A-pillars that slanted back from the cowl at a 57-degree angle and blended seamlessly into the roofline. While having different windshields for each car was briefly considered, Porter's design was eventually selected for both the Firebird and the Camaro, as was his team's design for the rest of the upper body, including the roofline, the B-pillars, and the back glass.

Although Chevrolet and Pontiac executives might have been attempting to reduce production costs through the development of common parts that could be used on both cars, history has shown this simply isn't the case. Outside of a common windshield and roofline, there were few shared components between the second-generation Camaro and Firebird. Each had different doors, fasciae, grilles, headlight bezels, hoods, fenders, etc.

While there's no mistaking the common overall aesthetic between these cars, it is worth noting that each design team took enormous pride in the product their division produced, so much so that every subsequent Camaro and Firebird model since has contained these same subtle differences, despite the significant added production cost incurred by General Motors to build each model separately.

The Camaro's New Interior

In much the same way that Bill Mitchell had outlined his expectations to Henry Haga concerning the second-generation Camaro's exterior, interior designer George Angersbach was provided some specific guidelines before starting work on its interior. In the book *The Great Camaro* by Mike Lamm, Irv Rybicki explained the design expectations from which the interior evolved: "A lot of time on the interior was spent on 'human engineering.' We were aiming at something that was close to the Corvette in terms of ride and handling and ease of operation. This had to be a driver's car, with the shift lever correctly placed relative to the steering wheel—all the controls just right."

Angersbach was no stranger to the Camaro. As the assistant chief of interior design, he had been responsible for development of the original Camaro's interior (under the direction of Interior Design Chief Don Schwarz). His work on that car

As with its exterior, the evolution of the second-generation Camaro's interior started with a series of design drawings and full-scale models. This image depicts some of George Angersbach's design work during the development of the car's dashboard. While both models seen here include elements that would become part of the final design, the interior continued to evolve in conjunction with its exterior, as each needed to complement the other. (Photo Courtesy General Motors LLC)

had been praised for its ability to make the driver feel that he or she was connected and in control of a powerful and precise machine. He had also been previously involved in the interior designs of the Corvette, Corvair, and Chevy II. He understood the expectations, and he knew how to deliver what had been asked of him and his team of designers.

Gauges

As work on the interior got underway, Angersbach turned to the cockpit of the third-generation Corvette for inspiration. Like the Corvette, the Camaro's speedometer and tachometer were grouped around the steering column, providing the driver an unobstructed view of each. Unlike the Corvette, the secondary gauges were mounted to either side of the primary gauges: the engine temperature and fuel to the left and the oil pressure and battery voltage to the right.

The entire instrument cluster was intentionally developed to ensure the driver had easy and immediate access to pertinent information during vehicle operation. Likewise, Angersbach placed control switches, including the car's wipers and headlights, within easy reach of the driver's fingertips for the same reason.

Center Console

The center console assembly was also inspired by the Corvette, although no common parts (or styling) was borrowed from Chevrolet's flagship sports car. For the 1970½ Camaro, Angersbach had the center console start behind the driver and passenger seats and extend all the way to the instrument panel near the radio housing. The shift selector (automatic) or the transmission shifter (manual) assemblies were mounted below the radio and placed far enough back to ensure they were comfortably within reach of the driver, ensuring a more connected driving experience whenever shifting was required. A covered storage bin was also integrated into the center-console assembly, along with an ashtray for the rear occupants—remember, this was the 1970s!

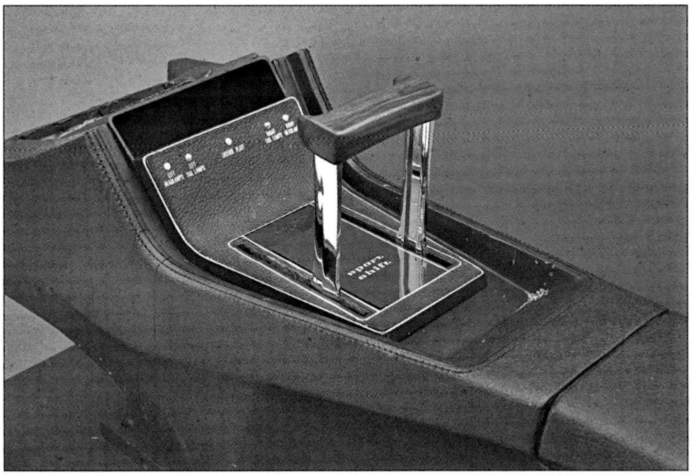

This design mock-up shows the Camaro's "horseshoe" automatic-transmission sport shifter and center console. (Photo Courtesy General Motors LLC)

Seating

Angersbach, working in conjunction with the Fisher Body Division, introduced new bucket seats constructed entirely out of foam for the 1970½ model year. Each seat featured a low back and an adjustable headrest that provided greater rear visibility. Despite lacking metal springs for cushioned ride support, the seats were surprisingly comfortable. The same seat design was shared with the Firebird for its inaugural year. While foam seat pads are an industry standard today, the Camaro (and Firebird) were the first to use it.

A significant amount of plastic was used in the fabrication of the Camaro's interior. This enabled Angersbach's team greater flexibility in configuring the dashboard, the center console, and even the driver and passenger door skins to accommodate the ergonomics of the driver and passenger. Every design decision, from the placement of each and every interior component to the types of materials used, followed the "human engineering" edict prescribed above.

Another full-scale mock-up of the Camaro interior shows that this model includes many of the aesthetics/styling elements that would be used in the production model, including the dashboard layout and general configuration of the air ducts, glove box, and radio. Even so, there are several components, including the steering wheel, the passenger air vents, and the overall contour of the dashboard itself, that was updated prior to being ready for production. (Photo Courtesy General Motors LLC)

A Masterpiece of Proportion

The second-generation Camaro (and Firebird) arrived in dealer showrooms on February 26, 1970. Given its late arrival (most new model year cars were/are introduced in the late summer/early fall of the previous year), they were marketed as a 1970½ model. Interestingly, the second-generation Camaro was only offered as a 2+2 coupe.

As Bill Mitchell had directed at its inception, the new exterior aesthetic included a fusion of European styling elements combined with classic pony-car proportions. It featured a long hood, a low cowl, and a steeply raked windshield, all of which harkened back to the more exotic lines of cars being built by the likes of Ferrari and Maserati.

A convertible option was briefly considered during the second-generation Camaro's development but was abandoned due to the added costs and the waning sales of other convertible-optioned vehicles, including the Chevy Corvette. This one-off, special-edition 1970½ Camaro, featuring a fully removable top, was specially built by Chevrolet for entertainer Glen Campbell. (Photo Courtesy General Motors LLC)

The second-generation Camaro is frequently referred to as a "1970½" model. This is because production of the second-generation Camaro did not begin until November 1969. The Fisher Body company, which produced the body panels for the Camaro, experienced issues stamping the new quarter panels, which delayed the new Camaro's launch date by nearly four months. (Photo Courtesy General Motors LLC)

The 1970½ Camaro shared the same 108-inch wheelbase as its predecessor, but it was 2 inches longer (188 inches total length), 0.4 inch wider (74.4 inches), and 1.1 inches lower (50.1 inches) than the first-generation model. It had a wider track width by 1.7 inches out front and 0.5 inch in rear, and (as planned) its doors were 5 inches longer.

The second-generation Camaro continued the tradition of offering multiple engine and trim packages for would-be consumers. The base-model Camaro came standard with a 250-ci 6-cylinder engine and included baby-Moon-like hubcaps, exposed flat black windshield wipers, bright single bezels around each headlamp assembly, and a straight-across bumper. If the 350-ci engine was selected as an alternate to the standard six, the car was fitted with unique engine identification plates on each fender.

RPO Z21 Trim Package

For an additional $52.70, consumers could order a Camaro with the optional Z21 trim package, which included bright moldings for the roof gutter, the trailing edge of the hood, and an additional trim ring around each of the four taillamp assemblies. It also included color-matched body handles.

RPO Z22 RS Package

The Rally Sport (RS) trim package (Z22) was available for an additional $168.55. The RS trim included the Z21 upgrades,

Camaros equipped with the Rally Sport (RS) option (RPO Z22) featured a distinctive front end/bumper treatment, round front parking lights, hidden wipers, and other assorted trim. The RS package could be added to any model of Camaro. When combined with an SS, the car was badged as an RS/SS (as seen here) or as an RS/Z28 when combined with the Z28 package. (Photo Courtesy General Motors LLC)

plus it included a free-standing grille, a color-matched urethane grille frame, chrome bumperettes, parking lamps mounted between the headlights and the grille, hidden wipers, and special "RS" badging on the fenders.

RPO Z27 Super Sport Package

For those consumers looking to transform their Camaro into a track-capable sports car, the Super Sport (SS) option (Z27) was offered for an extra $289.65. Unlike the earlier packages, which offered consumers upgrades solely to the car's exterior, the SS package included a 350-ci V-8 engine standard, with the option to order either the beefier L34 or L78, which were a pair of 396-ci V-8 engines.

The SS package also included a special black grille, hidden wipers, power brakes, bright engine trim, special hood insulation, 14x7-inch wheels wrapped with F 70-14 bias-belted white-letter tires, chromed dual exhaust tips, and SS badging. When consumers upgraded to the SS 396 package, they also received an upgraded F41 suspension package to accommodate the added engine weight, and their trunk lids were painted black.

The Camaro Super Sport package (RPO Z27) offered consumers improved performance and included a 300-hp Turbo-Fire 350 (L34) standard as well as an optional 350-hp (L34), 375-hp (L78), or 396-ci (displaced to 402 ci) big-block engine. The SS also received special badging on its steering wheel, fenders, and grille. (Photo Courtesy General Motors LLC)

RPO Z28 Performance Package

Lastly, the Z28 package was offered to consumers looking for a singular-purposed track car. For the 1970½ model year, the Z28 Camaro included the LT1 engine (360 hp and 380 ft-lbs of torque) that has remained one of the most coveted and sought-after engines of all time. The 1970½ Z28 Camaro was also equipped with front disc brakes, front and rear anti-roll bars, new front suspension, improved seats, and a better insulated body. An optional Turbo Hydra-Matic transmission was also offered as an option for the first time.

"The second-generation F-Body was much more of a designer's car," said Henry Haga in *The Great Camaro* by Michael Lamm. "It had the proportion, it had the dash-to-axle, it had the low cowl, and it had these things because it was specific and didn't have to share anything with any other vehicle."

The second-generation Camaro (along with the Firebird/Trans Am) has remained one of the most iconic models of the brand in its 55-plus-year history. Bill Mitchell was particularly fond of the second-generation model, and he often claimed that the key to its long-term commercial success stemmed from the decisions that were made during its initial design phase. "They ran for 10 years because I got the right dash-to-axle [and] the right cowl height," he said.

The 1970½ Camaro Z28 Special Performance Package (RPO Z28) was intended for consumers looking for serious performance from their cars. It came equipped with a 350-ci, 360-hp V-8 engine based on the Corvette's LT1 engine. (Photo Courtesy General Motors LLC)

1967 XP-873 Mini-Camaro

Notwithstanding the Camaro's near-overnight success in the mid-size sports car arena, General Motors had begun feeling the pressure from the inexpensive European and Japanese imports that now littered the U.S. automotive marketplace. Many of these cars, such as the Volkswagen Beetle, the Honda S500/600, and the Datsun 510, offered consumers fairly reliable small cars that were also exceptionally good on gas. While Chevrolet offered consumers an assortment of smaller automobiles (including the Corvair and the Nova), it had nothing that could directly compete with these imports in terms of affordability or fuel economy.

The design team in Studio X was tasked by Pete Estes and Bill Mitchell with developing the XP-873, a four-passenger Mini-Camaro that was intended to help expand the Corvair name into its own marque. The project was helmed by designers Roy Lonberger and Geza Loczi with input from Larry Shinoda and (occasionally) Dave Holls. (Photo Courtesy General Motors LLC)

This is an early, full-size, side-view tape drawing of the XP-873 Mini-Camaro GT concept as a two-door hatchback coupe. Interestingly, the hatchback became a standard feature on the third-generation Camaro 15 years after it was first proposed as an option on this concept. (Photo Courtesy General Motors LLC)

In early 1967, a young designer named Roy Lonberger from Haga's Chevy Studio Two sketched an automobile design that he dubbed the "Mini-Camaro GT." At the direction of Chevrolet President Pete Estes, Bill Mitchell reassigned Lonberger to his Studio X, along with fellow Designer Geza Loczi, to develop Lonberger's Mini-Camaro GT design (now officially designated project XP-873) into a miniaturized coupe that could compete against the VW Beetle.

This early rendering of the XP-873 by GM Designer Geza Loczi depicts the XP-837 with retractable headlights. Much of the early design work on the second-generation Camaro (including the Mini-Camaro GT) was borrowed from the nearly completed third-generation Corvette, which, like the XP-873, was designed in Bill Mitchell's Studio X. (Photo Courtesy General Motors LLC)

Designers Geza Luczi and Roy Lonberger continued the hatchback motif throughout the evolution of the XP-873. Its taillights, on the other hand, were revised repeatedly from the teardrop design shown here to a more conventional pair of taillight lenses somewhat reminiscent of those found on the original Ford Mustang (though oriented horizontally instead of vertically). (Photo Courtesy General Motors LLC)

The following quote is from a 2011 interview with Roy Lonberger conducted by Susan Skarsgard (Global Industrial Design Manager) and Christo Datini (Chief Archivist, GM Design Archives) at the GM Heritage Center:

"It was intended to be the size of (and cost less to manufacture than) the Volkswagen Beetle," Lonberger said. "Fellow designer Geza Loczi was assigned to the studio, along with several modelers, and a tech stylist. Larry Shinoda would consult, and occasionally Dave Holls would stop by. As before, concepts were presented weekly as full clay models in the courtyard of the dome, and all design decisions were made by Mr. Mitchell."

Mitchell insisted that the XP-873 would accommodate four or five passengers. Given its compact size along with its low, swept-back design, most of the concept models ended up being more of a 2+2 design instead of a genuine five-passenger car. Early iterations of the car included a massive back hatch that extended well into the rear quarter panels. As the design evolved, a single-piece, forward-opening front-end bonnet (comprised of the hood panel, fascia, and front fenders) was briefly considered.

A pair of single, exposed-but-recessed headlight assemblies appeared on later-design iterations of the XP-873. Although this rendering still depicted a sharp-edged beltline and Coke-bottle front fenders like those found on the Corvette, the design work introduced on the Mini-Camaro established motifs that would be echoed in other GM designs throughout the 1970s and beyond. (Photo Courtesy General Motors LLC)

Unknown to Lonberger at the time, Mitchell was directing the XP-873's development to help resurrect and expand the Corvair brand into a stand-alone marque under the Chevrolet banner. Even with the criticisms and growing safety concerns circling the Corvair in the mid-1960s, there were still many within General Motors who believed in the brand's long-term viability. What's more, Mitchell (along with designer Shinoda) designed the popular 1962 Monza GT Corvair concept, and it was believed by all involved (save Lonberger) that the XP-873 Mini-Camaro might become the fully realized version of that earlier concept.

As the design work continued, a fair amount of friction developed among Mitchell, Loczi, Lonberger, and Chief Designer Irv Rybicki. Each had his own viewpoint on how the XP-873 was to evolve. While Loczi and Lonberger envisioned a more aggressive-looking automobile synonymous with the Camaro, Mitchell and Rybicki were pushing for a car built upon the popularity of the other Corvair models.

> "A YOUNG DESIGNER NAMED ROY LONBERGER FROM HAGA'S CHEVY STUDIO TWO SKETCHED AN AUTOMOBILE DESIGN THAT HE DUBBED THE 'MINI-CAMARO GT.'"

An early full-size clay model (circa March 1967) of the XP-873 is parked next to a Volkswagen Beetle in the courtyard of Studio X. Chevrolet's Pete Estes wanted to develop a Camaro that was the same size as (and cost less than) the Beetle to help General Motors compete with the smaller, less expensive cars routinely being imported from Europe and Asia. (Photo Courtesy General Motors LLC)

Though considerably smaller than the first- and second-generation Camaros, the XP-873 GT shared many of the same design motifs as its larger counterparts. Lonberger and Loczi borrowed elements from Jaguar, Aston Martin, and the second-generation Camaro clay models (still under development) while creating the look of the Mini-Camaro. (Photo Courtesy General Motors LLC)

Although the Mini-Camaro never evolved past the clay modelling phase, many of the styling elements showcased on the car were repurposed and used on other GM models. For example, an elongated version of its taillight assembly was first introduced on the 1970 Pontiac Firebird and, later, on the 1974 Camaro. (Photo Courtesy General Motors LLC)

Chevrolet experienced a notable year-over-year drop-off in total Corvair sales between 1965 and 1967 after the publication of consumer advocate Ralph Nader's book *Unsafe at Any Speed* in November 1965. The book's fist chapter "The Sporty Corvair" outlined the serious dangers of the Corvair's swing-axle suspension. It also inferred that General Motors had not taken the proper measures to correct this serious design

This was one of the final concept models of the XP-873 on display in the courtyard of GM's design studios. As noted earlier, the profile of the Mini-Camaro shared more than a passing resemblance with the 1972 Aston Martin Vantage, although its front grille and headlight assemblies were more closely related to the Jaguar E-Type. There is no denying that Chevrolet "borrowed" many of the Mini-Camaro's exterior styling elements while developing the 1970 Chevy Vega. (Photo Courtesy General Motors LLC)

flaw. Although a 1965 redesign of the Corvair addressed this issue, the Corvair's reputation had been irrevocably damaged.

The XP-873 project was summarily canceled in the summer of 1967 once General Motors elected to discontinue the Corvair platform entirely.

Interestingly, the XP-873 Mini-Camaro resurfaced a few years later, at least from a design perspective, as the XP-973 Chevrolet Vega. While their development was separated by nearly a half decade, there's no denying that the Vega shares more than a passing resemblance to Lonberger's Mini-Camaro concept design.

1970 Camaro Kammback

The 1970 Camaro Kammback (or more accurately, the Kammback F-Body) was a concept created by GM Designer Bob Ackerman in the late 1960s. Ackerman's design was based on a "shooting brake" architecture that he'd first observed on Aston Martin automobiles of that era, and one that he started experimenting with in his own design work while attending the ArtCenter College of Design.

After graduation, Ackerman gained employment as an automotive designer at the Chevy Studio Two. Ackerman joined Henry Haga's team in August 1967 and was tasked with cleaning up the look of the 1969 Camaro. In addition, he helped develop the bodystyling for the second-generation Camaro, which was to be introduced as a 1970 model. It was during this

A full-size clay model of the 1970 Kammback Camaro is shown on display in the courtyard of the GM design studios. Although this model wears Camaro badges, the Kammback F-Body treatment was seriously considered for both the Camaro and the Pontiac Firebird. (Photo Courtesy General Motors LLC)

Early color rendering of the Kammback Camaro by GM Designer (and Director of Design for General Motors of Europe) Dick Ruzzin. Ruzzin's design was an evolution of Ackerman's original sketch (not shown) depicting a non-specific sports car (Camaro or Corvette) with a pair of Coke-bottle fenders and a dramatic, swept-back Kamm-tail assembly. (Photo Courtesy General Motors LLC)

time that Ackerman, recounting his earlier fascination with the shooting-brake concept, first sketched a Camaro with its quarter glass rolled into the roof and touting a Kammback profile.

For reference, a "Kammback" rear end (also known as both a "Kamm tail" and a "K-tail") is an automotive engineering element first introduced in the 1930s by German aerodynamicist Dr. Wundibald Kamm. Simply put, the rear of the car slopes downward before ending abruptly with a near-vertical trailing edge. Dr. Kamm successfully demonstrated that this type of rear end minimized drag while also maintaining a practical profile.

Impressed by Ackerman's illustration, Haga encouraged the young designer to create a full-size tape drawing of the car. Ackerman was happy to oblige. He immediately set to work on the project and soon decided that a full rendering of the car (and not just a tape drawing) would provide the detail needed to communicate his vision of the car more accurately. Anxious that interest in his design might wane if he took too long to complete it, Ackerman decided he'd complete his rendering in a single day and present the finished drawing to Haga the following morning. He worked tirelessly until 1:30 a.m. and then returned to the studio a few hours later to witness people's reaction to his design.

In an article published on the website "Deans Garage," Ackerman commented on the response his car received: "Hank's reaction was worth the lack of sleep. His first excited words were all expletives, as he ran to the phone to call Dave Holls, executive director. Holls had the same reaction and put a call into Bill Mitchell's office . . . . After viewing the rendering, (Bill) ordered that work should start on a full-size clay (model)."

Development of a Kammback Camaro clay model began at once. The model incorporated the same front-end styling previously introduced on Bill Mitchell's all-new, as-yet-unreleased Rally Sport (RS) Camaro design. Eager and excited to see his design come to life, Ackerman (who had previously worked as a technical stylist on other clay models prior to his becoming a designer) spent a considerable amount of his time assisting the clay sculptors with many of the more technical aspects of the car.

Ackerman's Kammback Camaro received so much favorable attention that a significant portion of Chevrolet's Studio Two was allocated for its continued development. The studio became known as "the Kammback Studio" by the designers working on the project. The models seen here show the evolution of the rear hatch assembly. The car on the left featured the narrower upper hatch with fixed taillamps, while the example on the right introduced a single-piece hatch assembly that included the taillamps and rear decklid panel. (Photo Courtesy General Motors LLC)

The full-scale fiberglass model of the Kammback Camaro was finished in a yellow-gold paint and was fitted with Borrani wire wheels. The completed model sat just 50.1 inches high, which is more than 3 inches lower than the current-generation Camaro. (Photo Courtesy General Motors LLC)

As the model evolved, GM executives decided that a Firebird version of Ackerman's Kammback concept should be developed simultaneously, so they directed John DeLorean, Pontiac's general manager, to visit Haga's design studio. Mitchell was furious when he learned that DeLorean was paying them a visit. He instructed the plaster shop to develop a "fake" front end casting to conceal the clay model's Rally Sport fascia.

Preliminary aerodynamic studies of the Kammback F-Body were performed by Styling Aero Department Manager Kent Kelly. Kelly's work indicated that the Kammback had a lower coefficient of drag (CD) than the coupe. This was a significant discovery for two reasons: 1.) a lower CD meant the car could slip through the air more easily and 2.) lower drag meant better fuel economy, which equaled consumer savings at the gas pump.

Kelly's favorable evaluation of the Kammback's aerodynamics further increased interest in the car's development, and it wasn't long before the employees of Haga's Chevy Studio Two started calling it the "Kammback Studio." There was even a brief period where Ackerman and Mitchell considered developing a GT version of the car, but that idea was abandoned when former race-car driver and team owner Roger Penske campaigned an American Motors Javelin for the 1970 Trans-Am season.

A fiberglass model of the Kammback Camaro was created from the full-size clay model. The car shared the same RS

The profile of the Kammback Camaro includes a slight-but-notable arching taper from the windshield line back. The arched roofline was developed to improve fuel efficiency, which had been a common issue in traditional flat, squared-off station wagons. (Photo Courtesy General Motors LLC)

Although the Kammback Camaro was always meant to include a hatch assembly to allow access to the car's rear storage compartment, this early model of the car also included a rear fascia assembly that contained the taillights and license-plate housing. Its presence created a physical hurdle when attempting to enter the car from the back. (Photo Courtesy General Motors LLC)

The interior of the Kammback Camaro received minor updates from the production model. While the gauge cluster and controls remained mostly unchanged, the Kammback was equipped with a steering wheel from the Chevy Caprice, wood-grain trim, and restyled bright yellow vinyl finishes on the interior door panels and seats. (Photo Courtesy General Motors LLC)

Allegedly based on Bill Mitchell's desire for his dogs to have easier access to the car's rear compartment, the Kammback's rear hatch was reworked to include the taillights and license-plate housing as part of the assembly. This enabled everything above the rear bumper to open as a single unit and allowed the easier ingress/egress that Mitchell had been looking for. (Photo Courtesy General Motors LLC)

The taillight assemblies on the fiberglass model were eventually redesigned and relocated to the C-pillars. As before, a concerted effort had been placed on maximizing accessibility of the car's rear compartment. However, their relocation in this instance was due to federal requirements that mandated the placement of taillight assemblies on a fixed section of the vehicle. (Photo Courtesy General Motors LLC)

front end and featured a rectangular, V-shaped, egg-crate grille framed by a single round headlight at each corner of the front fascia. A wraparound chrome bumper divided the grille into upper and lower sections and added to the car's aggressive, sporty look.

The Kammback F-Body sat just 50.1 inches tall (more than 3 inches shorter than the sixth-generation Camaro) at its highest point, which happened to be along the roofline just behind the A-pillars. From there, the roofline sloped back toward the rear of the car before ending abruptly at the Kammback's top-hinged rear hatch/rear window assembly. Framing the back end of the car was a pair of fixed round taillights and a second full-length (though much less dramatic) chrome bumper.

Chevrolet commissioned a series of drawings/paintings that demonstrated the versatility of the Kammback Camaro to would-be consumers. This first image by artist Bill Molzon depicts a pair of skiers headed to the slopes. While creative marketing, it does pose the question of whether General Motors figured out a way to make a Camaro drivable in the snow. (Photo Courtesy General Motors LLC)

This rendering by George Gallion depicts the Kammback Camaro being used for a run to the grocery store, which once more demonstrated its versatility as a practical-but-fun family car. While this type of marketing might be considered sexist today, it helped attract female buyers in the 1970s. (Photo Courtesy General Motors LLC)

From snow to surf, the versatility of the Kammback Camaro was to be one of its strongest selling points. The fiberglass model of the car was frequently displayed at car shows and marketing events with a pair of surfboards strapped to its roof. (Photo Courtesy General Motors LLC)

It has been reported that during the Kammback Camaro's development, the rear, round taillights were eventually removed from the fiberglass model and replaced with rectangular taillamps mounted in the car's C-pillars. This was allegedly done at Bill Mitchell's direction. He wanted to increase the size of the rear hatch opening so that his dogs could more easily access the rear compartment.

The completed fiberglass model was painted light gold and fitted with a set of Borrani wire wheels. It was also equipped with a ski rack and a pair of skis (mounted backward to better align with the car's profile) to showcase the car's versatility.

Both Chevrolet and Pontiac management wanted to move forward with a production version of the Kammback F-Body. Ironically, it was their combined interest in this concept that brought its production to an untimely end. The Camaro and Firebird models, while similar in appearance, used none of the same body panels. The character lines on each car were separated by more than 1 inch, and the Firebird included a "bone line" (a hard, often sharp line that runs the length of most modern automobiles) that was absent on the Camaro.

A production budget was developed that allotted for (and required) the use of common door and quarter panels on both models. Had the Chevrolet and Pontiac leadership been able to strike a compromise in the design of each car, the Kammback F-Body may well have moved to production. Unfortunately, neither was willing to change their car's outward appearance. Chevrolet management considered producing the car as a Camaro-only model, but the cost of the extra tooling required for its production was deemed too expensive, and the project was abandoned.

A new Kammback station wagon concept (based solely on the Pontiac Firebird this time) was originally introduced by designer Jerry Brochstein at the 1977 Chicago Auto Show as a potential 1978 production model. Like its predecessor, the

In 1977, Pontiac developed a Kammback version of the Firebird called the K-Back concept. The K-Back was designed by GM Studio Stylist Jerry Brochstein. Pininfarina built two prototypes based on Brochstein's design. (Photo Courtesy General Motors LLC)

The 1977 Pontiac K-Back Firebird concept toured the auto show circuit for several years and was generally well received by enthusiasts. Unfortunately, as with the earlier Kammback Camaro, the car's high production costs proved to be too expensive for the niche market it was intended to fill, and future development was permanently discontinued. (Photo Courtesy General Motors LLC)

Kammback Firebird used a two-door station wagon configuration, but this version featured a pair of gull-wing-style rear windows on either side of its cargo area. Bill Mitchell, in one of his final acts as GM's vice president of design, approved the construction of two Kammback concept models from a pair of production Firebirds. The cars, which became known as both the "Type K" and the "K-Back" Firebirds, were assembled by Pininfarina in Italy. One was finished in gold paint with a beige interior, while the other was painted silver with a red interior.

It is unclear what happened to the gold Kammback Firebird model, although it was reportedly destroyed by General Motors after a brief stint on the auto show circuit. The silver car, on the other hand, eventually received an updated front end from a 1979 Trans Am. It continued to gain popularity on the auto show circuit and after making an appearance on the *Rockford Files* television series.

Given its popularity, it seemed certain the car would be developed into a production model. That is, until it was identified that General Motors would need to sell the cars for approximately $25,000 each. Because of the car's high cost, combined with the fact that both Chevrolet and Pontiac were well into the development of a third-generation F-Body model, General Motors elected instead to abandon the Kammback program for a second time.

1971–1973 Can-Am ZL1 Camaro Berlinetta

Not long after the launch of the second-generation Camaro, Bill Mitchell opted to have one of the early preproduction models personalized to his unique specifications. Mitchell ordered the creation of numerous custom automobiles (many of them Corvettes) over the course of his career at General Motors. He enjoyed these cars for his personal use while simultaneously using them to showcase the latest styling and technology in GM automobiles.

Developed under the direction of Bill Mitchell, the Camaro Berlinetta concept underwent several transformations during its almost-decade-long development. This iteration, which was unveiled in 1973, established many of the design motifs for the 1978 Camaro. (Photo Courtesy General Motors LLC)

1971

This Camaro, which Mitchell branded as a "Berlinetta" early on (likely due to his personal affinity for European sports cars) was equipped with a Corvette-derived, all-aluminum block, 427-ci ZL1 engine paired to an automatic transmission. Its exterior was fitted with molded front and rear lower fender spats, a custom-built LT1-style hood, a covered/concealed hood-mounted tachometer (repurposed from a Pontiac GTO), and European-style fog lamps, the last of which was a favorite styling element of Mitchell's. The car rode on a set of custom-designed, crossed-spoke steel wheels. A version of these same wheels would be used on the 1978 Camaro Berlinetta production model.

The word "Berlinetta" is Italian for "little saloon." The term became synonymous with sports/race cars in the early 1950s due in large part to the popularity of the 1952 Ferrari 225 S Berlinetta.

The Camaro's front grille and rear taillamp panel were each fitted with special badges denoting the car as a Can-Am ZL1 model. Both rectangular badges depicted the flags of

Mitchell's Berlinetta was constructed to his personal specifications from a preproduction, second-generation Camaro. In its earliest form, the majority of its modifications were found beneath its hood, including its all-aluminum block, 427-ci engine. It received a custom fabricated hood with a hood-mounted tachometer. (Photo Courtesy General Motors LLC)

Known for constantly revising and redefining his own designs, Mitchell returned the Camaro ZL1 Berlinetta to his design studios. There, it was fitted with integrated front and rear fender skirts that were molded into exterior body panels (versus the bolt-on skirts found on many late-model Z28 Camaros and Pontiac Trans Ams.) (Photo Courtesy General Motors LLC)

Mitchell had special badging added to the car's front grille and rear decklid assemblies that identified the car as a "CAN-AM ZL-1." The badging was intended to pay homage to the Can-Am race series. (Photo Courtesy General Motors LLC)

In addition to its front and rear "CAN-AM" badging, Mitchell insisted on having special "Berlinetta" badging placed on the car. Mitchell selected the Berlinetta moniker in reference to his decades-long passion for European sports cars. (Berlinetta is a common Italian term used to identify sports coupes). Prior to joining General Motors, Mitchell had been closely tied to the Automobile Racing Club of America (ARCA), later known as the Sports Car Club of America (SCCA), and had frequently raced European sports cars. (Photo Courtesy General Motors LLC)

Mitchell originally selected Mulsanne Blue as the paint color for his 1971 Camaro Berlinetta. This color choice was interesting given that Mitchell's preferred color palette was traditionally hues of red and/or silver. As we'll see in the following images, he returned to his traditional paint colors with the next reimagining of the Berlinetta, which took place the following year. (Photo Courtesy General Motors LLC)

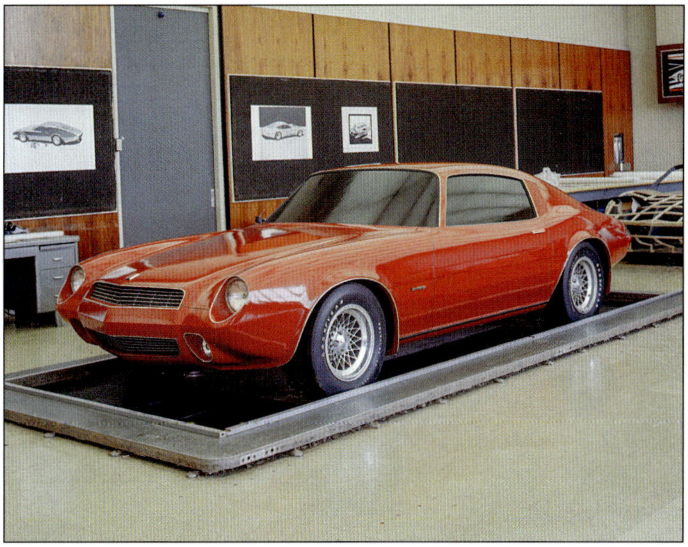

In 1972, Mitchell's studio designed a single-piece, urethane front-fascia assembly. This significant update to the Camaro's styling placed the steel bumper behind the fascia, eliminating the need for the Camaro's exposed two-piece split bumperettes. Though delayed by production issues, the popularity of this design found its way onto the production-model Camaros in 1974. (Photo Courtesy General Motors LLC)

Canada and the United States, followed by the "CAN-AM" designation to the right of the flags. Below each, a separate ZL1 badge had been installed. Although the car was not intended for the racetrack, the unique moniker paid homage to the Can-Am race series, for which the ZL1 engine had originally been developed.

Mitchell's Can-Am ZL1 Berlinetta Camaro concept was finished in Mulsanne Blue paint with matching interior trim. It toured the auto show circuit as a 1971 model-year concept car. In early 1972, it returned to Chevy's design studios for several Mitchell-directed modifications.

1972 and 1973

To give the car a more swept-back appearance, Mitchell's design studio created a new Endura front fascia/bumper with a sloped grille and sloped headlamp assemblies. The single-piece fascia was constructed of a soft urethane material. In lieu of chrome bumperettes (like those found on the production-model Camaro), the updated ZL1 concept had concealed metal bumpers mounted behind/beneath the fascia. Although manufacturing costs prohibited the advancement of Endura fascia as a factory option for several more years, a less-complex version of the sloped grille was first commercially produced for the 1974 Camaro.

Mitchell's Can-Am Camaro concept was overhauled again in 1973. This time, the car was fitted with an updated roof assembly and wraparound rear glass. It also featured a more streamlined hood with a pair of integrated pods that replaced the original single tachometer assembly. As before, the car was badged with the Can-Am and ZL1 badges. Unlike its predecessor, this version also wore "Berlinetta" badges on its broad B-pillars.

Moving to the back, the car's factory-installed round rear taillights were replaced with grooved rectangular lenses that framed the back license plate and wrapped around the rear corners of the car before tapering to a point along the Camaro's character line. Aesthetically, the ZL1's taillight lens assemblies were similar in appearance to those introduced on the 1974 Pontiac Firebird/Trans Am models. A shortened version of the Can-Am's taillight lenses was also included on all 1974–1978 production-model Camaros. A longer, three-tone (red, amber, and white) lens was introduced for the 1979 model year, and these more closely matched the length and unique contour of Mitchell's earlier design.

Like the front end, the rear fascia was comprised of a single-piece Endura bumper/fascia assembly that was far more subtle than anything found on most cars from that era (due mostly to government guidelines that regulated specific bumper standards on production vehicles). Although it was probably not legal, the rear fascia added to the aerodynamic look of the car. A pair of rectangular exhaust tips, similar to those used on the third-generation Corvette, were one of the only features that broke up the otherwise fluid lines of the car's back end.

Bill Mitchell: GM's Second Vice President of Styling

In the history of automotive design, there are few stylists in the world more celebrated than Bill Mitchell. Over the course of his 40-plus-year career with General Motors, his signature designs were directly responsible for many of the company's most iconic automobiles, including the 1955–1957 Bel Air, the 1961–1976 Corvette, and the 1970–1981 Camaro. His work directly influenced the creation of more than 72.5 million GM production automobiles, and many of his signature styling elements can still be found on GM's current lineup of automobiles, especially the Chevy Corvette and Camaro models.

Bill Mitchell remains one of the most prolific automobile designers of all time, spending the entirety of his 42-year career at General Motors. During his tenure there, he was responsible for designing or influencing the design of more than 72.5 million production vehicles built by the automaker between 1935 and 1985. (Photo Courtesy General Motors LLC)

A young Bill Mitchell is shown working as a graphic designer. His artistic talents combined with his passion for fast cars helped launch his career into high gear, especially after a friend took notice of Mitchell's automobile designs and presented his work to Harley Earl at General Motors. (Photo Courtesy General Motors LLC)

Born the son of a small-town Buick dealer and automotive enthusiast from Greenville, Pennsylvania, William L. "Bill" Mitchell literally grew up surrounded by automobiles. From an early age, young Bill had shown an interest and aptitude for drawing cars, especially those of the sporty variety. By the time he was 10, he developed an obsession with race cars and driving fast.

On July 2, 1927, 15-year-old Mitchell secured his first job in the art department of the Baron Collier agency in New York City. Working part time at first, he built a design portfolio that captured the attention of the company's owner. After graduating from high school, he was offered a full-time position at the agency. He also enrolled in the Art Students League of New York to further improve his skills as an artist.

While working at the agency, Mitchell met and eventually befriended Sam and Miles Collier, Barron Collier's sons. The brothers introduced Mitchell to European-style road racing, a sport they'd already been promoting for years across the United States. Together, Mitchell and the Barron brothers raced whenever/wherever they could, including at the family's Pocantico Hills Estate. In 1933, the brothers established the Automobile Racing Club of America (ARCA), which became more famously known as the Sports Car Club of America (SCCA) a few years later.

When he wasn't actively driving a sports car around the racetrack, Mitchell sketched the beautiful European-built racers, all the while pondering why American automobile manufacturers had yet to build anything comparable to the compact, sporty cars that repeatedly roared past him. It was this question that led Mitchell to begin designing his own sport and race cars.

Mitchell's work caught the attention of Walter Carey, an insurance executive who worked with the Collier family and who also happened to be a friend of Harley Earl, GM's first vice president of styling. Carey shared some of Mitchell's work with Earl. Earl was impressed with the young artist's abilities. In December 1935, he offered Mitchell a position in his Art and Colour Section at General Motors.

Mitchell quickly ascended through the ranks in his early years at General Motors. By 1938, he was named chief engineer of the Cadillac Studio. It was in this capacity that he designed the 1938 Cadillac 60 Special, which was the first "youthful" Cadillac in the history of the brand. While GM's brass loved everything about his latest addition to the Cadillac lineup, it left Mitchell longing to return to the sports cars of his youth.

A fortuitous business trip with Harley Earl in the summer of 1941 introduced Mitchell to several independent coach builders, all of whom were fabricating and selling American-made race

As GM's second vice president of Design and Styling, Bill Mitchell transformed the Corvette program by creating a series of radical concept cars that included the Sting Ray Racer, the Mako Shark, and the Manta Ray. He did the same for the Camaro nearly a decade later when he established the guidelines from which the styling of the second-generation model would evolve. (Photo Courtesy General Motors LLC)

Originally dubbed the "Madam X," Mitchell's Pontiac "Phantom" was surreptitiously developed in the basement of the ultra-secret Studio X. Mitchell recruited Designer Bill Davis to develop the car as an homage to Mitchell's decades-long career at General Motors. Mitchell had hoped the concept would be fully developed by General Motors as a retirement present to himself. (Photo Courtesy General Motors LLC)

cars! What's more, the demand for these cars was overwhelming. How was it that none of the major manufacturers in Detroit had even considered building a sports car when the sport of racing cars was thriving on both coasts?

Despite these frustrations, Mitchell's career continued to flourish. During World War II, he produced several U.S. Navy training manuals for General Motors, including one that taught pilots how to fly their aircraft solely using their instruments. After the war, he returned to Cadillac and successfully ran the design department there throughout the remainder of the 1940s.

On May 1, 1954, Harley Earl named Mitchell GM's director of styling. Earl had developed the Chevy Corvette a year earlier, and he needed Mitchell to manage the design programs for Chevrolet's 1955 lineup so that Earl could keep his focus on the continued development of his two-seat sports car. Additionally, Earl was nearing retirement age, and Mitchell proved he had the goods to succeed Earl as GM's next vice president of design. When Harley Earl retired on December 1, 1958, he named Mitchell as his successor.

In the years that followed Mitchell's promotion to vice president of GM's Styling Department, Mitchell worked to differentiate his automotive styling cues from the design motifs made famous by Earl. He replaced the large tailfins and excessive chrome flourishes from yesteryear with automobile designs that were more streamlined in appearance and more aerodynamic on the open road.

A chance encounter with a mako shark while on a fishing trip in the Bahamas provided Mitchell with the inspiration, and the future look, of both his Mako Shark concept car and the 1963 Corvette split-window coupe. The cars, which were mostly designed by Larry Shinoda (with direction from Mitchell), became the first cars to feature the aggressive and muscular Coke-bottle styling that became synonymous with many of GM's cars from that era, including the first Camaros.

In response to the 1973–1974 energy crisis, Mitchell led GM's styling and design efforts to downsize many of its mid- and full-size automobiles. He remained involved with both the Chevy Corvette and Camaro programs for the remainder of his career with General Motors, often using his influence to defend the continuance of Chevrolet's V-8 powerplant program, both as the only viable engine for the Corvette and as a must-have option for the Camaro.

The last car he designed for General Motors was the 1977 Pontiac Phantom concept. It has been alleged that he conceived the car as a retirement gift to himself. Unfortunately, the car was never equipped with a powertrain. The Pontiac Phantom is currently on display at the Sloan Museum in Flint, Michigan.

Bill Mitchell retired from General Motors in July 1977. In the years following his career at General Motors, Mitchell opened "William L. Mitchell Design," a private design consulting firm that he successfully operated from 1977 to 1984. On September 12, 1988, Bill Mitchell passed away at the age of 76 from heart failure at William Beaumont Hospital in Royal Oak, Michigan.

According to automotivehalloffame.org, the man responsible for the Corvette Stingray, Oldsmobile Toronado, Buick Riviera, Pontiac Firebird, and Chevy Camaro operated under a single guiding principal: "It is a sin to design an ugly car. The cost of designing, engineering, and manufacturing are virtually the same: beautiful or ugly."

Mitchell's Can-Am Camaro underwent one final overhaul in 1973. The urethane fascia was redesigned with squared-off headlamps, its round taillights were replaced with longer rectangular assemblies, and its upper assembly was replaced with an updated roof assembly that included a wraparound rear window and narrower B-pillars. (Photo Courtesy General Motors LLC)

The 1973 Berlinetta Can-Am Camaro is shown parked in the courtyard outside of GM's Design Dome in Warren, Michigan. Now finished in a deep crimson with gold accents, it served as one of Mitchell's personal cars until his retirement from General Motors in 1977. (Photo Courtesy General Motors LLC)

The interior of Mitchell's Can-Am Camaro featured a fusion of Pontiac and Chevrolet design elements. It used a stock Camaro dashboard and instrument cluster, but it also included a Pontiac Trans Am steering wheel. Additionally, the shifter, seats, and interior door panels were updated to Mitchell's unique specifications. (Photo Courtesy General Motors LLC)

The heavily modified ZL1 Camaro Berlinetta concept was repainted a brilliant, translucent crimson, which was one of Bill Mitchell's favorite colors. It was adorned with subtle gold pinstriping around its grille, headlamp assemblies, front fender skirts, and more. Additional gold pinstriping was also installed along its character line. The gold trim culminated in a flourish of pinstriping on the car's hood and rear decklid assemblies.

The ZL1's interior was also reimagined for the updated concept car. Wrapped almost entirely in faux leathers/vinyl dyed Neutral Grey, the interior borrowed from the interiors of both the late-model, second-generation Camaros and Firebirds. It used a factory, three-spoke Firebird steering wheel paired with the traditional Camaro dashboard and instrument cluster. New appointments, such as deeper-set bucket seats and European-inspired map pockets, gave the interior a more sophisticated flare, which was Mitchell's intent.

Camaro Berlinetta

Mitchell's unique Camaro concept toured the auto show circuit for much of the 1977 season. This time, however, special focus was paid to the car's upgraded interior and exterior. While the Can-Am badging was still present, greater emphasis was placed on the "Berlinetta" moniker.

The reason? Chevrolet was in the process of developing

The taillights on the Can-Am Berlinetta were a fusion of the stock Camaro and Firebird assemblies. While the taillamps featured a wraparound outer corner similar to the lamps on the Camaro, the horizontally striped lenses shared more than a passing resemblance with the taillights on the late-model Firebirds and Trans Ams. (Photo Courtesy General Motors LLC)

a production-version of the Camaro that was to be branded the "Camaro Berlinetta." Unlike the SS and Z28 models, both of which promised blistering speed and unbridled horsepower, the Berlinetta models were specifically targeted at customers (especially women) who wanted a quieter, more luxurious driving experience. While a bit of an outdated marketing strategy by today's standards, the second- and third-generation Berlinetta Camaros were equipped with more luxurious trim, softer suspension, and (presumably) more sound insulation for a quieter ride.

The Camaro Berlinetta went on sale as part of the 1978-model lineup and was produced for the duration of the second-generation era. A third-generation Camaro Berlinetta was introduced in 1982 as part of the next-generation Camaro lineup (which will be discussed in Chapter 3).

The 1973 version of Mitchell's ZL1 Berlinetta concept laid much of the groundwork for the 1978 Camaro. In Michael Lamm's book *The Great Camaro*, Chevrolet designer Jerry Palmer explained, "Bill Mitchell's ZL1 Berlinetta show car . . . had the soft front and rear, (which) proved to be a very useful tool for doing the 1978 models—not only in design but also to help sell the ideas to our management. The 1973 Berlinetta became sort of a theme car for the 1978 model. Not that it was initially intended to come out that late. We'd originally hoped to have it out for 1976, then 1977, and we finally made it in 1978."

Although its exact whereabouts are unknown, it is believed that Bill Mitchell's ZL1 Camaro concept car still exists today.

The 1972 TASC4GT Concept

The following narrative about the General Motors "X" Car program, the TASC program, and especially about the TASC4GT, evolved from a collection of memoirs originally written by Dick Ruzzin, former chief designer of GM's International Studio, and Gary Witzenburg writing for *Collectable Automobile* magazine.

To appreciate and understand the purpose behind GM's Total Automotive System Concept (TASC) and X-car programs, it is first necessary to review the global factors that are attributed to their creation and development.

In the late 1960s (and into the early 1970s), many of the world's top oil-producing/oil-extracting countries had reached peak production. These production peaks, which included Germany in 1966, Venezuela and the United States in 1970, and Canada in 1974, created spikes in oil prices that adversely impacted financial markets in other parts of the world.

Not long after reaching its own oil production peak, the United States began to suffer the same per-barrel price hikes as its dependency on imported oil increased. In addition to increasing oil prices, the Arab members of the Organization of Petroleum Exporting Countries (OPEC) had begun threatening an oil embargo that had the potential to reduce/stop the flow of oil into the United States.

It was for these reasons that Clare MacKichan (then director of the Overseas Design Studio) along with executive engineers Jim Juif and Chuck Torner began campaigning GM management in the winter of 1969 to re-evaluate the current production lineup in favor of manufacturing more fuel-efficient vehicles. Except for the Chevrolet Chevette, an Opel-derived automobile, GM's domestic fuel-efficient offerings were extremely limited. It left many (including MacKichan) worried about the company's long-term viability in the marketplace if a genuine fuel crisis occurred.

The pending fuel crisis threat was formally addressed in an internal report that was presented during a GM European Strategy Board meeting in Brazil. It outlined the looming concerns being threatened by the Middle East oil cartels, and it detailed how these fuel supply shortages could adversely impact the company financially. The message was clear: it was time for a change.

During his time as the European director of design, MacKichan earned the respect of his German colleagues. Even as he prepared to return to the United States, he was asked to remain involved with the design group and to collaborate on the advancement of smaller fuel-efficient vehicles for each of the GM marques.

Now back in the United States and serving under Bill Mitchell as GM's executive in charge of the Advanced Design Studios (which included GM's Oversea Studio), MacKichan

This is the full-scale clay model of the TASC4GT concept coupe. This image was taken on the viewing road at GM's design studios in Detroit shortly before the model was destroyed. (Photo Courtesy General Motors LLC)

developed a new internal design staff training program aimed at establishing innovative design criteria for the evolving automotive market. Under the watchful eye of Ed Cole and with support from Mitchell, MacKichan's efforts quickly gained traction within the design studios. It wasn't long before others, including the Chevrolet division, the engineering staff, GM's research laboratories, and GM Europe, started supporting it as well.

Around that same time, a new group at GM Design was formed that could leverage customer input to influence design and marketing. Under the direction of Ken Pickering, this group gathered data by hosting customer-attended product clinics. Prior to the formation of Pickering's group, another group had been established within the design studios that evaluated and applied the latest aerodynamics to many of GM's products. It was from the formation of these groups that the first TASC programs evolved. Many advancements—including reductions in drag, engine cooling, water management, and sound reduction—were invented through these programs, and many of these technological advancements are still used today.

In May 1971, MacKichan instructed the engineering and design staffs at the Overseas Studio to begin work on the TASC concept, which General Motors originally called the World Car program. As development of the World Car got underway, its design scope expanded rapidly into a multi-vehicle platform, all of which shared one of three different body widths and a variety of different lengths. Each version would use the same space-saving, fuel-efficient, front-wheel-drive engine, along with a variety of other interchangeable braking, suspension, and steering components.

According to a January 21, 2011, article by GM Designer Dick Ruzzin, as the TASC Program gained momentum, GM executives began looking at it as the "proposed FWD International platform replacement for all GM sedans, wagons, coupes and future mini-vans and sports cars."

It was believed that the TASC program, and the X-car program that evolved from it, revolutionized the automotive development process by enabling multiple vehicles to be constructed from the same interchangeable components. Moreover, these components were inexpensive and lightweight, which also meant that the TASC cars would achieve levels of fuel economy previously unseen in GM vehicles.

Over the course of his 50-year career with General Motors, Clare MacKichan worked as an automotive designer both for Chevrolet in the United States and Opel in Germany. He was involved with many of GM's most successful marques, including the Opel GT and the Chevy Corvette. MacKichan was later promoted to executive in charge of Advanced Design and Engineering. Although he passed away in 1996, he was posthumously inducted into the Corvette Hall of Fame in 2011. (Photo Courtesy General Motors LLC)

The TASC4GT Takes Shape

About the same time that the TASC program was getting underway in the United States, GM Designer Dick Ruzzin had been tasked with developing a mid-engine, rotary-powered Opel sports car for German race car driver Erich Bitter. In May 1971, Ruzzin had started a six-month assignment at the Opel Studios in Germany to gain a greater appreciation for European design practices.

Now, with just weeks to go before he returned to the United States, he landed an exciting opportunity to develop

This early thumbnail sketch by Dick Ruzzin depicts a highly streamlined profile of the not-yet-named TASC4GT. Ruzzin had been instructed to design the vehicle as a rear-engine coupe, which explains the car's disproportionately short front end in this sketch. (Photo Courtesy General Motors LLC)

a "special projects" sports car designated as the Opel GTR. Over the next four weeks, Ruzzin worked feverishly on his design proposal for a three-door hatchback coupe. His design submission was approved and became the basis of design for the German-built 1973 Bitter CD, a front engine, V-8-powered sports coupe.

Despite his early involvement with the Opel program, Ruzzin's assignment in Germany had ended, and he was reassigned to Bill Mitchell's Detroit-based Studio X in December 1971. Shortly after his return, Ruzzin sketched a small, rear-engine, rotary-powered sedan that incorporated many of the components being developed by the TASC program.

MacKichan saw the sketch and was impressed with Ruzzin's efforts, both with the rotary-powered sedan and his work on the Opel/Bitter project. Moreover, MacKichan was aware that the current TASC development program did not have a platform for GM's popular F-Bodied Camaro and Firebird models, as up to that point at least, the F-Cars had all used a front engine, rear-wheel-drive configuration. It was with this in mind that MacKichan approached Ruzzin and asked him to create a coupe version of his most recent design using the same, rear-engine platform.

Ruzzin was elated at the request. He immediately set to work and created a variety of thumbnail sketches. From these, he selected several of his favorites and created quick, full-size tape drawings. MacKichan loved everything he saw and instructed Ruzzin to begin work on a scale model at once but without indicating which design he preferred. Effectively, he had given Ruzzin complete creative control over the look of the new coupe concept.

It was at this point that Ruzzin decided to name his project the TASC4GT. "TASC" because his concept incorporated components being developed by that program, albeit in a different configuration than anything developed by the TASC group to-date, "4" since the car was to be a four-passenger coupe, and "GT" because of its direct connotation to "high-performance cars."

"AS DEVELOPMENT OF THE WORLD CAR GOT UNDERWAY, ITS DESIGN SCOPE EXPANDED RAPIDLY INTO A MULTI-VEHICLE PLATFORM, ALL OF WHICH SHARED ONE OF THREE DIFFERENT BODY WIDTHS."

Ruzzin's early concept sketches were so well received by Clare MacKichan that he gave the designer nearly complete creative control over the car's future development. Both the quarter- and full-scale models that followed closely matched the aesthetic of the car seen here. (Photo Courtesy General Motors LLC)

In addition to showing passenger and luggage placement, this full-scale cutaway view of the TASC4GT includes a transverse-mounted rotary engine. The Wankel rotary engine, which was under development by General Motors around the same time as the TASC4GT, was paramount to the car's future success. There is no doubt that GM's inability to develop a viable rotary engine contributed significantly to the downfall of the TASC4GT program. (Photo Courtesy General Motors LLC)

Ruzzin might just as well have called the program the TASC Camaro/Firebird concept, but given its departure from the F-Body's current front-engine, rear-wheel-drive architecture, the TASC4GT name seemed more appropriate during this early stage of development. Besides, the name also gave his design a bit more mystique. It was something new and exciting and not just a reimagining of an existing vehicle platform.

Ruzzin settled on the centerline profile and body sections detailed in his first sketch as the basis for the scale model. He employed Ray Hildebrant, assistant chief modeler in the Overseas Studio, to create a clay model from his designs. As the pair fabricated the centerline section of the styling buck (upon which the clay model was eventually assembled), both men recognized that the TASC4GT would be an electrifying, aggressive-looking sports car.

As the model took shape, Ruzzin noted that the TASC4GT concept was slightly shorter, lower, and wider than the second-generation Camaro. Despite this, both cars offered the same front seating capacities, but the TASC4GT offered its occupants more spacious rear seating and greater luggage capacity.

GM Chief Modeler Ray Hildebrant (left) and GM Engineer Nate Hill examine the quarter-scale TASC4GT clay model in the basement of Studio X. Hill would use this model, along with Dick Ruzzin's drawings, to create full-size foam body panel templates for the 1:1-scale concept model. (Photo Courtesy General Motors LLC)

It took Ruzzin and Hildebrant roughly two weeks to advance the quarter-scale model of the TASC4GT concept to a point where it could be presented for review. The model featured a finished front end with four recessed headlamps and a rear end with corner-mounted taillights and center-mounted exhaust pipes. To better showcase Ruzzin's multiple design ideas, the car's driver's and passenger's sides each contained unique styling elements.

On the driver's side, the car featured squared-off wheel openings and a wide, triangular B-pillar that swept back toward the rear of the car. This side (along with front and rear ends) was finished entirely in red paint. The passenger's side included rounded wheel openings, a narrower, nearly vertical B-pillar, and a two-tone paint scheme. Like the other faces of the car, the upper portion was painted red. Below the character line, the car was finished in silver. The contrasting paint colors on the passenger's side were separated by a narrow, black bodyside molding.

The quarter-scale model of the TASC4GT included two separate design proposals. The driver's side of the car included concave door and fender panels; squared-off fender openings with flared fenders; and a large, triangular B-pillar behind the driver's door glass. (Photo Courtesy General Motors LLC)

The passenger's side of the quarter-scale model included convex fenders and door panels; rounded wheel openings; less-aggressive fender flares; a two-tone paint scheme; and a narrow, black body molding that ran the length of the car's character line. (Photo Courtesy General Motors LLC)

MacKichan loved the design and congratulated Ruzzin for getting it assembled so quickly. He directed Ruzzin to move forward immediately with the development of a full-size clay model. The challenge was that there simply were not any available resources within the current studio to complete a project of this size within conventional timelines.

Not to be deterred, Ruzzin assured MacKichan that he could complete the work on time, provided he could continue to utilize Ray Hildebrant. MacKichan agreed. He also assigned GM Engineer Nate Hall to the team. It was also decided that the TASC4GT project should be relocated to the old Studio X building, where Ruzzin's team could work in greater privacy until the full-scale proposal was ready to be presented to Bill Mitchell.

Nate Hall joined Ruzzin and Hildebrant, and together they relocated the entire TASC4GT design operation (from the quarter-scale model to the full-size tape drawings) into the farthest corners of the Studio X basement. Once they set up everything, the trio set to work on the full-size model.

Working in Studio X

As Dick Ruzzin had previously stated in his memoirs about building the TASC4GT, there was a certain mystique about working in Studio X. He wrote, "We soon discovered that the design shops thought we were working directly with Bill Mitchell because we were in Studio X. That was not so; our boss was Clare MacKichan."

Using the quarter-scale model for reference, Hildebrant and Hall completed the necessary drawings to create a full-scale styling buck. The drawing set was delivered to GM's fabrication shop, and within a few days the team had a dimensionally accurate wood buck upon which they'd build the clay model.

To expedite the creation of the clay panels, Hall engineered a panograph, a tool that enabled him to create full-scale

Hall (left) works to create a full-scale drawing from the quarter-scale rendering of the TASC4GT while Hildebrand (center) and Ruzzin (right) look on. This trio was almost solely responsible for the development of this spectacular concept car. (Photo Courtesy General Motors LLC)

drawings from the quarter-scale TASC4GT's clay body panels. Using Hall's drawings for reference, Hildebrant started sculpting foam templates. Once these subassemblies were mounted in place, the team started priming each of the foam panels with clay until an adequate thickness was achieved.

Although Ruzzin and Hall lacked the skills to sculpt with the precision necessary to create a finished body panel, each worked to support Hildebrant throughout the process. Typically, Ruzzin and Hall spent their mornings revising/re-engineering various components for the car while Hildebrant toiled alone on the clay model. But by lunchtime, the trio came together and spent their afternoons/evenings working on the model, often for several hours each day. This process continued for several weeks.

Late into the build, Ruzzin received a phone call that Bill Mitchell was headed to Studio X to evaluate the TASC4GT model. Mitchell, accompanied by GM president Ed Cole, examined the clay model. Much to everyone's relief, he stated that he was satisfied with what he saw. When Cole learned that the TASC4GT would be powered by a rotary engine, he also gave the team an enthusiastic thumbs-up. After all, Cole had issued the mandate that rotary Wankel engines were to be used in all future GM automobiles.

It took the team approximately six months to complete the full-size clay model of the TASC4GT. The completed model was transported from the basement of Studio X to the outdoor design patio. After making a few final corrections, MacKichan came out to see the car. His enthusiastic response to the car alleviated any concerns that Ruzzin had about the design. However, the car still had to pass muster with Bill Mitchell. Despite his favorable response to the car during his earlier visit, his reaction to the finished model would dictate whether the project would advance or be terminated entirely.

They needn't have worried. Mitchell's enthusiastic response to the clay model was the only vote of confidence the

One of several promotional images of the TASC4GT clay model was taken on the viewing road at GM's design studios. While the model was sufficiently developed to obtain design approval from GM's management, it is worth noting that the passenger's side of the car lacks detail (note the absent passenger taillamp assembly). Full-scale clays were frequently finished in this fashion to save fabrication time/cost. (Photo Courtesy General Motors LLC)

The full-size clay model of the TASC4GT is under development in the Studio X workshop. This model evolved over a period of several weeks, with Hildebrant working the clay while Ruzzin and Hall advanced assorted design elements on paper. Note the assortment of tape drawings and the scale model behind the full-scale model. (Photo Courtesy General Motors LLC)

This is another photograph of the TASC4T full-scale clay model. This time, it was photographed in front of GM's Design Dome. As before, the car is photographed from the completed driver's side. (Photo Courtesy General Motors LLC)

project needed. After Mitchell's review, MacKichan phoned Ruzzin and said simply, "Keep going!" The model was brought back into the studio and the passenger's side, which had only been partially blocked in when presented, was completed. A full-size plaster cast was made from the clay model. This, in turn, was used to create fiberglass body panels.

Unfortunately, Ruzzin had been reassigned to Irv Rybicki in the Advanced Oldsmobile Studio to begin work on another project: the Four Fendered Farkle. The completion of the fiberglass prototype was reassigned to Hall with additional styling support coming from a different designer.

Too Radical for Its Time?

Ruzzin's reassignment to Oldsmobile at the height of the TASC4GT's development was probably the earliest indicator that the project was in trouble. Although the concept was well received by all involved, its sporty architecture was likely seen as being too exotic for its time. Moreover, the TASC4GT had been developed to use a Wankel rotary engine. While considerable efforts had been made by Ed Cole and his team of engineers to develop the rotary engine as a viable powerplant for General Motors in the early 1970s, the program was indefinitely postponed due to ongoing emissions and fuel-economy deficiencies.

The TASC4GT concept was briefly displayed in the lobby of the design staff building. It was also showcased as the TASC program's answer to the Camaro/Firebird. Not long after the TASC car program implemented by GM's corporate management, the TASC4GT was put into storage and forgotten about. Sometime later, the model was unceremoniously destroyed when the storage space it occupied was needed for other vehicles.

The Evolution and Success of the TASC Program

During the time that Dick Ruzzin and team were developing the TASC4GT concept, MacKichan continued to develop the TASC program across the corporation. As it gained momentum, he added 15 of his former colleagues from the Overseas Studio to the TASC team to support the rapidly expanding program. GM Designer Leo Pruneau, who is perhaps best known for his work on the Holden Commodore and the 1965 Impala hardtop, was named MacKichan's design assistant upon his return from Holden to the United States.

The Advanced Design Studios were reorganized, and a new, larger International Studio was created in conjunction with the start of the first official "TASC X" production program. Under his leadership, MacKichan's TASC X team grew to more than 70 people. This included Ruzzin, who was assigned to the TASC program on March 4, 1974, and Bob Eaton, who was named TASC X's chief engineer at MacKichan's recommendation and with Ed Cole's approval. Throughout its development, MacKichan maintained control of the TASC X program, which was later rebranded the "X-Car Program."

Much like the TASC program before it, the focus of the X-Car Program was to produce a unibody platform that could accept transverse, small-displacement engines and offer significant improvements in the areas of fuel economy, cabin space, and production costs. Its success resulted in a massive change to GM's product portfolio, giving rise to the Chevy Cavalier, the Buick Skyhawk, the Pontiac Sunbird, and the Oldsmobile Cutlass Ciera—to name a few.

Although the TASC4GT concept car no longer exists, there are hints of Dick Ruzzin's radical concept car still visible on several GM production models. While every designer brings an individual style to his or her work, it is difficult to believe that Ruzzin's incredible design never influenced other designers (or their designs) within GM's studios.

In Ruzzin's memoirs on the TASC4GT, he stated, "The front-end theme was used on a Firebird Facelift." The recessed headlights found on every Firebird and Trans Am built between 1979 and 1981 are certainly reminiscent of those found on the TASC4GT. Similarly, the car's gull-wing door and pocket-window side glass assemblies are reminiscent of those found on the DeLorean DMC-12.

Even if the similarities between these elements and Ruzzin's concept are pure coincidence, the TASC4GT was a car that, in Ruzzin's own words, "demonstrated a new proportion

Although the TASC4GT never made it to production, several design elements introduced on the car eventually found their way onto other GM products. Perhaps the best example of this is the concept car's headlamps. A slightly reimagined version of these same headlamp assemblies was introduced on the 1979–1981 Pontiac Firebird and Trans Am models. (Photo Courtesy General Motors LLC)

and form language, one that Bill Mitchell described as 'a combination of round forms and sharp peaks. It was a great effort, we learned a lot and helped move the corporate design culture forward. The whole effort was a great time for us."

1976 Camaro Europo Hurst

The Camaro Europo Hurst is a one-of-a-kind concept designed and built by Italian automobile designer Pietro Frua. Frua was commissioned by Chevrolet to transform a stock 1976 Camaro into his unique vision for a modern Italian redesign of the American pony car. This rebodied, coach-built Camaro was first introduced at the Turin International Auto Show in November 1976. It made its American debut the following year at the Greater New York Auto Show.

Born May 2, 1913, in Turin, Italy, Pietro Frua developed a passion for designing automobiles at an early age. At age 17, Frua joined Stabilimenti Farina, an Italian automotive coachbuilder, and began designing car bodies for the Fiat Automobile Company. At age 22, he was named the director of styling at Stabilimenti Farina. During his tenure there, he met Gionvanni Michelotti, a talented artist who went on to become one of the most prolific sports car designers of the 20th century. Michelotti succeeded Frua in 1939 as head of styling after Frua decided to leave Stabilimenti Farina and start his own design studio.

Frua's automotive design work was impeded by the start of World War II. He was forced instead to design electric ovens, kitchen units, children's toys, etc. It was during this time that Frua also (allegedly) designed the original Vespa Scooter. He purchased a bombed-out warehouse in 1944, transformed it into a functional factory, and established Carrozzeria Frua. It was there that he designed the stunning, soft-topped Fiat 1100C Spider, a car that wowed the Italian automobile community at its public debut. Frua rose to even greater prominence in 1963 with his design for the Maserati Quattroporte, the car that helped establish Maserati as a luxury automobile manufacturer.

Upon his acceptance of the commission, Chevrolet shipped a 1976 Camaro to Frua's studios in Turin, Italy. Frua incorporated many of the latest styling elements being showcased on European sports cars from that era. Starting at the front end, Frua lengthened the hood and replaced the Camaro's signature pointed nose with a black squared-off fascia that housed two pairs of rounded headlights. At the back of the car, he incorporated a large, sloping hatch assembly, a European-style rear bumper, and Firebird-inspired taillights. Once completed, the car looked more like a Ferrari Dino 308 GT4 than a Chevy Camaro.

The Camaro Europo appeared to be noticeably longer than the Camaro donor car from which it had been created. In reality, Frua's completed concept car was nearly identical in length. The "extra" length was an illusion created by the addition of side glass panels behind the B-pillars, combined with the expansive sheet of glass that made up the rear hatch window. Together, these elements gave the car's back end a far

The 1976 Camaro Europo Hurst emerged from the imagination of famed Italian Coachbuilder and Automobile Designer Pietro Frua. While Frua is more famously remembered for cars such as the 1974 Maserati Quattroporte, his vision for the Camaro garnered considerable attention when it was unveiled at the Turin International Automobile Show in 1976. (Photo Courtesy Karissa Hosek)

The Camaro Europo Hurst was equipped with a 347-ci V-8 and a 4-speed manual transmission. Per the original specifications, the carbureted 5.7L V-8 was rated at a modest 165 hp when new. (Photo Courtesy Karissa Hosek)

While the Camaro Europo Hurst may have been all Chevy Camaro beneath the surface, there was nothing about the car's exterior that looked like a production Camaro. Even the Chevy bowtie at the center of the car's front grille was reworked to include the following statement: "Camaro restyling by P. Frua," with the "P. Frua" moniker prominently centered within the bowtie in a raised gold font. (Photo Courtesy Karissa Hosek)

The 1976 Camaro Europo Hurst was auctioned without reserve at RM Sotheby's during its week-long auction event in September 2020. The car, which was expected to fetch close to $100,000 when it crossed the auction block, sold for a modest $31,900. (Photo Courtesy Karissa Hosek)

more prominent (and longer) appearance than the single-piece, rounded rear glass window found on production Camaros from that era.

Although its exterior was transformed into something completely new, the undercarriage and mechanical components of the Europo remained virtually unchanged from the 1976 Camaro donor car. It was still powered by the same 165-hp, 347-ci, small-block V-8 engine and 4-speed manual transmission. It used the same A-arm front suspension and solid leaf-spring rear suspension. Even the car's interior was essentially the same, with one notable exception: the dashboard, trim panels, and carpeting were dyed a different color, and the seats were recovered in a cream-colored vinyl/leather.

It is believed that only one example of the Camaro Europo Hurst was ever built, although the car underwent some notable changes between its initial unveiling at the Turin International Auto Show and its U.S. introduction in New York on January 29, 1977. The most significant of these changes included the addition of 10-spoke Vincent wheels and "Hurst Hatches," which were a pair of removable T-top panels mounted into the roof panel above the doors. Still, the car displayed at both events shared the same seafoam green exterior and the same cream-colored upholstery. Moreover, a small portion of the original black roof moldings remained visible at the edge of the T-tops, indicating that these panels were cut in later as an addition to the original concept.

The 1976 Camaro Europo Hurst was presented at the New York Auto Show by Multi-Passenger Export Inc., a New York City–based firm that claimed it would begin marketing conversion kits to consumers looking to transform their stock Camaros into an exact replica of Frua's show car. The company further claimed that the kits would be offered through General Motors as the "Camaro Europo," as well as through Hurst Performance Parts as the "Europo Hurst."

Later that same year, Standard Motors of Miami ran an advertisement that claimed it was the exclusive distributor of Frua's conversion kit. It remains unclear to this day whether Standard Motors had negotiated a deal with Multi-Passenger Export to distribute the original kit or if the company had engineered a duplicate of its own. It is also unknown whether either company ever produced a replica of Frua's original Camaro Europo. If a duplicate does exist, then it has remained a well-kept secret, as no known photographic evidence has ever surfaced of a second Camaro Europo sports car.

Automobile appraiser and car curator/collector Dennis Mitosinka acquired the Camaro Europo in 1990. While in his possession, he occasionally exhibited the car at various Southern California car shows near his home, including the Huntington Beach Concours d'Elegance and Concorso Italiano. The mostly unaltered car remained part of his private collection until his passing in August 2020, at which point it was sold as part of the Mitosinka Collection via an online-only auction hosted by RM Sotheby's.

According to rmsothebys.com, a total of 31 of Mitosinka's cars and "more than 400 lots of automobilia, collectibles and ephemera (all offered without reserve)" were sold between September 16 and 25 to online bidders from 32 different countries. While the collection raised $1,819,225, the Camaro Europo sold for a surprisingly modest $31,900, which is far below the estimated $80,000 to $120,000 the car was expected to earn when crossing the auction block.

The 1980s

The arrival of 1980 marked a turning point within the automobile industry. The Middle East oil embargo and ensuing energy crisis of the 1970s forced manufacturers to begin developing smaller, less powerful automobiles. Downsizing became the new standard, and it had a global reach. Cars equipped with big, powerful V-8 engines sat unsold in dealership showrooms. Included with these was Chevrolet's flagship Corvette and the immensely popular Camaro.

Fortunately, corporate leadership at Chevrolet recognized the apparent waning interest in horsepower and the fuel shortages of the late 1970s for what they were: temporary impediments that eventually passed. Just the same, federal mandates for increased fuel economy and stricter emissions forced the company to evaluate the types of powerplants it was placing in its cars. To satisfy these mandates while simultaneously satiating those consumers who desired more horsepower, the division elected to introduce an assortment of optional V-6 and V-8 engines for the 1980 Camaro.

In the 1980 model year, the Camaro's 250-ci (4.1L) inline-6 was replaced with a 229-ci (3.8L) V-6 engine (and a 231-ci [3.8L] in California). An assortment of V-8 engines were also offered, including the 120-hp, 267-ci L39; the 155-hp (165 hp in the Z28), 305-ci LG4; and the 190-hp, 350-ci LM1.

Chevrolet turned to technology to ensure the small-block V-8's continued viability. It invested heavily in the development of new computer-controlled induction systems. The automaker knew that this technology needed to advance quickly and exponentially if Chevrolet hoped to meet the standards set by the government and satisfy consumer demands. While the current-generation Camaro might not benefit from these technological advances, the third-generation model would be dependent on it, which meant the clock was ticking.

1980 Camaro Ultra Z

Even as the world celebrated the start of a new decade, Chevrolet was hard at work on an entirely new Camaro. The second-generation Camaro was now 10 years old, and it was showing its age. Even so, Chevrolet knew that the next-generation model was still a few years from being ready, due in large part to changes in leadership and internal disagreements around the next-generation's powertrain configurations.

Although most of Chevrolet's engineering and design departments were focused on developing the next-generation car, a limited number of resources were tasked with finding new and interesting ways to keep the current car appealing to would-be consumers.

It was from this latter group that the 1980 Camaro Ultra Z concept car emerged. Although the car started life as a stock Z28, the Ultra Z concept was developed to show consumers that, even amid stricter government regulations, Chevrolet could produce a Camaro that offered amazing performance.

The Camaro Ultra Z concept was equipped with an experimental, custom-built, all-aluminum, 350-ci V-8 engine fitted with electronic fuel injection and a specially developed turbocharger. The engine was paired

The 1980 Camaro Ultra Z is seen here parked beside a stock Z28 Camaro hardtop coupe. The Ultra Z was equipped with a custom-built, all-aluminum, fuel-injected, and turbocharged 350-ci V-8 engine. It also featured a unique hood, an upgraded whale-tail rear spoiler, and custom hood and fender vents. (Photo Courtesy General Motors LLC)

The 1980 Camaro Ultra Z concept started makings its rounds as a show car in the late fall of 1979. Its formal unveiling took place in February 1980 at the 72nd Annual Chicago Auto Show. (Photo Courtesy General Motors LLC)

This early rendering of the Camaro Ultra Z was drawn and colored by GM Designer Randy Wittine. Although he is most famously remembered for his work on the Corvette, Wittine's contributions to the Ultra Z design helped propagate new styling elements for the last of the second-generation Camaros. (Photo Courtesy General Motors LLC)

Despite being a fan favorite at the 72nd Annual Chicago Auto Show, Chevrolet ultimately opted not to advance the Camaro Ultra Z beyond its conceptual phase. There have been a number of reasons given explaining why, but it's generally agreed that the Ultra Z never made it to production due mostly to the high production and certification costs. (Photo Courtesy General Motors LLC)

Although many of its styling elements were a direct carryover from its production counterpart, the Camaro Ultra Z's sleek silver paint, blue-gray decals, updated hood and fender vents, and updated rear spoiler all helped give the car the contemporary flare that had been growing increasingly stagnant on other late-model Camaros prior to its arrival. (Photo Courtesy General Motors LLC)

to a bolstered automatic transmission. Although the engine was rated at just 278 hp (which is timid by today's standards), it was still a massive improvement over the stock 350-ci V-8's modest 190 hp.

Outwardly, the 1980 Camaro Ultra Z concept was essentially a stock Z28, save for its distinctive whale-tail rear spoiler, unique hood with dual air vents, front fender louvered air extractors (though these appear to be the same as those found on the 1979 Z28 model), a custom two-tone silver-and-blue paint job, and special "TURBO" and "ULTRA Z" badging affixed to its front fascia and front fenders/door panels, respectively. Although it was an available option on all 1980 Camaros, the Ultra Z concept was also equipped with removable T-top panels.

Chevrolet originally introduced the Ultra Z concept in late 1979 at a limited number of select venues. It made its auto show debut at the 72nd-annual Chicago Auto Show on February 23, 1980. The car was an instant favorite with spectators, many of whom wanted to place an order for the car on the spot. Unfortunately, given the limited number of cars that could be produced combined with the high-cost requirements to certify the car for production, Chevrolet leadership elected not to manufacture the car.

However, Chevrolet did grant famous road racer and Chevrolet dealer Don Yenko permission to build and sell an Ultra Z of his own. Yenko, along with Kim Mason, his dealership's general manager, saw the opportunity such a car might bring into their dealership. Borrowing heavily from the specifications provided them by General Motors, they developed the 1981 Yenko Turbo Z. Just 19 examples were built by the dealership, making it the rarest Yenko Camaro of them all.

Although General Motors only built a single example of the Camaro Ultra Z show car, Chevrolet granted the Yenko car company exclusive rights to build a car inspired by the original Ultra Z concept. Known as the 1981 Yenko Turbo Z, this modified Camaro featured familiar styling elements that appeared to be lifted from the earlier concept car. It also received several custom embellishments, most notably its modified front fascia. (Photo Courtesy Mecum Auctions LLC)

A total of just 19 Yenko Turbo Zs were built during the 1981 model year due to the high $11,000 Stage I and $17,500 Stage II price points. (Photo Courtesy Mecum Auctions LLC)

CHAPTER

3 THIRD GENERATION (1982–1992)

"WHEN THE ALL-NEW THIRD-GENERATION CAMARO CAME OUT AT THE DAWN OF 1982, THE Z28 WAS THE SLICKEST PIECE OF WORK ON THE ROAD: NOSE DOWN, TAIL UP, STRIPED AND BE-SPOILERED LIKE A MUSCLE MACHINE BUILT A DOZEN YEARS PREVIOUS MIGHT'VE BEEN. . . . IT WAS A SIMPLE STATEMENT AND HAD A GREAT STANCE. JUST PARKED, IT LOOKED LIKE IT WAS READY TO LAUNCH, A REAL STREET FIGHTER."
— JERRY PALMER, CHIEF STYLIST OF THE THIRD-GENERATION CAMARO

A second-generation and third-generation Z28 Camaro are parked side-by-side in the courtyard of GM's design studios. While there's no denying the common ancestry of these cars, the third-generation model was a huge leap forward in terms of technology, drivability, and design. (Photo Courtesy General Motors LLC)

Although the profile of these Camaros is strikingly similar, the third-generation model had a shorter wheelbase (101 inches versus 108 inches), was longer (192 inches versus 188 inches) and taller (50.2 inches versus 49.2 inches) but weighed significantly less (2,855 pounds versus 3,310 pounds). The third-generation Camaro also featured a steeper windshield rake (62 degrees) than its predecessor, although a similarly raked windshield was originally proposed on the second-generation model. (Photo Courtesy General Motors LLC)

When the third-generation Camaro went on sale in December 1981, it set a new standard for how pony cars would be built around the globe. Everything about it (from its sleek styling to its now-iconic sports-car stance) boldly stated to the world that this was a Camaro for a new generation. It also challenged almost every rule General Motors had established to govern how these cars were supposed to be built.

General Motors (along with most Detroit-based automobile manufacturers) had always lived by the mantra that the next-generation model of any vehicle should be longer, wider, and heavier than its predecessor. The 1982 Camaro followed that edict—sort of.

Yes, it was longer than the previous model, but its wheelbase was nearly 7 inches shorter (101.1 versus 108 inches). It was also narrower (72.8 inches compared to 74.4 inches). But perhaps the most significant difference of all was that the third-generation Sports Coupe (base model) had a curb weight of just 2,855 pounds, making the new Camaro more than 400 pounds lighter than the outgoing 1981 model.

However, that was just the start. The third-generation's windshield was mounted at a dramatic 62.5 degrees, thereby exceeding GM's previous rule that stated all windshields should have a maximum incline of 60 degrees (or less). Additionally, the early third-generation Camaros were only offered as a hatchback model (although a convertible option was reintroduced in 1987). The hatch assembly featured a large, complex, curved rear glass panel affixed to the rear decklid. The entire assembly opened, allowing owners access to the car's spacious storage area and foldable rear seats, which were both firsts for the Camaro.

Despite its dramatically reimagined exterior, the most controversial aspect of the third-generation Camaro was its choice of engines. For the first time in the brand's 15-year history, the Camaro could be purchased with an inline 2.5L 4-cylinder engine. Known as the "Iron Duke," the 151-ci powerplant produced a modest 90 hp.

Its inclusion as the standard engine in the 1982 Camaro lineup had everything to do with GM's needs to satiate the ever-increasing federal mandates governing fuel economy. Fortunately for General Motors, offering a 4-cylinder engine satisfied the requirements of that mandate. Unfortunately for General Motors, Camaros equipped with the Iron Duke engine accounted for a meager 12 percent of all units sold in 1982.

The selection of the Iron Duke 4-cylinder engine by Chevrolet's motor division was likely incorporated as the Camaro's base powerplant to appease GM's managerial hierarchy after it elected to forego building the third-generation Camaro as a front-wheel-drive model in favor of producing a car that could be equipped with a more robust V-8 engine. In fact, the third-generation Camaro marked another milestone in the history of the brand: it was the first generation to offer the Sports Coupe, the Berlinetta, and the sensational Z28 models simultaneously during its freshman year.

And yet, it almost didn't happen.

Engine Placement: Front, Back, or Middle

Preliminary design work on the third-generation Camaro began in July 1975, deep inside of the GM Design Center in Warren, Michigan. Advanced One Studio Chief Designer William L. "Bill" Porter, along with his assistant and two junior designers, began creating a collection of preliminary F-Body sketches that depicted a variety of front-wheel-drive, rear-wheel-drive, and mid-engine sports cars.

In *Camaro: The Third Generation* by Michael Lamm, Bill Porter explained, "We had no idea what the next-generation Camaro and Firebird was going to be like, so we looked at rear-engined proposals, mid-engined proposals, conventional layouts, and ultimately proposals that involved front-wheel drive with transverse engines, as in the X-Car."

The X-Car platform (the Chevy Citation, Oldsmobile Omega, Buick Skylark, and Pontiac Phoenix) was seriously and extensively considered for the next-generation F-Body. Management reasoned that both the X- and F-Body platforms

Beginning in July 1975, Jerry Palmer's Chevy III and Bill Porter's Advanced One Studios began creating a variety of next-generation Camaro proposals. Since designers did not know if the car would be front-wheel drive, rear-wheel drive, or even a mid-engine platform, they generated dozens of designs like the one seen here. (Photo Courtesy General Motors LLC)

One of the recurring themes on the early Camaro designs was a severely raked windshield and one-piece (or two-piece as seen here) oval-shaped side glass that dipped below the beltline. (Photo Courtesy General Motors LLC)

could share a common chassis and powertrain. Moreover, it was thought that the new Camaro might benefit from either a front-wheel-drive or mid-engine configuration. GM's engineering staff even developed a concept car (briefly referenced toward the end of "The 1972 TASC4GT Concept" section in Chapter 2) that used the same transverse-mounted powerplant that had been developed for the X-Car platform.

Thoughts around building a mid-engine platform were abandoned early in the third-generation's development. This

This rendering, created by Jerry Palmer's assistant Theodore "Ted" Schroeder, depicts a probable mid-engine configuration. As before, note the large side glass design extending below the beltline. (Photo Courtesy General Motors LLC)

Jerry Palmer created several unique designs for the Camaro even before he started working on the third-generation model. This example, which was part of the early batch of third-generation styling studies, also appears to be a mid-engine-platform design. Note the sloped hood line (which would severely limit engine size and placement) and the forward position of the driver's seat in relation to the rear axle. (Photo Courtesy General Motors LLC)

was due mostly to space limitations inside the rear of the cockpit. Simply put, a mid-engine Camaro lacked the real estate to adequately accommodate rear passengers. Front-wheel drive, on the other hand, continued to gain momentum for several more years, resulting in a barrage of both front- and rear-wheel-drive concept models from GM's Advanced One studio.

Early in the third-generation's development, there was consideration given to building the new F-Car on the proposed X-Car platform. Management reasoned that the new F-Car could use the same front-wheel-drive powertrain and body plan as the proposed X-Car. Although this idea was abandoned early on, the front-wheel-drive/rear-wheel-drive debate continued through much of the third-generation's evolution. (Photo Courtesy General Motors LLC)

Although the idea of building a Camaro based on the X-Car platform was short-lived, this full-scale model of the proposed 1976 F/X Camaro concept shared more than a passing resemblance with many of the X-Car production models, especially the 1980 Chevy Citation. (Photo Courtesy General Motors LLC)

The F-Car Advanced Project Center

The sheer number of unique F-Body designs that emerged between the fall and winter of 1975 and the first half of 1976 caused executive leadership to intervene. It was decided that parameters needed to be established that would dictate what the next-generation Camaros and Firebirds should be. Engineers from Chevrolet, Pontiac, and General Motors Central Engineering divisions were assembled to accomplish this significant undertaking.

Each division worked independently from the others. By November 1976, Chevrolet's engineering division had established the "F-Car task force" with the express purpose of establishing the formal dimensions for the next-generation F-Body. Recognizing the need to create synergy between the divisions, the separate engineering groups were pooled, and an engineer from each was selected. This trio of individuals (Chevrolet Chassis Engineer Robert J. Haglund, Pontiac Engineer Robert. H Knickerbocker, and GM Design Staff Engineer/Designer Hulki Aldikacti) were assembled with the Advanced One Studio's development room. Two weeks later, the F-Car Advanced Project Center was formed.

The trio of F-Car Advanced Project Center engineers worked together in earnest. They partnered with designers from Advanced One, Chevrolet's Production Studio Three, and Pontiac's Studio Two to establish the dimensions, the character, and a timeline for developing the future Camaro and Firebird models.

The F/A-Car Camaro concept (seen here behind a second-generation Camaro) was built around the same platform as the Chevrolet A-Cars (the Malibu). While the debate continued to rage as to whether the next-generation Camaro would be front- or rear-wheel drive, the F/A-Car concept was based on a front engine, rear-wheel-drive configuration. Interestingly, this model shared nearly the same dimensions as the 1982 Camaro. (Photo Courtesy General Motors LLC)

From the start, the third-generation Camaro was designed with its bumpers integrated into the front and rear fascia assemblies. Integrated bumpers first appeared on the 1978 Camaro, four years after they were introduced on the Chevy Corvette. (Photo Courtesy General Motors LLC)

> "Many believed that the continued use of rear-wheel drive in the next-generation Camaro was old fashioned."

On January 24, 1977, the F-Car Advanced Project Center's engineers hosted a special meeting inside the design staff auditorium. During that meeting, they presented three potential solutions for the future F-Body program:

1. The new F-Body sports car would be based on the upcoming front-wheel-drive X-Car, which was a notion that had been previously entertained prior to the formation of the group.
2. The new F-Body sports car would be based on the rear-wheel-drive A-Body platform (which included the Chevy Chevelle, Pontiac Tempest, Oldsmobile Cutlass, and the Buick Skylark).
3. The new F-Body sports car would use a midship engine placement and X-Car components.

After reviewing the data, which included sketches and clay models of each proposed solution as well as estimated fuel-economy data, straight-line performance, braking, etc., the individuals in GM's divisional leadership voted for the solution that made the most sense to them. The majority agreed that the future F-Body program should be built around the A-Car platform and, in doing so, use A-Car hardware. This meant that the future Camaro and Firebird would once more feature a front-engine, rear-wheel-drive configuration.

Not everyone within General Motors agreed with this decision. On one hand, the argument was made that rear-wheel drive provided several benefits, including better cornering and a more balanced distribution of weight. It also allowed for a broader range of engine choices. Conversely, many believed that the continued use of rear-wheel drive in the next-generation Camaro was old fashioned. They argued that a new Camaro should be innovative and not simply rely on the same tried-and-true convention of past generations.

The Case for Front-Wheel Drive

Despite these differences of opinion, work resumed at GM's Advanced One Studios following that meeting. The new F/A-Car program (as it quickly became known among the design and engineering teams) progressed at a respectable pace for the next several months until May 9, 1977. That day, General Motors hosted its first-ever corporate Future Product Conference and brought the F/A-Car program to an immediate end.

The Future Product Conference was an idea conceived by GM president Elliot "Pete" Estes to address the federal government's 1980–1985 Corporate Average Fuel Economy (CAFE) requirements. As part of the new CAFE mandate, the government was calling for manufacturer fleet fuel-economy averages to increase to 27.5 miles per gallon by 1985.

Aerodynamics was a key element in all the designs being presented for the next-generation Camaro. This model, which was presented in early 1976, features "softer" surfaces than those that appeared on the 1982 production model. Still, some of the third-generations design architecture begins to emerge from this (and other) models. (Photo Courtesy General Motors LLC)

The conference, which was hosted by GM's worldwide product-planning staff, called the fuel economy of every current and future GM vehicle, including the Camaro, into question. By its conclusion, it was decided that all GM automobiles would be downsized, and that the Camaro would be a small, front-wheel-drive F-Car for the 1980/1982 model year that incorporated parts from the X-Car and J-Car platforms.

Five months of design sketches and clay models were abandoned almost overnight. The Advanced Projects Center and GM's design studios both struggled to find an acceptable platform for a front-wheel-drive F-Car. Worse still, Bill Mitchell was quickly approaching retirement after 19 years as GM's vice president of design. It left many feeling uncertain about the future direction of the design studios, and a great many more questioning if there would even be an F-Car program once he was gone.

Pontiac Shows the Way

Bill Mitchell retired from General Motors on July 31, 1977. He was succeeded by Irvin W. "Irv" Rybicki, who took Mitchell's place the very next day. Rybicki had shared much of Mitchell's enthusiasm about the F-Car program, and less than two weeks after assuming the role of vice president of GM's design staff, he started taking steps to revitalize the floundering program.

Rybicki tasked Chevy Studio Three Chief Designer Jerry Palmer and Pontiac Designer William L. "Bill" Porter with gathering each studio's best full-size clay models in the viewing yard outside of the design staff auditorium. In addition to Palmer and Porter, Rybicki invited design executives Chuck Jordan, David Holls, Jack Humbert, Stanley R. Wilen, and Edward R. Taylor to attend the showcase of assorted Camaro concepts.

After examining each of the clay models, Rybicki provided the team with valuable feedback that would ultimately govern the future (and final) look of the third-generation Camaro and Firebird models.

The following Irv Rybicki quote from the book *Camaro: The Third Generation* by Michael Lamm, explained, "At the time, the 1980 program had gone toward cars with large rear quarter windows, like the new J-Car fastback coupe and the Toyota Celica liftback. The rule that I laid on the chaps at that viewing was that the 1982 F-Car would have 1-piece side glass, period (no quarter windows), like the second-generation F-Car. I wanted the '82-model Camaro and Firebird to be associated more with the Corvette than anything else.

"The earlier clay models had hard edges in their roofs, quarter panels, and front fenders, and I stopped all that on that day, too," Rybicki continued. "The car would be softer in character, but certainly not as soft as the previous model because the new package was so much smaller. . . . That really started the development of the 1982 Camaro as it was released."

Of all the models presented by Palmer and Porter that afternoon, there was one example that had exuded Rybicki's styling directives. It was a swept-back, glass-roofed, front-wheel-drive Pontiac Firebird concept originally conceived in October 1976 by Roger Hughet. Hughet, who had served as an assistant designer to Bill Porter, had previously

The attempts to develop a viable third-generation F-Body architecture soon became a combined effort among Jerry Palmer, Bill Porter, and John Schinella. This model of the F/A-Car Camaro included unique styling elements that differentiated from its Firebird counterpart (below). (Photo Courtesy General Motors LLC)

While the Firebird model featured a different front and rear fascia, less-pronounced side glass, and an assortment of other unique styling elements, it still shared much of the same overall bodystyling as the Camaro (above). (Photo Courtesy General Motors LLC)

Pontiac designer Roger Hughet created this rendering of a front-wheel-drive F-Body early in the third-generation's development. This image (along with the clay model based on this rendering) was originally abandoned when the decision was made to move forward with rear-wheel drive. (Photo Courtesy General Motors LLC)

presented his model in 1976 when front-wheel drive was still being considered for the F-Car program. After the F/A-Car program mandate dictated the Camaro and Firebird both be rear-wheel drive, Hughet's model was unceremoniously abandoned to one of the design center's warehouses.

Hughet's model set the tone for the third-generation F-Body program, especially for the Pontiac Firebird, which carried many of the concept's design motifs all the way to production. Several aspects of the production Camaro's styling could also be attributed to Hughet's concept, especially its single-piece, wraparound, rear glass window as well as its minimalist B-pillar assembly. Hughet's concept also exuded the Corvette motif, just as Rybicki had directed. It is probable that Hughet's concept influenced Palmer's styling efforts while designing the fourth-generation Corvette.

FWD versus RWD Is Settled

Although a consensus had been reached regarding the future look of the F-Car, there was still considerable debate among its designers related to powertrain type and configuration. On December 20, 1977, GM's top management assembled at the GM tower in Detroit to settle the front-wheel-drive/rear-wheel-drive debate. The meeting was held in Pete Estes's 14th-floor office. Several compelling presentations were delivered by the same divisional engineers and designers who had spent the past several months working on the F-Car project.

Based on their collective recommendations, it was decided that the 1982 Camaro and Firebird should be built as rear-wheel-drive automobiles. A month later, GM's Product Policy Group made the same endorsement but with an

Pontiac Designer Bill Porter (left) and Advanced Design Executive Dave Holls admire a glass-roofed scale model of Hughet's 1976 Firebird concept. Although this layout had originally been dismissed, Holls convinced management that it should become the design theme for the third-generation Camaro and Firebird. (Photo Courtesy General Motors LLC)

Even after establishing the basic look of the F-Body, there was still considerable debate as to whether the next Camaro would be rear-wheel drive (as seen here) or front-wheel drive. Designers continued to design the car with both powertrain configurations through the end of 1977. (Photo Courtesy General Motors LLC)

This rendering of a front-wheel-drive Camaro was created by Theodore "Ted" Schroeder. Given that this full-scale drawing included the signature "Schroeder '78", it is assumed that this rendering must have been completed very early in the year, as the final decision to move forward with a rear-wheel-drive platform had been decided on December 20, 1977. (Photo Courtesy General Motors LLC)

added stipulation: GM's design staff had to present a full-size clay model of the 1982 Chevy Camaro for final management approval.

Chevrolet and Pontiac: Separate but Together

With a deadline of less than a year, not one but two of GM's elite design studios started the sizable task of transforming Hughet's concept into a viable, full-size clay model that corporate management would approve for production. Jerry Palmer's Chevrolet Studio Three and John Schinella's Pontiac Studio Two along with input from Hughet worked concurrently to advance the design while simultaneously ensuring that the Camaro and Firebird models remained separate and unique from one another. But because Schinella's staff was also occupied with completing design updates to Pontiac's J2000 automobile, much of the Firebird's early styling was developed by Palmer and his team of designers.

Jerry Palmer was responsible for designing many of the third-generation Camaro/Firebird's key components, including its 62-degree windshield, roof assembly, rear-glass liftgate, and doors. However, there were several other designers, including Palmer's assistant Ted Schroeder, Senior Designer Randy Wittine, Studio Chief Engineer George McLean, Chief Modeler Al Tholl, and relative newcomers John Cafaro and John Adams, who contributed significantly to giving the third-generation cars their final outward form.

At the same time, Schinella's team, with considerable support from Pontiac General Manager Alex C. Mair, was responsible for giving the Firebird its signature hidden-headlights feature. Schinella had previously campaigned for recessed headlights on the second-generation Firebird, but his efforts had been thwarted by Pontiac's financial accountants, who claimed that development of such a feature was overly cost prohibitive. This time, he insisted on the feature, arguing that it served as a significant differentiator between the Camaro and Firebird models.

While there is no denying that Roger Hughet's design established the theme for the third-generation F-Body cars, it was Jerry Palmer (and his Chevy Studio Three) who gave the Camaro its signature look and developed the design to a point where it could be transformed into a production automobile. (Photo Courtesy General Motors LLC)

Of course, it was not just Palmer who formalized the look of the third-generation Camaro. Chevy Designer John Cafaro also provided significant contributions to the car's aesthetic. His rendering of the Z28 Camaro (seen here) helped Chevy III's efforts to define the look of the brand's top-performance package. (Photo Courtesy General Motors LLC)

This is a sketch of the third-generation Camaro taillights by John Cafaro. This drawing and countless others like it were created throughout the Camaro's development to help define and/or provide important design details for each of the car's numerous components. (Photo Courtesy General Motors LLC)

Palmer's team, meanwhile, developed the Camaro with exposed headlights without a separate headlight bezel (as had been the standard on every Camaro before it). The headlights mounted to structural supports hidden under the hood but were framed only by the car's front fascia and the hood panel itself. The benefit of this design was that it enabled the Camaro to feature a wedge-shaped front end. Ironically, both the Camaro and the Firebird shared common structural components despite the dramatic differences in the appearance of their front ends. The use of common substructures saved money and likely allowed for the inclusion of the pop-up headlights on the third-generation Firebird.

Jerry Palmer (Chevy) and John Schinella (Pontiac) vowed to work together to keep the Firebird and Camaro as different as possible. Early resistance from GM's financial department to keep production costs down originally had both cars sharing the same exposed lamps and front end. Schinella insisted that the Firebird should include retractable, hidden headlamp assemblies. (Photo Courtesy General Motors LLC)

Truth be told, the exterior aesthetics of the third-generation Camaro and Firebird were independently developed by the two design studios. While they communicated with each other throughout the design/refinement process, Palmer and Schinella agreed that each car should have its own distinctive look. GM's leadership was resistant to this idea, arguing that the cars needed to share more interchangeable parts to reduce production costs.

In the end, Palmer and Schinella successfully argued their case, and additional budgets were allotted for the development of each car. In fact, the only common exterior components shared between the two cars are the windshield, roof panel, rear glass, and doors.

The Camaro Arrives with a Bang

It took every bit of the allotted 10 months for Palmer's studio to finalize its full-size clay model of the 1982 Camaro production concept. While conventional practices were used by the studios, development of the third-generation Camaro was aided considerably by advances in computer-aided design technologies.

Even as the clay model was being developed, the studio engineers and designers collaborated on much of the car's design through computer-rendered models. These models

Here is a full-scale clay model of the Camaro Berlinetta coupe inside the Chevy design studio. This model was close to the production design, but it demonstrates how even small changes can affect the look of the car. Note the following: this model includes round fog lamps in the front fascia, has different, non-color-matched sideview mirrors, is missing the front hood emblem, and has the "CAMARO" fender badge mounted above the accent line (not below it, as found on the production models). (Photo Courtesy General Motors LLC)

This full-scale mock-up of the 1982 Z28 Camaro's front-end shows the placement and style of the hood vents on this model. The scoops used on the production model were narrower, recessed into the hood, and mounted closer together. As with the previous example, this model demonstrates how scale models helped designers advance the styling on a project. (Photo Courtesy General Motors LLC)

used extensive, preloaded engineering data (such as wheelbase, overall length, height, engine location, fuel-tank placement, etc.) to ensure that the exterior aesthetic could accommodate the car's mechanical and structural components.

> "THE NEW CAMARO CONCEPT CREATED SUCH A SENSATION THAT IT ALLEGEDLY CAUSED ONE OBSERVER TO WRECK HIS OWN CAR."

Even with the assistance and extensive use of computer-design technologies throughout its development, Palmer's studio worked diligently for those 10 months to finalize the look of each body panel on the new Camaro. During this period, Roger Hughet was reassigned from Pontiac's Advanced Studio One to Studio Three. He became Palmer's assistant and worked closely with him to finalize the look of the Camaro prior to the studio's December deadline.

On December 11, 1978, Jerry Palmer and Roger Hughet unveiled the 1982 Camaro clay to GM's top brass. As the car emerged from Studio Three into the courtyard for its first "public" viewing (viewing by GM staff not directly involved with its development), the car received enthusiastic approval from everyone who saw it. The executive management signed off on the design almost at once while openly praising Palmer and his team for their outstanding work.

In the 15 months that followed that auspicious meeting, Palmer and Hughet advanced the third-generation Camaro

The full-scale model of the 1982 Camaro hatchback coupe is parked in the courtyard of GM's design studios. The rear decklid design underwent additional revisions and was more squared off by the time the Camaro went to production. A version of this taillamp treatment was introduced on the 1985 Z28 model, although it had narrower gridlines. The rectangular tailpipes didn't appear on a production car until the 1992 Corvette and the 1993 (fourth-generation) Camaro. (Photo Courtesy General Motors LLC)

The clay mock-up of the 1982 Z28 Camaro included a more accurate representation of the taillamp assemblies. Upon closer examination, you'll also note that the rear spoiler is actually split down the car's centerline and consists of two half assemblies, each of a different style and height. Styling models frequently featured contrasting elements like this to evaluate how well each worked on the car compared to the other. (Photo Courtesy General Motors LLC)

The front end of the Camaro Z28 is shown in its final configuration. Even at this late stage in the design process, the clay model features air scoops with color-matched louvers. The 1982 production model included similarly shaped air scoops, but the louvers were not offered as a factory option until the 1985 model year when the Camaro underwent its first mid-generation redesign, and these came in a matte black finish. (Photo Courtesy General Motors LLC)

This GM media photo features the 1982 Camaro Z28 parked next to the outgoing second-generation Z28 model. The third-generation Camaro started production on October 12, 1981, and went on sale in December that same year. It was the first Camaro to have a hatchback and fuel injection and be offered with a 4-cylinder engine (in the base model). (Photo Courtesy General Motors LLC)

from a clay model to a fiberglass mock-up in February 1979 and finally to a fully realized, running prototype in March 1980. For the remainder of 1980, the Camaro prototype was exposed to a variety of wind-tunnel and driving tests, including an extended stint at GM's Milford Proving Grounds.

Then, in December 1980, while being showcased at a corporate ride-and-drive event near Phoenix, Arizona, the new Camaro concept created such a sensation that it allegedly caused one observer to wreck his own car. The story goes that a pair of third-generation Camaro prototypes were being driven in the open on the streets around Phoenix. The said observer, who happened to be driving his own 1981 Camaro, spotted the new cars coming toward him. As they passed, he recognized them as the new Camaros and craned around to get a better look. As he did so, he smashed into a stopped car in front of him.

In Lamm's book *Camaro: The Third Generation,* Design Chief Charles Jordan, who happened to be at that fateful event, explained, "Here was this poor guy . . . sitting there, the glass all broken out of one headlight, the grille smashed, and I felt really sorry for him. On the other hand, I thought, 'Well, that's the mark of a successful design if you can get a guy to smash his car just craning to look at the new one. That's a real testimonial.'"

The side view of the full-scale 1982 Camaro Z28 clay model is in the courtyard of GM's design studios. This model features an air duct mounted in the fender behind the front wheel opening. This feature was abandoned on the Chevy Camaro but was included on all third-generation Firebirds and Trans Ams built between 1982 and 1992. (Photo Courtesy General Motors LLC)

Jerry Palmer

GM Designer Jerry Palmer is best known for his design work on the third-generation Chevy Camaro (1982) and the fourth-generation Corvette (1984). In 1986, Palmer was promoted to executive designer of GM's Advanced Design division. He was promoted again in 1990 and served as the director of the Thousand Oaks Concept Center. He finally earned the title of executive director of design for GM North America in 1992. (Photo Courtesy General Motors LLC)

Jerry P. Palmer was born in Detroit on October 22, 1942. The son of a successful Pontiac salesman, young Jerry grew up around cars, which helped fuel his fascination with automobiles. He filled his school notebooks with drawings of cars and trucks (many of his own design) instead of transcribing the notes and schoolwork that his teachers assigned. While some of his teachers had likely expressed concern about his lack of focus in class, others recognized Jerry's drawings for what they really were: the burgeoning talents of a future automobile designer.

After graduating high school in 1961, Palmer enrolled at Detroit's Society for Arts and Crafts (known as the College for Creative Studies [CCS] today), a Detroit-based private art school with degree programs for aspiring artists and designers. His instructors included famous Detroit-based designer Homer C. LaGassey Jr. and Tucker/Ford stylist Alex Tremulis.

While studying at the Society for Arts and Crafts, Palmer secured employment with a pair of companies that would help advance his appreciation of the automotive industry. His first position was at Gus Pernack's Applied Industries, a Detroit-based tool-and-die shop. While there, Palmer learned how to machine prototype parts for Ford, Chrysler, and General Motors. Later, he went to work at Creative Industries, a Detroit design firm, where he helped develop the futuristic United States Steel *Innovari*, a concept car fabricated from high-strength alloys.

During his junior year, Palmer was selected to participate in a summer design internship at General Motors. That internship helped pave the way for his future, long-term employment with the company. After graduating from the College for Creative Studies in 1966, Palmer secured a full-time position as a junior designer in GM's Detroit-based design studios. He was the first graduate of the Center for Creative Studies ever to be granted a permanent position at General Motors.

Not long after joining the company, Palmer was transferred to GM's Advanced Studio Four. His first major assignment there was to help design the newly envisioned boattail Buick Riviera. This garish-looking Buick interlaced the lower half of a late-1960s Riviera with the upper body styling of the second-generation Corvette Sting Ray. Despite his personal disinterest in the project, Palmer's work was well received by management. It also caught the eye of Bill Mitchell, who appreciated Palmer's form and attention to detail.

In 1967, Palmer joined Henry Haga's team in the Chevy Design Studio Two. Haga had just finished design work on the 1970½ Camaro. Under Haga's direction, Palmer helped design the 1970 Camaro Kammback station wagon and aided in the styling of the second-generation Z28 package. However, his primary assignment was to design the Chevy Vega.

Palmer became Haga's assistant around the same time that Chevy Studio Three became interlaced with Chevy Studio Two. When this happened, Haga (and in turn, Palmer) became involved with several of Chevrolet's key design projects at once, including aesthetic refinements to the exterior of the Camaro and Corvette as well as continued development of the Chevy Vega and Monza models.

Mitchell appointed Palmer assistant chief designer of the Chevy Studio Three in 1971. At Mitchell's request, Palmer (alongside Haga) became involved with the four-rotor Aerovette concept Corvette design program. By Palmer's own admission, designing the Aerovette was one of the most challenging assignments of his career. However, his design served as the inspiration for the fourth-generation Corvette, a car that Palmer was tasked with developing after his promotion to Chevy Studio Three's chief designer in 1974. Beginning with the 1975 model year, Palmer was also responsible for all of the second-generation Camaro styling updates.

On August 1, 1977, Irv Rybicki replaced Bill Mitchell as the vice president of GM's design staff. Just two weeks after assuming his new role, Rybicki tasked Palmer (along with designer Bill Porter) to present their best full-size F-Body clay models in the design studio's outdoor viewing yard. Rybicki examined each model in turn and offered the designers feedback that outlined his expectations for the future development of the F-Body program. In a very real sense, it was after this fortuitous meeting that Jerry Palmer started defining the look of the third-generation Camaro.

A young Jerry Palmer poses with his full-scale rendering of a proposed 1973 Camaro concept car. His lavish designs captured the attention of his superiors and created opportunities for him to work on a variety of other cutting-edge projects, including the four-rotor Aerovette concept, which allowed him to join (and eventually lead) the Camaro and Corvette design studios. (Photo Courtesy General Motors LLC)

Irv Rybicki (left) and Jerry Palmer evaluate a full-scale rendering of the third-generation Camaro. Rybicki played a pivotal role in defining the character of the 1982 Camaro. It was from his instruction, along with Roger Hughet's scale-model Firebird concept and Jerry Palmer's masterful design talents, that led to the genesis of the third-generation production model. (Photo Courtesy General Motors LLC)

Palmer was soon named chief stylist of the third-generation Camaro. His designs were responsible for much of the 1982 Camaro's (and Pontiac Firebird's) exterior aesthetic. It was Palmer's Chevy Studio Three, working in conjunction with John Schinella's Pontiac Studio Two, that ensured the third-generation Camaro and Firebird each reflected Palmer's designs. Several design studio up-and-comers, including Chevy's own John Cafaro (who would go on develop the look of the fourth-generation Camaro a few years later) and John Adams, began their careers working with Palmer on the third-generation Camaro program.

In addition to his design work on the third-generation Camaro, Jerry Palmer was also tasked with developing the look of the fourth-generation Corvette. Although it was physically smaller than the Camaro, the styling motif between the two cars is unmistakable, especially when parked beside one another.

Palmer was named executive designer of GM's Advanced Design division in October 1986, director of the Thousand Oaks Advanced Concepts Center in April 1990, and ultimately, executive director of design for GM's North American Operations in 1992. In this role, he was responsible for overseeing the interior and exterior design for all of GM's production vehicles.

On September 1, 2000, Jerry Palmer was inducted into the Corvette Hall of Fame under the GM/Chevrolet category for his many significant design contributions to various GM products, including the Camaro and the 1987 Chevy Beretta but mostly for his work on the fourth-generation Corvette.

He retired from General Motors in 2002.

As the executive designer of the Advanced Design division, Palmer played a significant role in the development of the fourth-generation Camaro F-14 Tomcat concept (see Chapter 4). He discovered and mentored GM Designer John Cafaro (not pictured) to take over the Advanced Design Studios upon his promotion to director of the Thousand Oaks studio in 1990. (Photo Courtesy General Motors LLC)

1985 and 1993 Camaro GTZ Concept

While the following information on the Camaro GTZ was obtained from a variety of sources, a fair amount of the content and all of the quotes in this section came from an article written by Jim Hall and originally published in *Motor Trend* magazine in June 1985.

Designed by Jerry Palmer and Charles "Chuck" Jordan, the Camaro GTZ is a highly stylized concept car built on the third-generation Camaro platform. The car was developed by the Chevrolet design studios as a showpiece for the 1984 SEMA Show in Las Vegas. (Photo Courtesy General Motors LLC)

The paint color developed by Ed Ketterer for the GTZ included specific chemical components that were deemed too dangerous by OSHA to be sprayed inside a factory environment. As a result, this color was never introduced on a production automobile, and it likely never will. (Photo Courtesy General Motors LLC)

Despite the relative newness of the third-generation model, Chevrolet wasted no time beginning development of several fourth-generation Camaro conceptual designs. While most of these early designs/styling models never made it beyond the interior of Chevrolet's design studios, the handful that did served one of two primary purposes: 1) they were either displayed at auto shows to gauge public interest of GM's latest design

Many of the elements introduced in the Camaro GTZ's front-end styling found their way onto the third- and fourth-generation Camaro production models. A version of the car's louvered hood was reimagined for the 1985 Z28/IROC-Z Camaro, while the side scoops in the front fenders were introduced on the 1990 Camaro. (Photo Courtesy General Motors LLC)

The Camaro GTZ was equipped with 16x10-inch Jongbloed Racing modular wheels at all four corners. Palmer and Jordan selected these wheels to contrast the softer "Eurosnob" styling that they'd created for much of the car. Palmer felt the car needed an aggressive "real men drive Camaros" stance that would allow it to look at home drag racing on the streets of Detroit or touring around the French Riviera. (Photo Courtesy General Motors LLC)

The GTZ's front fenders and rear quarter panels were widened and their contours softened to give the car a more muscular appearance. Although the rear end needed to be immediately recognizable as a Camaro, its lines were also softened/rounded to complement the rest of the bodystyling. (Photo Courtesy General Motors LLC)

standards or 2) they were used to showcase new technologies being developed by General Motors.

The 1993 Camaro GTZ, a highly stylized Camaro concept created by Jerry Palmer and Charles "Chuck" Jordan, was developed to do a bit of both.

Chevrolet had just finished development of its most advanced 90-degree V-6 engine to date (the 262-ci 4.3L engine) as an available powerplant for its 1985 model year lineup. To help give it a proper introduction, GM's marketing team elected to unveil the new engine at the 1984 Specialty Equipment Manufacturers Association (SEMA) Show in Las Vegas, Nevada. Given the success of the third-generation Z28 Camaro after its first two years of production along with growing consumer excitement around the impending 1985 IROC-Z model, Chevrolet management decided that a Camaro would be the ideal sports car in which to display its new 4.3L powerplant.

Once the decision had been made, GM Director of Design Chuck Jordan was tasked with getting a Camaro show car ready in time for the following year's SEMA Show. Jordan, in turn, handed the assignment over to Jerry Palmer (the chief designer of Chevrolet's Studio Three) along with his assistant Roger Hughet. Having just finished development of the third-generation Camaro and the fourth-generation Corvette, Jordan knew beyond doubt that Palmer and Hughet could produce a show car worthy of SEMA.

Palmer was excited by the opportunity.

"At the Chevy studio [Three], we have a special affection for the Camaro," he said. "Any assignment to rework the car is never a chore. I believe it's because the basic form responds so well to rethinking from a design standpoint."

The Camaro GTZ started life as an early 1985 IROC-Z Camaro, which made its transformation into a one-off show car extremely challenging for Palmer. Traditionally, when an automotive stylist begins designing a new concept car, he or she generally works without considering things such as driver/passenger comfort, government safety regulations, or even luggage space. Their completed designs often border on the extreme, as they evolve solely from the imagination of the designer. It's quite literally "design without limits."

In the case of the GTZ, Palmer began with an existing car that already undergone years of production development from his original conceptual design. In many respects, the IROC-Z model was the epitome of his original third-generation Camaro design. It made his task of transforming the IROC into something new and noteworthy that much more daunting.

At the same time, Palmer saw the GTZ concept as an opportunity to adapt several styling elements that had been previously abandoned during the development of the original 1982 Z28 Camaro and the 1985 IROC-Z production models. He also recognized that the GTZ could be used as a styling showcase for some of the fourth-generation design elements that they'd been developing in Chevy Studio Three.

Hughet was tasked with creating much of the original concept art for the GTZ. Using Palmer's design objectives as a guide, he sketched a Camaro with large National Advisory Committee for Aeronautics (NACA) air ducts cut into the hood. These were framed by air fences along the hood's outer edges. While Palmer appreciated how the hood enhanced the look of the car, he felt that Hughet's early styling was not "wild enough."

Nearly all the early GTZ sketches depicted a stock Camaro with a limited assortment of more-aggressive styling elements. Palmer argued that the third-generation F-Cars (both the Camaro and Firebird) were "wheel-oriented cars," which meant that the strength of the car's graphics and outward aesthetics were dependent on wheel size. Simply put, the production Camaro wheels were too small for the GTZ show car.

"The 16-inch alloys from the IROC production look like production wheels," Palmer declared. "While that's okay for a car in a showroom or at the signal next to you, it just isn't the stuff show cars are made of."

Instead, Palmer elected to use a set of Jongbloed Racing 16x10 modular wheels wrapped in Goodyear Eagle VR50 P255/50V16 tires on the GTZ. The addition of the larger, wider wheels improved its overall stance and added to the car's overall aesthetic, as did the louvered hood (which remained an integral part of the GTZ's styling throughout its development). However, in Palmer's estimation, the rest of the car's styling was still too conservative.

Even as Palmer and Hughet struggled to establish a satisfactory look for their Camaro show car, it was decided that fabrication of the GTZ's exterior would be outsourced to Diversified Glass Products in Pontiac, Michigan. Diversified Glass had previously worked closely with several of GM's design studios, and it had repeatedly demonstrated that it had the infrastructure to quickly transform the Chevy Studio Three designs into a fully realized fiberglass prototype. As work on the GTZ got underway, early efforts further proved Palmer's concerns about the car's styling.

Determined to separate the GTZ from the production IROC, Palmer widened the car's front fenders and rear quarter panels while simultaneously softening the production Camaro's sharp body contours. It gave the car a wider, meaner, and more muscular appearance. In addition to widening the car, Palmer also incorporated a pair of interior air extractors into the leading edge of each of the car's B-pillars.

The GTZ's front end was also reworked. Given that it only needed to house a 6-cylinder engine beneath its massive front-end assembly, the GTZ's nose was lowered and given a more rounded contour analogous to the front-end styling introduced on the fourth-generation Camaro. The openings for the recessed headlights were lengthened slightly and rounded to match the contour of the fenders. They were fitted with a pair of smoked headlight covers. The front turn signals, fog lamps, and front license-plate mount were eliminated entirely and replaced with a single, centrally located air-inlet assembly.

A pair of air scoops were incorporated into the lower front and rear fender assemblies just ahead of the wheel openings. A similar version of these same scoops were added to the exterior styling of every Camaro beginning with the 1991 model year.

As Palmer's team implemented each of these changes to the design, the team at Diversified Glass added them to the evolving show car's shell. From the rear quarter panels forward, the car finally started to exhibit the radical styling that Palmer was looking for. However, when Design Chief Chuck Jordan inspected the car, he openly expressed his dissatisfaction with the car's back end. He argued that the GTZ's back end looked too much like the production Camaro and detracted from the aesthetic that Palmer (and team) had developed for the rest of the car.

Jordan returned to the studio and worked with Palmer and Hughet to design a rear end that was more befitting the rest of the car. The trio worked quickly and devised a radically redesigned back end that featured a single, wedge-shaped taillamp assembly that was noticeably narrower than the production cars. Like the rest of the car, the rear end's contours were also softened and rounded. The rear license-plate pocket's placement was relocated from between the taillights and molded into the lower third of the rear fascia assembly. Below the new license-plate pocket, the car's extended side rocker panels wrapped around the back of the car where they merged to form a flow-separator spoiler.

To finish the car's exterior appearance, a flattened, wing-type, wraparound spoiler was integrated into the rear decklid assembly. While Palmer's original design for the spoiler began at the middle of the sail panel and traced the lower edge of the car's rear glass, the reimagined version began at the bottom edge of the rear window just behind the B-pillar and extended back along the rear decklid assembly, following the profile contour of the car's stylized front fenders. Supported by a pair of narrow posts affixed to the trailing edge of the decklid, the spoiler looked like a free-floating wing akin to something found on military aircraft. The popularity of this styling element led to its inclusion on the GTA Trans Am and Formula Firebird models beginning in 1985.

Now that Jordan and Palmer were satisfied with the look of the car, they turned their attention to color choice. Both agreed that the car should be finished in a bold color, and they mutually settled on yellow. Ed Ketterer, the GM Design staff's color technologist, was tasked with selecting/creating a shade of yellow that would best accentuate the aggressive-looking GTZ. Ketterer spent a decent amount of time and effort formulating the right hue of yellow. The color palette he settled on was a clearcoat pearl over bright yellow with gloss black wheels to accent the car's bright exterior.

The Ultimate V-6 Camaro?

Although the GTZ Camaro was developed with the assumption that it would showcase Chevrolet's latest 6-cylinder engine offering, there was a period during its development when the use of a 2.8L V-6 engine was also considered.

> "THE GTZ'S 4.3L ENGINE PRODUCED A MORE ROBUST 230 HP, WHICH WAS MORE HORSEPOWER THAN THE 5.0L V-8 ENGINE OFFERED IN THE Z28 AND IROC-Z CAMAROS FROM THAT SAME ERA"

Conceptually, the GTZ was meant to be the ultimate expression of the Z28 Camaro. As such, all involved believed that the introduction of GM's newest 90-degree V-6 would best represent the car's transition from the more robust 90-degree V-8 engines that had powered every Z28 Camaro since its earliest iteration. The V-8 had been an integral part of GM's engine programs since 1955. If General Motors was going to make a reduction in the number of cylinders in its engines, it also needed to do everything possible to ensure that the smaller, 6-cylinder powerplants produced a comparable amount of horsepower and torque.

The GTZ was developed so quickly that GM paint shops were unable to paint the car in time for the 1984 SEMA Show. Instead, the car was shipped to Jessy's Auto Body, a collision repair shop just south of GM's design center in Warren, Michigan. (Photo Courtesy General Motors LLC)

The Camaro GTZ crossed the Barrett-Jackson Scottsdale auction block in 2009 and sold for just $22,000. Reportedly, it was purchased by the owner of a GM dealership in Duncan, British Columbia, and was showcased for several years in the dealer's showroom. The car has also been displayed at the National Corvette Museum. (Photo Courtesy General Motors LLC)

The conventional 4.3L V-6 engine found in most Chevy products of that era used a heavy iron block, had throttle-body fuel injection, and produced a modest 130 hp at 3,600 rpm. The engine that was developed for the GTZ used an aluminum casting of that same iron block, a prototype air-mass-sensing port-injection fuel-delivery system, a bolstered crankshaft, a distributor-less ignition system, and a set of aluminum splayed-valve heads. Designated the XPV-6, the GTZ's 4.3L engine produced a more robust 230 hp, which was more horsepower than the 5.0L V-8 engine offered in the Z28 and IROC-Z Camaros from that same era.

The rest of the GTZ's chassis remained largely unchanged. The front suspension was lowered by 2 inches, in part to account for the lighter-weight engine (the 4.3L XPV-6 weighed nearly 200 pounds less than the donor car's original V-8). Outside of that, the GTZ used the same T-5 BorgWarner manual transmission, the same 3.73:1 rear axle, and the same front and rear ventilated disc brakes.

It's been stated that if the design team had been given more time to create the GTZ Camaro, additional consideration may have been given to bolstering these other components. However, there simply hadn't been enough time to work through all those additional details. Besides, the Camaro GTZ was intended to be a show car, which meant it would spend much of its time under the bright lights of events, such as SEMA. It needed to look fast, not *be* fast.

SEMA and Beyond

When the Camaro GTZ was officially unveiled at the SEMA Show in October 1984, it was praised by automotive enthusiasts and critics alike for its aggressive stance and futuristic styling. Perched atop a rotating, circular display table, the car left many wondering if the GTZ Camaro might be an early iteration of the GM80. GM80 was an internal GM designation that had become synonymous with the next-generation Camaro program and which, for many automotive enthusiasts of that era, became something of a unicorn in the early days of the fourth-generation's development.

Palmer was quick to denounce any such rumors.

"The GTZ is just a show car," he said. "We don't have any plans to put it into production."

Despite his claim, there is no denying that the third-generation GTZ contained design elements that were, at the very least, reminiscent of the styling from which the fourth-generation Camaro evolved nearly a decade later. After its introduction at SEMA, and its subsequent 1985 tour across the United States, many in the automotive community denounced Palmer's earlier denial that the GTZ was just a show car. The car became known first as the 1988 Camaro GTZ, suggesting that 1988 would be the year Chevrolet unveiled its fourth-generation Camaro. After 1988 had come and gone, the car became known as the 1993 Camaro GTZ, once more indicating a correlation between the concept car and the pending arrival of a next-generation model.

Interestingly, when the fourth-generation Camaro was unveiled in 1993, automotive critics were quick to point out the similarities shared between the production model coupe and the GTZ concept. What's more, several of Chevrolet's earliest press images of the fourth-generation Camaro depicted the car with its headlights concealed behind smoked covers like those on the GTZ. The 1993 Camaro also included a flattened, integrated spoiler that wrapped around the rear decklid before blending with the rear quarter panels. While nowhere near as dramatic as the spoiler introduced on the GTZ, there was no denying the concept car's influence on the design.

In July 2009, Chevrolet sold the 1993 Camaro GTZ concept at the Barrett-Jackson auction in Scottsdale, Arizona. The car was advertised by Barrett-Jackson as being a concept vehicle, and it was accompanied by several strict stipulations as a condition of its sale. For instance, the auction stated that "the vehicle [was] not certified to comply with any federal, state, or local laws, rules, or regulations." Additionally, the vehicle "could not legally be driven on any public roads."

Listed as lot 1507 when it unceremoniously crossed Barrett-Jackson's auction block, the Camaro GTZ was sold with a scrap title for the modest sum of just $22,000.

The GM80 F-Body

Despite its 20-year success as a traditional front-engine, rear-wheel-drive sports car, there were those at General Motors who believed the next-generation Camaro and Firebird platforms ought to be constructed as front-wheel-drive vehicles. GM's success selling cars such as the Citation, Cavalier, and Sunbird supported its position that consumers would embrace and purchase a front-wheel-drive F-Body platform. Moreover, GM's engine programs had developed smaller, less-expensive-to-build, 4- and 6-cylinder engines capable of producing the same amounts of horsepower previously reserved for the small-block V-8 engines that were being used in the third-generation models.

To be clear, General Motors never intended on lessening the quality or performance that consumers had come to expect from its F-Body sports cars. Instead, it was looking to build a technologically advanced automobile that could be produced at a lower cost, that shared the same engine platforms as other cars in GM's current lineup, and that allowed for greater interchangeability among various exterior designs by using lightweight, plastic body panels (like those first introduced on the Pontiac Fiero).

At the order of CEO Roger B. Smith, and under the direction of Chevrolet Chief Engineer Fred Schaafsma, General Motors launched the GM80 development program in the spring and summer of 1984. The program's primary focus was to develop a fourth-generation, front-wheel-drive sports car to replace both the Camaro and the Firebird. Additionally, a third GM80 concept would be developed as the all-new Oldsmobile Silhouette Sport/Touring Coupe.

Two powerplants were developed for the GM80 program. The first was Oldsmobile's Quad 4, which was a dual-overhead-cam (DOHC), inline 4-cylinder engine that produced an estimated 150 to 190 hp (depending on the source). The second was GM's 24-valve, "Twin Dual Cam" 3.4L V-6 engine. This engine, which had been derived from Chevrolet's 60-degree V-6 engine family, originally produced an estimated 285 hp. Unfortunately, General Motors had yet to develop a front-wheel-drive transaxle that could handle that much power,

The GM80 F-Body concept was developed by General Motors as a cost-efficient, front-wheel-drive replacement to the third-generation Camaro. Because of increasing uncertainty around gas prices and the Big Three's need to compete with Japanese automakers in the late 1980s, General Motors also planned to eliminate the Camaro's V-8 engine completely and replace it with 4- and 6-cylinder options. (Photo Courtesy General Motors LLC)

The GM80 concept was shorter and lighter than its predecessors. GM's engineers reasoned that a lighter platform paired with smaller, higher-revving engines would provide consumers with a similar driving experience to the ones they'd known previously. Fortunately for General Motors, Ford's failure with the Probe sent a clear message that the Camaro might suffer a similar fate if the traditional engine/powertrain programs were eliminated. (Photo Courtesy General Motors LLC)

Had the GM80 F-Body concept advanced to a production model, it would have been manufactured in the same assembly plant as the Pontiac Fiero. Unfortunately, complications ranging from overly expensive body panels to weight-reduction challenges caused the car's development budget to spiral out of control. The program was canceled in late 1986. (Photo Courtesy General Motors LLC)

so the engine was detuned to a more manageable (though less impressive) 200 hp and 215 ft-lbs of torque. A limited-slip differential was also specified as standard equipment.

While both proposed GM80 powerplants offered more horsepower than those found in the third-generation Camaro (the 1985 LQ9 4-cylinder engine produced a mere 88 hp, the LB8 2.8 V-6 produced 135 hp, and the more robust L69HO V-8 produced just 190 hp), the GM80's front-wheel-drive configuration produced less torque, which adversely impacted acceleration.

To counteract this loss in performance, the dimensions of the GM80 were reduced, and a variety of weight-saving materials were considered. First, the GM80 was designed around a 96-inch wheelbase, which was a full 5 inches shorter than the current F-Body's wheelbase. Second, General Motors planned to introduce the GM80 as its first high-volume, plastic-bodied car (although, as history shows, this distinction ultimately went to the Pontiac Fiero). Several materials were considered for the car's chassis and frame assemblies, including tubular steel, extruded aluminum, and fiberglass.

The decision to mount plastic body panels to a composite chassis was especially appealing to General Motors given the potential savings in production costs, the significant reduction in corrosion, and the ease of modifying the structure for future vehicle platforms. Moreover, having a composite frame would reduce weight while also improving structural rigidity, while the front-wheel-drive configuration would improve vehicle handling.

As planned, three unique GM80 concepts were developed. The first two (the Camaro and Firebird versions) shared many of the same design elements with one another, and it is apparent that both cars inspired their fourth-generation, rear-wheel-drive production counterparts. From its front fascia to its taillights, the GM80 Camaro looked remarkably like the 1993 Camaro production model that arrived nearly a decade later. The GM80 Firebird's front-end on the other hand looked more like a Pontiac Fiero, although the rest of the car closely matched the styling of the 1993 Firebird Trans Am. Each had futuristic styling (for the time) with a wedge-shaped front end and a large rear hatch with dramatically contoured glass.

The third concept (Oldsmobile's GM80 model) was unique in that it had a more defined roofline with sidelights cut into the B-pillar and a separate rear window. It was also the

Even though the GM80 F-Body program was deemed a critical and costly failure, the styling introduced on the Chevrolet variant of the GM80 F-Body (seen here) is remarkably like the styling featured on the fourth-generation Camaro that arrived a few years later. (Photo Courtesy General Motors LLC)

only example to include a rear decklid instead of a glass hatch.

The development of these cars proceeded in earnest. Over the next 18 months, several GM80 test cars were produced and driven extensively on GM's test tracks and the open road. Assorted spy photos of these GM80 test mules started appearing in automotive magazines such as *Automotive Week* and *Metalworking News*, along with claims that it would be released as either a 1989 or 1990 model.

One article, published on March 30, 1986, in the *Cincinnati Enquirer*, expressed concern around whether General Motors planned to continue manufacturing the Camaro and Firebird at its Norwood, Ohio, plant once the GM80 model officially replaced the current F-Body cars. While the article conceded the point that "GM [had] not officially acknowledged the existence of the GM80 project," it still seemed to the world that GM's front-wheel-drive sports car was most definitely on its way.

Four months later, the GM80 project came to a grinding and irrevocable stop.

In an article distributed by the Newhouse News Service on July 30, 1986, it was announced that "General Motors Corp. [would] delay indefinitely a $1 billion investment in a revolutionary, plastic-bodied car." On August 3, 1986, just four days after the announcement that the project had been suspended, an article in the *Detroit Free Press* reported that GM Chairman Roger Smith (along with the rest of the brass) made the decision to fully terminate the project after learning its budget "might top $2 billion."

Although General Motors had initially projected that it would build more than 350,000 examples of the GM80 Camaro and Firebird "twins," the complex and costly process of fabricating plastic body panels at that scale, along with the equally sizable costs associated with the technology packages being developed for each car, caused the project's budget to spiral out of control. Additionally, it was reported that the cars were far heavier than originally planned, and they performed poorly during crash tests.

There is no way to know exactly how much money General Motors invested into the GM80 platform, but given that the car had been nearly two years into its development when CEO Roger Smith terminated the program, it is reasonable to assume that the sum was considerable. Despite this, history has shown that Smith made the right decision. Given the unprecedented number of Camaro and Firebird owners who have continued to demand high-horsepower V-8 engines combined with the traditional front engine/rear-wheel-drive setup in their cars, the GM80 program may well have brought about the untimely end of the F-Body program.

A fair amount of speculation still exists around what happened to the GM80 prototypes. Most historians agree that the cars were destroyed (as is common practice at General Motors when a concept/development program is canceled). However, some believe that these same prototypes were temporarily repurposed to serve as the basis of design for other GM marques, including the Chevrolet Beretta, the Oldsmobile Cutlass Supreme coupe, and the Buick Reatta, before they were sent to the crusher. While this is mostly hearsay, there is no denying the styling similarities between the GM80 concepts and these other cars.

CHAPTER 4

FOURTH GENERATION (1993–2002)

"HAVING A LOW FRONT END WAS IMPORTANT TO THE DESIGN. IT REALLY WORKED WITH THE HIGH DECKLID REAR SPOILER TO ENHANCE THE APPEARANCE OF MOTION. ALL THESE YEARS LATER, IT STILL LOOKS CONTEMPORARY—AND FAST!"

— KIRK BENNION, CHEVROLET CAMARO EXTERIOR DESIGN MANAGER ON THE EXTERIOR DESIGN OF THE FOURTH-GENERATION MODEL

On May 30, 1993, the brand-new, fourth-generation Camaro Z28 served as the official pace car for the 77th running of the Indianapolis 500. It marked the fourth time in the brand's history that the Camaro served this honor. Previous Camaro pace cars (seen here) included a 1967 SS convertible, a 1969 RS/SS 396 convertible, and a 1982 Z28 coupe. (Photo Courtesy General Motors LLC)

Best remembered as one of the most dramatic examples of "cause and effect" within the last 50 years, there is no question that the introduction and unparalleled sales success of the original 1964½ Ford Mustang led to the genesis and the evolution of the Chevy Camaro less than three years later. It is all the more ironic then that another decision made by the Ford Motor Company more than 20 years later would have the exact opposite effect and would effectively save Chevrolet from making a major mistake during the development of the fourth-generation Camaro.

Chevrolet General Manager Jim Perkins gives spectators a big thumbs-up as they admire the new Camaro Z28 during the weekend festivities at Indy. (Photo Courtesy General Motors LLC)

In much the same way that General Motors had given serious consideration to producing a front-wheel-drive Camaro throughout much of the third-generation model's early development, Ford had also begun working on an entirely new sports coupe with longtime Japanese partner Mazda. Based on Mazda's MX-6 sport coupe, the compact, front-wheel-drive Ford Probe was originally intended to replace the fourth-generation Fox-Body Mustang. But when *Auto Week* published a story verifying the existence of the "ST-16 Mustang" concept coupe in April 1987, Mustang owners voiced their strong objections. By the time the car reached dealership showrooms, it had been rebranded as the Ford Probe.

After witnessing the overtly negative response Ford received to the ST-16 Mustang announcement, General Motors refused to make the same mistake with the Camaro. Although Chevrolet had started offering its consumers an ever-increasing assortment of front-wheel-drive vehicles throughout the 1980s, the company recognized the decades-long success of the Camaro's front-engine/rear-wheel-drive platform both on and off the racetrack. If nothing else, Ford's failure with the Probe had quelled any debate as to whether a front-wheel-drive option should even be considered for GM's next-generation pony car.

Instead, it was decided (at least internally) that the design studios should start developing an entirely new interior and exterior for the next-generation model that could pair with an updated version of the current model's chassis. In lieu of employing a smaller transverse-mounted engine, the new Camaro offered improved aerodynamics incorporated into its exterior architecture that could increase performance while simultaneously improving fuel efficiency.

Jim Perkins Saves the Camaro

Even as GM's design studios busied themselves with potential next-generation F-Body designs, there were sizable concerns being expressed within GM's hierarchy on whether or not the Camaro program should even continue beyond the third-generation model.

Under the leadership of Chairman and CEO Roger Smith, General Motors had undergone a tumultuous transformation in the mid- to late-1980s. Essentially, Smith had redirected each of GM's car divisions to consolidate into strategic joint ventures with Japanese and Korean automakers. The first step in this strategic realignment had been Smith's creation of two divisional "super groups": Buick-Oldsmobile-Cadillac (BOC), which was tasked with building larger vehicles, and Chevrolet-Pontiac-Canada (CPC), which built the smaller coupes and sporty cars. The Saturn corporation and the Geo marque both emerged as byproducts of Smith's realignment initiatives.

The newly formed BOC and CPC super groups created massive confusion throughout GM's hierarchy. Product quality suffered and, as a result, so did GM's reputation and sales volume. Smith's mandatory cost-savings strategies also brought the Camaro's (and Corvette's) continued development under serious scrutiny.

In fact, had it not been for Chevrolet General Manager Jim Perkins's efforts to save both marques in the late 1980s, it is likely that neither car would still exist today. Perkins's efforts provided the catalyst that saved both cars.

The Meteoric Rise of Jim Perkins at General Motors

A graduate of Baylor University, Jimmy C. Perkins joined Chevrolet in 1960 as a parts sorter in a Chevrolet warehouse. His success in that early role opened a floodgate of opportunities for him across the United States. Some of these roles included San Diego zone manager, Dallas zone manager, and director of marketing policy and dealer relations for all of General Motors, to name but a few.

His meteoric rise through the company afforded him career opportunities in the top positions of three famous car companies (Buick, Toyota, and Chevrolet) and made him one of the most powerful, most recognizable, and most popular automotive executives in North America (if not the entire world).

Perkins had been serving as the assistant general sales manager for Buick when he decided to leave General Motors to accept a position with the Toyota Motor Corporation. In early 1984, Toyota had approached Perkins about serving as senior vice president of Toyota's new Lexus luxury brand division. The opportunity had been too good to ignore. For the next four and a half years, Perkins helped Lexus rise to prominence. However, when he received word that Chevy general manager Bob Burger was retiring, he sought out the opportunity to return to General Motors to fill that role.

His return to Chevrolet in 1989 began with a battle to save the company's most iconic sports car marques: the Chevy Camaro and the Corvette. Perkins had always believed that image-enhancing sports cars enticed consumers into showrooms, even consumers who were looking to purchase an automobile that was more conventional, more affordable, or more family friendly than those sports cars offered. Now, he stood mostly alone on that front. Although he argued that the continuation of such brands would "excite the press" and "get people talking about Chevrolet and GM" in a favorable way (something that both needed desperately), there were few within the corporation's hierarchy who were prepared to listen.

In an excerpt from the book *Camaro: An American Icon* by Gary Witzenburg, Jim Perkins explained the challenges the Camaro (along with the Corvette) was facing during that time

"There was a real undercurrent at CPC and at high levels of GM to kill the project," Perkins said. "They didn't see the volume opportunity or the investment paying back. Corvette was going through the same thing; we had a battle on two fronts."

Despite the considerable resistance he received, Perkins continued to drive the fourth-generation Camaro program forward. He recruited CPC Engineer Dave Hansen to assume the design responsibilities previously managed by Chevrolet's chief engineer, a role which had been mostly dissolved as part of Smith's consolidation efforts a half-decade earlier. He challenged Hansen with developing the best Camaro possible. As Hansen went to work on the Camaro project, Perkins redoubled his efforts to build the necessary business justifications he needed to convince the CPC to keep building the car.

"Because it was a performance car, there was a Corporate Average Fuel Economy (CAFE) issue, the matter of where we would build it, and issues with union concessions that would have to be made," Perkins said. "But we kept grinding on it until we got the volume where we needed it [120,000 for Chevrolet], built a case that made sense, and got the car approved to be built in Canada—given the exchange rate, Canadian labor rates and its composite [body] materials."

It is generally agreed that Jim Perkins's return to General Motors in 1989 as Chevrolet's general manager provided the catalyst that kept the Camaro and Corvette from being discontinued completely. It was because of Perkins's actions, which included allocating funds to have prototypes of both sports cars assembled and marketed to would-be consumers, that these programs survived.

After retiring from General Motors in 1996, Perkins remained an active part of the automotive community. He joined Hendrick Automotive Group's network of 100 dealerships and served as its CEO until 2005. Perkins transitioned to leading Hendrick's racing and retail operations, where he also oversaw the development of specialty products for classic and high-performance Camaros, including the fifth-generation model. (Photo Courtesy General Motors LLC)

Conflicting Exterior Designs

The evolution of the fourth-generation Camaro (and Firebird) exterior really began with the creation of three unique concept cars: the 1987 Camaro F-14 Tomcat, the California Camaro, and the Pontiac Banshee. Although we delve into the history and evolution of each of these concept cars later in this chapter, it is worth noting here that their combined influence on the form and function of the fourth-generation F-Body cars was significant.

It is also worth noting that while each of the aforementioned concept cars was developed by an array of talented automotive designers and engineers, it was three men (Exterior Designer John Cafaro, Interior Designer Pat Furey, and Chief Engineer Ted Robertson) who were most directly responsible for leading the design and development of the production model Camaro that was first introduced by Chevrolet in 1993.

John Cafaro's Chevrolet Studio Two based much of the fourth-generation Camaro's exterior aesthetic on a full-scale, fiberglass model of the 1987 Camaro F-14 Tomcat concept car. The Tomcat Camaro concept had been presented to Chevy's Studio Two to help inspire the look of the production model even before Cafaro's team had been given the assignment. Given its dramatic, sweeping lines and its fighter-jet-inspired stance, it seemed more than reasonable that Cafaro's team would refine the concept car's somewhat radical styling into a more viable, production-capable design.

What no one in the Chevy Studio Two (including Cafaro) realized was that another concept car, the California Camaro, had been simultaneously developed in secret by GM's Advanced Design Studios. It was only presented to Cafaro's team after most of the design work on the production Camaro had been completed.

Per Cafaro, Design Vice President Chuck Jordan presented the California Camaro to the Studio Two team to show how the design "ought to have been done." Although Cafaro wasn't at the studio when Jordan reviewed the production car's final design with the Chevy Studio Two design team, it has been stated that Jordan severely criticized the design and insisted that his California Camaro would have made a much better design than the car they developed.

In Gary Witzenburg's book *Camaro: An American Icon*, John Cafaro shared the following about Jordan's response to his team's design.

"He said our car sucked, we didn't know what we were doing, and this was the way to go," Cafaro said. "But that car [the California Camaro] was an Advanced Design cartoon with gigantic wheels and no engineering criteria. It was great, but not doable, and that ruffled a lot of feathers . . . . The only thing we did incorporate from the California Camaro were those mirror pods where the mirrors are built into the fenders."

One of the later iterations of the full-scale Camaro F-14 Tomcat concept clay models is shown in the courtyard of GM's design studios. This model was presented to John Cafaro's design studio and provided most of the styling cues that Cafaro's team incorporated into the production model. (Photo Courtesy General Motors LLC)

While the California Camaro concept may appear to closely resemble the fourth-generation car, this model was only introduced to Cafaro's team after it had completed design work on the new Camaro's exterior. Only the California concept's unique mirror pods were ever incorporated into the production model. (Photo Courtesy General Motors LLC)

The Camaro's Slippery Surfaces

Both the fourth-generation Camaro and Firebird are unique in that they were the first F-Cars in either brand's history to use body panels made from anything other than stamped steel. While it is true that the second- and third-generation models used rubber front and rear fasciae, these were cosmetic elements specifically designed to conceal the steel bumper assemblies mounted beneath them.

In contrast, the majority of the fourth-generation F-Car's exterior panels, including the doors, hatch, roof, and spoiler assembly, were made out of sheet molded compound (SMC), a material composed of chopped fiberglass and polyester resin. The remaining body panels were fabricated out of a polyurethane material, except for the hood and rear quarter panels, which were still made from stamped steel.

According to *Camaro: An American Icon* by Witzenburg, "Some of the panels were bonded on, [and] some were mechanically attached. And we had many issues with surface quality on the SMC panels, which cost us a lot of time and aggravation," said Ted Robertson, the CPC's F-Car platform engineering director.

Additionally, building the cars out of composite materials resulted in slower part production, higher per-piece manufacturing costs, and increased gaps between body panels due to contraction in colder temperatures. At the same time, it had allowed designers greater creative freedom when defining the look of the car's exterior, tended to be more dent resistant than conventional steel panels, and had lower per-unit tooling costs.

The fourth-generation Camaro had a "fast" windshield with an extreme, 68-degree rake, which was 4 degrees more inclined than the fourth-generation Corvette. To accommodate this steep angle, the windshield was mounted so far forward that its leading edge and the car's cowl were positioned above the back third of the engine. The rear glass shared a similar, steep angle and appeared almost horizontal in appearance when the hatch was in its closed position. Likewise, the car incorporated a low, pointed nose; a swept-back hood and roofline; and rounded panels on just about every exterior surface of the car.

The car's teardrop shape conveyed an immediate sense of speed, even when standing still. Even its rear end featured rounded, integrated taillights; a rounded rear fascia; and an innovative "floating" spoiler that was an integral part of the rear decklid. Moreover, it was unlike any spoiler found on any Camaro that came before it.

Engineering the Fourth-Generation Camaro

While Cafaro's team developed an entirely new exterior for the fourth-generation Camaro in Chevy Studio Two, F-Body Engineering Director Ted Robertson worked with CPC's process and product engineers in the old Fisher Body building to engineer the car's underpinnings.

Robertson felt that the successful development of the fourth-generation Camaro required a wholistic team approach made up of the best engineering and design talents within General Motors, all working collaboratively to build the best car possible. He also knew that restricted budgets and a consensus from upper management that Chevrolet's beloved sports car should "die on the vine" meant that frugality would rule the day if a new Camaro had any chance of becoming a reality.

Instead of starting from scratch, as he might normally have done, Robertson elected to reimagine and fortify the chassis from a 1992 Camaro. Although Robertson's chassis appeared nearly identical to that used on the outgoing Camaro, it was increased in length to 101.1 inches, which was 0.1 inch longer than the previous model. More significantly, Robertson's chassis was 23 percent stiffer than before.

From early in the fourth-generation Camaro's development, it was decided that the car would use an extreme windshield rake of 68 degrees. The "faster" angle of the windshield is immediately identifiable when compared to the windshield rake of the 1989 Camaro IROC-Z coupe to its left. (Photo Courtesy General Motors LLC)

"We formed this super team to do the new F-Car and decided to redesign the previous-generation rear-drive vehicle," Robertson said, according to *Camaro: An American Icon* by Gary Witzenburg. "We did a new front end and a whole new interior and exterior, and we strengthened the structure, so the rails were new. And it would be the first digital, all-math vehicle in General Motors . . . not just designing it but doing the analytics and everything else in math."

Much of the third-generation Camaro's rear suspension was also repurposed for the fourth-generation model. The front suspension, meanwhile, was almost entirely reimagined. Rack-and-pinion steering was introduced for the first time on any production Camaro, and a short/long control-arm (SLA) assembly replaced the previous model's strut setup. Both the front and rear suspension were equipped with de Carbon (so named for inventor Christian Bourcier de Carbon) high-gas-pressure shock absorbers.

Moving to the four corners of the chassis, the base Camaro model was equipped with a front disc/rear drum brake setup. The Z28 Camaro, on the other hand, included disc brakes at all four wheels, with 10.9-inch rotors out front and 11.4-inch rotors in the rear. All variants of the fourth-generation Camaro were equipped with anti-lock brakes (ABS) as standard equipment.

Just two powerplants were offered with the new Camaro. The base model was equipped with an L32 engine, a sequential fuel-injected (SFI) 3.4L V-6 that produced a modest 160 hp and 200 ft-lbs of torque. It also offered consumers some relief at the fuel pump, producing 19 mpg in the city, but 28 mpg on the highway. Paired to the L32 engine was either a 5-speed manual transmission (which was standard) or an optional 4L60 4-speed automatic transmission. Much like its first-generation counterparts, the base-model Camaro was intended for consumers who wanted economical but sporty transportation.

Completed in May 1988, this early iteration of the production-model Camaro exterior blends elements previously introduced on the Camaro F-14 Tomcat concept with design cues introduced by John Cafaro's Chevy Studio Two. (Photo Courtesy General Motors LLC)

Although construction of this full-size clay model was completed nearly a half-decade before production formally began on the fourth-generation Camaro, many of its design elements (including the recessed headlamps; the general shape of the hood, fenders, and front fascia; and the 68-degree windshield rake) advanced through the rest of the design process with only minimal changes to their overall aesthetic. (Photo Courtesy General Motors LLC)

One of the fourth-generation Camaro's most unique design elements was its integrated rear spoiler. The initial spoiler concept was designed by Ken Okuyama. It was incorporated into the Camaro F-14 Tomcat concept car and quickly evolved into an integral part of the production model's exterior aesthetic. The version of the spoiler seen here is remarkably like the one that was introduced on the 1993 production model. (Photo Courtesy General Motors LLC)

As is true with most cars, the fourth-generation Camaro's interior also evolved from a series of sketches and full-scale clay models, such as the one seen here. One of the unique differentiators between the 1993 Camaro and future fourth-generation models was the yellow-numbered gauges (as seen here). The 1993 Camaro was the only production model to include yellow gauges; all future models featured white numbering. (Photo Courtesy General Motors LLC)

The Z28 Camaro was another story entirely. A slightly detuned version of the Corvette's Gen II LT1 engine was selected for Camaro's flagship model. Rated at 275 hp (at 5,000 rpm) and 326 ft-lbs of torque (at 2,400 rpm), the LT1 could launch the Z28 Camaro from 0 to 60 in just 5.9 seconds and run a standing quarter mile in just 14.7 seconds at a speed of 97 mph. Although that is timid by today's standards, the LT1 offered would-be speed junkies of the early 1990s something to stand up and cheer about.

The 1993 Camaro Z28 Indianapolis 500 pace car was virtually identical to the production model, except that it was equipped with a special roll cage and custom lighting for the racetrack. A total of three official pace cars were assembled, and Chevrolet produced 645 replicas for the 1993 model year. Chevrolet General Manager Jim Perkins piloted the actual pace car during the Indianapolis 500 race event. (Photo Courtesy General Motors LLC)

Keeping Pace with the Competition

The evolution of the fourth-generation Camaro from concept car to production model had been an uphill climb for everyone involved in the project. Even as the car came into its own, there were still many arguments being made that denounced the investment that GM's design and engineering departments had made to develop the new F-Car. For starters, Camaro sales had slipped from 261,591 units in 1984 to just 70,007 units in 1992, indicating a 73-percent market decrease in less than 10 years' time. Additionally, market data showed that former Camaro owners were steadily moving toward truck and SUV ownership.

Still, GM management eventually relented and approved the fourth-generation Camaro for production as a 1993 model. In October 1992, the new Camaro (as well as Firebird and Trans Am models) were unveiled at the South Florida International Auto Show. Although the sneak-preview reveal was done without fanfare, Chevrolet received a large amount of favorable feedback about the new car.

In December 1992, it was announced that a 1993 Camaro Z28 coupe would serve as the official pace car at the 77th running of the Indianapolis 500. The announcement was made by Tony George, president of the Indianapolis Motor Speedway, and Jim Perkins. Finished in a two-tone, black-over-white paint scheme with stylized rainbow striping separating them, the new Camaro pace car received an overwhelmingly positive response from spectators when it led the field before (and during) the famous 500-mile race on May 30, 1993.

It appeared, for the time being at least, that the fourth-generation Camaro had captured the minds and hearts of would-be consumers, once more securing the car's reputation as a viable American pony car.

Concept Cars that Inspired the Fourth-Generation Camaro

As was discussed earlier, the evolution of the 1993 Camaro (and Firebird) began with a series of concept cars developed in the mid-1980s by several of GM's design studios. While it is impossible to know with any certainty how much influence each concept car had on the design and development of the others (if any), there is no denying that each of the following

John Cafaro

Although he's probably best remembered as the chief designer of the fifth-generation Corvette, John Cafaro's long-term involvement with the Camaro program, and especially with leading the development of the fourth-generation model, demonstrates the diversity of his design talents as well as his significant contributions to both of these iconic brands.

Cafaro's aspirations to become an automotive designer began after he discovered Bill Mitchell's Mako Shark II concept at the 1965 New York Auto Show. Mitchell's iconic concept car had served as the centerpiece of the Chevy exhibit at that year's show. When young John spotted it, its aggressive styling and sleek, streamlined exterior sparked a passion in him that defined the course of his life.

According to Corvette Action Center, John stated, "I made up my mind I wanted to get into car design and go to GM."

Throughout his formative years, Cafaro's passion for automotive design continued to grow. He collected Matchbox and scale models of the Chevy Corvette and spent countless hours drawing them anywhere he could, including on his school textbooks. After graduating from high school, John attended the Pratt Institute, a liberal arts college in Brooklyn, New York, from 1973 to 1977. He graduated with a degree in industrial design.

John Cafaro poses with a pair of GM studio sculptors, both of whom are in the process of creating the third-scale clay model of his fifth-generation Corvette styling proposal. (Photo Courtesy General Motors LLC)

Now armed with a degree and a portfolio of design drawings that he had created while at school, Cafaro turned his attention to securing a position at General Motors. During a 1996 interview with Wayne Ellwood of *Shark Quarterly* magazine, Cafaro explained his first experiences with General Motors.

"I hadn't really thought that getting a job at GM was possible," he said. "Even once I got the interview, I didn't think I had done very well. I had been interviewed by Stan Wilen, and I had brought lots of finished sketches and a design for a minivan, which was my major project in my final year [of college]. But I hadn't brought many working sketches because they generally don't look as good as a final rendering. Stan made me run home to my brownstone to get more working sketches just to stay in the process; it seems that he wanted to see how I worked, not just what the finished item looked like. I got a call the next day that I had won the job. I flew to Detroit the very next day and started immediately."

John's first assignments at General Motors included work for Pontiac and on the third-generation Camaro. It was while working on the latter that Jerry Palmer first took notice of the young but talented designer. Palmer was impressed with Cafaro's passion for design and his collaborative efforts as part of the third-generation Camaro's design team. Palmer invited the young designer to work under him on the fourth-generation

A young John Cafaro works on a full-scale rendering inside the Pontiac design studios (circa 1983). Cafaro's talents as a designer caught the attention of GM's higher-ups and afforded him opportunities to work on several key programs, including the Pontiac Firebird, the Chevy Camaro, and the Corvette. (Photo Courtesy General Motors LLC)

Corvette program. Later, when Palmer was promoted to GM's Advanced Studios, he helped his protégé secure the chief designer position at Chevrolet's Studio Three, which was the studio responsible for the Camaro and the Corvette.

As head of Chevy Studio Three, Cafaro's team was tasked with developing the production variant of the fourth-generation Camaro and with designing an entirely new Corvette. At the same time, General Motors was facing significant financial challenges, which put both programs at risk. Other factors, including Chuck Jordan's desire to bring other studios into the fold on these projects, further threatened Chevy Studio Three's, and in turn Cafaro's, involvement with these projects.

As history has proven, Cafaro's team succeeded on both fronts, eventually giving rise to the 1993 Camaro and more notably (for Cafaro at least) the 1997 C5 Corvette, the latter of which solidified Cafaro's reputation as a designer and his career at General Motors. On September 1, 2002, he was inducted into the Corvette Hall of Fame at the National Corvette Museum in Bowling Green, Kentucky, for his significant design contributions to the fifth-generation Corvette.

Fred Gallasch, board director at the North Carolina Center for Automotive Research, shared the following statement about John on the LinkedIn social networking website.

"Having worked closely with John during [the] design and development of the fifth-generation Corvette, I can confirm that John is an outstanding designer who understands and listens to the customers," Gallasch wrote. "He is also a great friend and colleague."

Today, Cafaro serves as the director of design for Chevrolet.

Today, John Cafaro works as the global director of small crossovers and global small and midsize cars at General Motors. While he may not be in the trenches of the design department anymore, his leadership role allows him to remain close to the creative process while also ensuring the continued success of GM's brands around the world. (Photo Courtesy General Motors LLC)

cars share at least some of the same styling attributes as their counterparts.

What is known is that designer John Cafaro used the first of these cars, the Camaro F-14 Tomcat, to advance the styling on the fourth-generation model that would go to market in 1993. Similarly, many of the styling elements introduced on the Pontiac Banshee gave rise to the fourth-generation Firebird as well as select design aspects of the fourth-generation Camaro. Even the California Camaro, for all the secrecy surrounding its development, shared styling elements that are reminiscent of the fourth-generation Camaro.

The remainder of this chapter is dedicated to these cars: the 1987 F-14 Tomcat Camaro, the California Camaro, and the Pontiac Banshee IV, and the talented individuals responsible for their creation.

1987 Camaro F-14 Tomcat

When the Paramount Pictures hit film *Top Gun* premiered in 1986, it inspired a generation of movie goers to literally reach for the skies. The movie resulted in a 500-percent increase in applications received by the U.S. Navy from young men and women who yearned to become naval aviators. It also made the navy's sweep-wing fighter, the F-14 Tomcat, an overnight superstar. Little did anyone know that the movie, and the jets featured in it, served as a source of inspiration for a designer who happened to be working at GM's Advanced Studios in the late 1980s.

Of course, history is replete with automobile designs inspired by military aircraft. Harley Earl pioneered the idea when he introduced his luxurious LeSabre coupe (appropriately named after the F86 Sabre fighter jet) in 1951. The trend of designing cars based on warplanes continued to gain popularity throughout the 1950s and 1960s. They not only shared a common name, as was the cast with the Ford Mustang, but actually "borrowed" styling cues from their sky faring counterparts as well.

In 1987, Jerry Palmer's Advanced Studios introduced the F-14 Tomcat Camaro concept. Along with the radical California Camaro and the Pontiac Banshee concepts that would be

The F-14 Tomcat Camaro concept is shown on display in the outdoor courtyard of GM's design studios in Detroit, Michigan. Developed by designers Clark Lincoln and Ken Okuyama, the Tomcat concept provided John Cafaro's team with a strong foundation from which to develop the look of the fourth-generation Camaro. (Photo Courtesy General Motors LLC)

This was one of Ken Okuyama's early renderings of the F-14 Tomcat Camaro. Although his design uses body lines that are more fluid than those introduced on the Tomcat concept car, Okuyama's drawings provided the catalyst for the future look of the fourth-generation Camaro and the C5 Corvette, both of which he helped design during his tenure at General Motors. (Photo Courtesy General Motors LLC)

introduced shortly after its introduction, the Tomcat Camaro provided many of the styling motifs that John Cafaro's Chevy Studio Two incorporated into the fourth-generation production Camaro design.

The F-14 Tomcat Camaro concept was developed by Chief Designer Clark Lincoln from a series of original sketches by Ken Okuyama, a young but promising designer in the Advanced Studios. It featured a fighter-canopy greenhouse and vestigial delta wings sprouting from its rocker panels. Early models of the Tomcat concept also included a split rear spoiler that harkened to the twin vertical stabilizers protruding from the rear of the U.S. Navy's premier fighter jet. Later iterations of the Tomcat concept abandoned the split spoiler in favor of a single, integrated rear spoiler. A version of this same spoiler would be introduced on the production Camaro a few years later.

One of the early, full-scale renderings of the F-14 Tomcat Camaro is shown inside of GM's design studios. Even at this early stage in the design process, the exterior aesthetic of the next-generation F-Body (Camaro and Firebird alike) begins to emerge. (Photo Courtesy General Motors LLC)

A third-scale clay model of the F-14 Tomcat Camaro is shown inside the GM design studios. At this stage, sculptors build the right hemisphere of the concept car and mount it against glass to present a complete car to the designers, management, etc. This process of building half of the car saves time and money as decision-makers evaluate which designs should advance and which should be rejected. (Photo Courtesy General Motors LLC)

The following details pay homage to the exterior of the Navy's F-14 Tomcat fighter jet: the delta wing protruding from the rocker panels; the split vertical-stabilizer spoiler; the pitched, wedge-style architecture; and even the two-tone aesthetic of the car's upper section. (Photo Courtesy General Motors LLC)

This was the first of the full-scale clay models of the Tomcat Camaro concept. Although its stance and some of its exterior features were considered to be too radical for a production-model Camaro, there is no denying that the Tomcat concept provided much of the design framework from which the fourth-generation production model evolved. (Photo Courtesy General Motors LLC)

During an interview about the Pontiac Banshee, Designer Jerry Palmer shared the following about the Tomcat Camaro.

"We also had another car going down in the advanced area, one called the Tomcat," he said. "The Tomcat was another [F-Car design] study, and it really came off a Ken Okuyama sketch. It did something that I thought [was] important to the production F-Car program. The Tomcat really set the windshield angle and the character of the upper, the area above the "beltline" [the windshield, A- and B-pillars, roof, etc.]. In that way, it helped package the vehicle."

The Camaro F-14 Tomcat (as well as the production Camaro that debuted as a 1993 model) featured a windshield set at a dramatic 68-degree angle. The steep rake of the windshield perplexed GM's engineers, many of whom argued that, if introduced, would give the Camaro a steeper windshield rake than the one previously introduced on the current Corvette (64.5 degrees). Engineers Harvey Bell and Ted Robertson contended that a 68-degree windshield was "much too fast/sloping" and that its inclusion would create several additional design issues, including wipers that would lift off the windshield at high speeds and improper airflow into the car's cowl. Adamant that the steeper angle was an essential element of the car's form and function, the design studios ultimately prevailed, and the 68-degree windshield remained a part of the final design.

In Witzenburg's book *Camaro: An American Icon*, Jerry Palmer explained the purpose behind the initial development of the Tomcat Camaro.

"I'm a firm believer that competition improves the breed, so we wanted to get a little competition going between the

The full-scale clay model of the F-14 Tomcat Camaro concept sits next to a 1988 IROC-Z edition third-generation Camaro in the courtyard of GM's design studios. Note the two separate design architectures on each hemisphere of the Tomcat Camaro model. This was often done to evaluate two unique designs at once and/or to aid in determining how well specific elements of a design worked with the overall package. (Photo Courtesy General Motors LLC)

Although the F-14 Tomcat Camaro was a dramatic reimagining of the third-generation Camaro platform, this side-by-side evaluation demonstrates that the concept car is an evolution of the brand and not a complete departure from it. (Photo Courtesy General Motors LLC)

Here's a front view of the F-14 Tomcat Camaro concept taken in the courtyard of GM's design studios in August 1988. This model, which now included fiberglass body panels and a fully realized interior, would be used extensively by Cafaro and his design studio throughout the development of the fourth-generation exterior styling. (Photo Courtesy General Motors LLC)

Unfortunately, little is known (at least outside of General Motors) as to the whereabouts of the original Camaro F-14 Tomcat clay models. Presumably, the models are still in storage at one of GM's design studios/warehouses, but it is also possible they were destroyed at some point after production of the fourth-generation Camaro began. (Photo Courtesy General Motors LLC)

advanced and production studios," Palmer said. "The production studio had its hands full, so we got a head start and did some studies of proportions and a very fast windshield."

The F-14 Tomcat Camaro concept advanced from its preliminary design sketches and scale models to a series of full-size clay models between the late spring/early summer of 1987 and the fall of 1988. A full-scale fiberglass model of the Tomcat concept was completed before Cafaro's Studio Two had started working on the production car. As such, the Tomcat Camaro served as the design inspiration for the fourth-generation Camaro program, which was originally slated for release as a 1992 model.

While much of the production car's styling would vary from the Tomcat concept, the integrated rear spoiler/decklid assembly advanced largely unchanged (minus the full-length brake light). Additionally, the lower, two-tone fascia with integrated exhaust ports (as seen here), would be repurposed on the Pontiac Firebird and Trans Am production cars. (Photo Courtesy General Motors LLC)

Many of the Tomcat's most extreme features had been refined and/or abandoned by the time that the fourth-generation Camaro was fully realized. The production model lacked the Tomcat's aggressive front and rear-end stance, included less angular doors, and incorporated side skirts that were devoid of the aforementioned vestigial delta wings. Nonetheless, several of the concept car's design elements transcended the concept car and appeared on the production model with only minimal changes to their design architecture.

Even though Jerry Palmer's 1989 California Camaro and Tom Peter's Pontiac Banshee were considered superior design concepts by the likes of Charles Jordan, there is no argument that the 1987 Tomcat Camaro played a pivotal role in the evolution of the fourth-generation Camaro.

It has also been claimed that the concept car influenced the exterior styling being developed for the proposed 1989 Pontiac Fiero redesign. Unfortunately, the next-generation Fiero project was abandoned when GM management decided to discontinue production of Pontiac's two-seat, mid-engine sports car at the end of the 1988 model year.

Advanced Concepts Center IROC-Z/ California Camaro Concept

In September 1983, General Motors established a new satellite design studio on the West Coast of the United States. Officially known as GM's Advanced Concepts Center, the small studio was opened in Newbury Park, a mostly residential area within the city limits of Thousand Oaks and just a few miles northwest of Los Angeles, California. It was the first of several such studios to emerge in that region. Although each of these studios belonged to a different American or Japanese automobile manufacturer, they all shared a common objective: to capitalize on the creative design trends being introduced on the West Coast.

The 1989 California IROC-Z Camaro concept car was developed in GM's California-based Advanced Concepts Center as an homage to West Coast lifestyles. (Photo Courtesy General Motors LLC)

Four years after its official launch, long-time Pontiac and Chevrolet Designer John Schinella was named director of the Advanced Concepts Center by Charles M. "Chuck" Jordan, GM's latest vice president of styling. Because of Schinella's earlier work on several of GM's most iconic automobiles, includ-

> "ESSENTIALLY, THIS MEANT DESIGNING A CAR THAT WAS MORE LIGHTWEIGHT, MORE FUEL EFFICIENT, AND MORE AGILE THAN THE CURRENT MODEL."

ing the original Camaro and the second-generation Pontiac Trans Am, it was thought that his leadership and vision would align perfectly with the avant-garde styling being nurtured and showcased in the West Coast studio.

GM Design Chief Charles Jordan was instrumental in the early development of the California Camaro concept program. At his direction, the 50-plus-person team at the Advanced Concepts Center transformed his ideas for a radical new Camaro into a fully realized, full-scale prototype. (Photo Courtesy General Motors LLC)

In 1989, Jordan approached Schinella and the Advanced Concepts Center with a unique assignment. He wanted Schinella's design team, which now consisted of more than 50 stylists, to create a new Camaro concept that would "stop people in their tracks when they saw it."

The car's design was to be based on some of the styling motifs already being considered for the fourth-generation model. Moreover, Jordan wanted to make certain that Schinella's team incorporated the latest West Coast design motifs. The car was scheduled to appear at many of the coming year's major auto shows to help corporate leadership gauge public opinion of the next-generation Camaro.

Schinella set his team to work on the project at once. He tasked Jim Bieck, chief designer, with developing the preliminary design for the California Camaro concept. It was decided from the start that the car should personify the West Coast lifestyle. Essentially, this meant designing a car that was more lightweight, more fuel efficient, and more agile than the current model. For Schinella, it also meant the car should allow its occupants to "soak in the California sun." This meant a design that incorporated an open, airy cockpit with large windows for unrestricted visibility.

Bieck's design evolved quickly. Under Jordan's guidance, Schinella and his team advanced the latest Camaro concept from full-scale drawings to both scale- and full-size clay models to a fully realized concept vehicle in a period of just six months, which was virtually unheard of when developing a functional prototype from scratch. The car, which was now being referred to as both the "1989 Chevrolet California Camaro concept"

From the beginning, the California Camaro concept was envisioned with quasi-gull-wing doors. Providing doors that swung up and forward would allow easier access into and out of the car's interior, especially for passengers accessing the car's rear seating. (Photo Courtesy General Motors LLC)

Under Schinella's direction, the Advanced Concepts Center's design staff developed several sketches of the 1989 California Camaro IROC-Z concept. These drawings provided a much-needed foundation from which the design evolved. (Photo Courtesy General Motors LLC)

Much of the California Camaro concept's exterior styling was repurposed during the development of the fourth-generation Camaro. While the final architecture of the fourth-generation model was somewhat less dramatic than the image seen here, there's no denying the relationship between this early rendering of the California concept car and the production model that was manufactured by Chevrolet between 1993 and 2002. (Photo Courtesy General Motors LLC)

and the "Advanced Concepts Center IROC-Z Camaro," was striking in appearance. It was also as a major departure from anything that had come before it.

Schinella's team had given the car an aggressive, forward-sloping, wedge-shaped profile. A single character line, beginning at the car's pointed nose and wrapping uniformly around the entirety of the car, essentially divided the wedge into upper and lower sections. The car's front and rear fasciae, which were both made of polyurethane, formed the only visible segment of the car's beltline. The rest (from the beltline down at least) was fabricated out of steel, which was virtually unheard of during this early stage of development.

Above its beltline, the car featured a steeply raked, wraparound windshield and a large, convex rear window, the latter of which was incorporated into the car's hatchback assembly. Between these two fixtures, the car's forward-opening, scissor-style doors each supported a single glass assembly comprised of side window glass paired to a flush-mounted glass roof panel. Except for the A- and B-pillars, and some minimal structural supports within the window/roof assemblies, the upper section of the California Camaro afforded vehicle occupants with virtually unobstructed views of their surroundings. In the March 12, 1989, article "Design Study Produces Concept Camaro," John Schinella explained that all that glass provided "lots of planned view(s) to take in the California sunshine."

When either door was opened, the entire massive assembly (which included the glass window and roof panel) rotated

When opened, the California Camaro's quasi-gull-wing doors rotated forward and outward at a 45-degree angle. Each massive door assembly was comprised of the lower door skin and substructure as well as an upper glass section supported by a portion of the roofline's metal structural assembly. (Photo Courtesy General Motors LLC)

The California concept was equipped with a full array of analog instruments, controls, buttons, switches, and a digital speedometer. Collectively, the driver's cockpit looked far more futuristic than any other vehicle being developed by General Motors at that time. One interesting item of note is the difference in color between the driver's seat and passenger's seat: the driver's seat is red, while the passenger's is black. (Photo Courtesy General Motors LLC)

forward at a 45-degree angle. Once fully opened, the driver and/or passenger could easily enter or exit the cockpit without being forced to contort their bodies to fit the space (a known issue that has plagued sports car owners for generations).

Upon entering the cockpit, occupants were introduced to a dramatically reimagined interior that included a full set of analog instruments paired with a digital speedometer; a high-mounted, short-throw gearshift lever; a smaller-diameter steering wheel with readily accessible control stalks for the wipers, cruise, lights, etc.; and a red driver's seat with high side bolsters. The passenger's seat, though similarly appointed, came finished in black.

Everything inside the cockpit was designed to enhance the overall driving experience. The driver's seat was mounted

Among the interior's many convenience features, the red driver's seat in the California Camaro concept swiveled outward to provide the driver improved access to the car's cockpit. The driver's seat could also be custom built to the specifications of the driver. (Photo Courtesy General Motors LLC)

on a swivel that, like the scissor-hinged doors before it, was designed to make entering and exiting the vehicle that much easier. The red driver's seat could also be custom fitted to accommodate the specific shape/body mass of a single driver, thereby offering the vehicle operator a more personalized interface between themselves and the car. Similarly, the steering wheel and the pedals could also be adjusted (moved forward or backward) to accommodate varying arm and/or leg lengths, ensuring greater overall ease of operation and more precise control. In fact, the layout of the California Camaro's interior was directly inspired by feedback from Formula One drivers.

Interestingly, an all-aluminum, DOHC 3.1L V-6 engine was selected as the powerplant for the 1989 California IROC Camaro concept car. Given California's stricter emissions standards and higher fuel costs, the engine choice probably made sense for the prototype. However, it left many Camaro enthusiasts across the United States concerned about the next-generation model's long-term viability, especially if Chevrolet elected to build the new model without an optional, 8-cylinder engine.

The Advanced Concepts Center IROC-Z/California Camaro concept was unveiled for the first time on January 7, 1989, at the Los Angeles International Auto Show. Finished in bright red and wearing both "Camaro" and "IROC Z" decals, the latest Camaro concept was a precursor of the production model that followed it just four years later. While many of its design elements, including the sideview mirrors, a less radical version of its front and rear fasciae, and its basic, overall aesthetic, were mostly repurposed for the 1993 Camaro coupe, the production model was approximately 8 inches longer, measuring in at 192 inches to the California Camaro's overall length of just 186.4 inches.

Why did General Motors elect to include the IROC-Z moniker on the car? Most likely, the automaker was attempting to garner added public approval for the California Camaro concept car by leveraging the popularity of the third-generation Camaro's involvement in the annual International Race of Champions (IROC) race series.

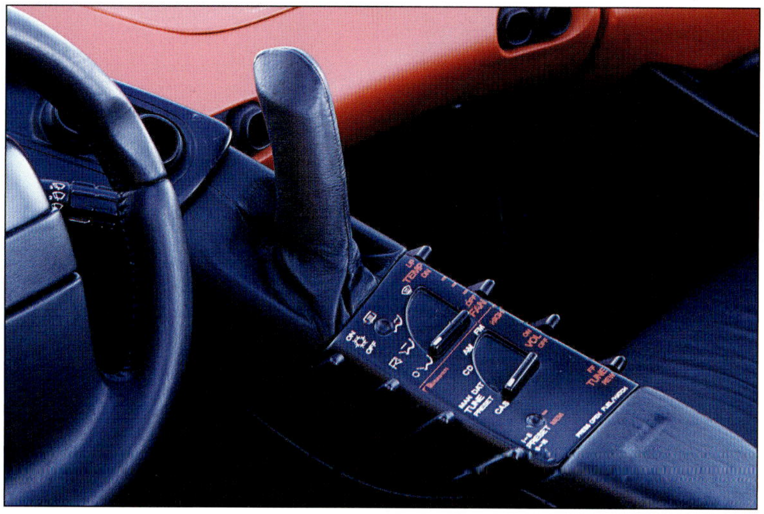

Nearly all the car's creature comforts could be managed through the controls mounted on the California Camaro's center console. Individual dials and levers were developed by GM's interior designers to allow ease of access when operating the radio, heating/air conditioning, fan speeds, and more. (Photo Courtesy General Motors LLC)

The California Camaro was fitted with a 3.1L, dual-overhead-cam V-6 engine as its sole powerplant. When the car was first introduced, it left many enthusiasts wondering/concerned whether a production version of the car would be offered with an optional V-8 engine. (Photo Courtesy General Motors LLC)

Although the Camaro California Concept (along with the Banshee IV) was introduced to help usher in a new aero-focused design motif, the car itself was deemed too radical to be considered for production. Many of its features, including its gull-wing doors, its unique driver's seat, its aviation-inspired gauges, and its integrated vacuum cleaner (not pictured), were all deemed to be nonstarters for a production model Camaro. (Photo Courtesy General Motors LLC)

Both "Camaro" and "IROC-Z" monikers were included on the California concept. While the engine installed in the concept lacked the horsepower requirements that many consumers demanded of any modern Camaro, the inclusion of the IROC-Z labeling led many to believe that a more powerful version of the Camaro would follow if the car moved to production. (Photo Courtesy General Motors LLC)

Pontiac Banshee IV

While this book is mostly devoid of the Pontiac-branded F-Body concept cars, the 1988 Pontiac Banshee IV was included here for several reasons. First, the Banshee IV was designed by Camaro Chief Designer Tom Peters (albeit before he officially carried that title). Second, the Banshee IV, along with the California Camaro, are collectively recognized as the "free expression" concepts that inspired the fourth-generation F-Cars.

Charles M. Jordan, former vice president of design for General Motors, was once asked during an interview to discuss the influence both concepts had on the F-Body program.

"The Camaro and the Firebird have always been partners," Jordan said.

Finally, the Banshee IV was one of several concepts developed by General Motors to help polish the company's tarnished reputation. While the Corvette has always served as Chevrolet's official "image" car, the F-Cars have always been recognized as image leaders as well, especially the Trans Am, which never lived in the shadow of the Corvette the way the Chevy Camaro did (an often still does).

The idea to create the Banshee IV began after the demise of the proposed GM80 front-wheel-drive F-Car program (introduced in Chapter 3). It was developed as one of five concept show cars for GM's 1988 Teamwork and Technology Trade Show that, like GM's Motorama shows of the mid- to late-1950s, was held at the Waldorf-Astoria Hotel in New York City. Its creation and introduction at the event served two basic but significant purposes: help strengthen the public's waning opinion of the Pontiac brand and provide consumers with a look at the styling being developed for the F-Body program, especially the 1993 Firebird.

The Banshee IV program was assigned to Pontiac Chief Designer John R. "Jack" Folden and Pontiac Interior Designer Will D. "Bill" Scott. As part of the assignment, the pair was tasked with developing a show car that would help consumers visualize what the next-generation Firebird might look like. In so doing, design management hoped to promote (and evaluate) customer enthusiasm for the evolving brand. Folden and Scott were encouraged to create a show car that took risks and tried very daring approaches.

Folden was no stranger to the Pontiac Firebird, having worked on the brand since the mid-1970s. He had previously worked on the second- and third-generation models and had been responsible for the mid-generation updates on each. Folden understood what the management team (which consisted of Jordan, Executive Designer Stan Wilen, and Design Director Dave Holls) was looking for, and he knew the right people within the Pontiac II Design Studio who could give them exactly what they wanted.

Folden tasked a young Tom Peters with creating the appearance and theme of the Banshee. Peters had recently been named the assistant chief designer of the Pontiac II Studio. His previous efforts on the 1986 Corvette Indy concept (a unique mid-engine concept Corvette created as an expression of pure design) made him an obvious choice for this assignment.

Peters began designing a new Banshee at once and by December 1987, he had created a series of sketches that embodied the aesthetic and the emotion that Folden had been hoping for. Peters's design fueled the imagination of other Pontiac II designers, and it wasn't long before his early sketches started to evolve, thanks to considerable input generated by the entire design staff, into a viable, fully realized concept model.

In a piece written by Michael Lamm called "Flying in Style—Tracing the Design Evolution of the Fourth-Generation Firebird," John Folden recounted how the studio rallied around the Pontiac Banshee's design.

"All our studio contributed, and we stayed in many a long night to get the work done," Folden said. "Dave Rand and Craig Janos also played key roles in the development process, as did all our studio sculptors and engineers. I feel we have one of the best and most creative teams in the business."

A full-scale clay mock-up of the Pontiac Banshee was displayed as part of Walt Disney's Epcot attraction "The World of Motion Presented by General Motors." The ride featured more than 170 animatronic figures and 16 GM cars (including the Banshee) and offered visitors a 14.5-minute history of transportation narrated by Gary Owens, a voice actor and American radio personality. An interesting footnote, General Motors was the very first sponsor of Disney's Epcot Center. (Photo Courtesy General Motors LLC)

While working for the Pontiac design studios, GM Designer Tom Peters was tasked with designing the Pontiac Banshee IV. This early rendering from August 1987 by Peters established the design motifs for the Banshee IV concept car program. (Photo Courtesy General Motors LLC)

By December 1987, Peters produced a more fully realized rendering of the Banshee IV (seen here). This highly stylized rendering enabled the studio to transform Peters's vision into a series of full-scale design drawings and to begin modeling the car out of clay. (Photo Courtesy General Motors LLC)

Complying with the F-Car's Architecture

By early 1988, GM's engineering division had determined the next-generation F-Car's basic architecture. The Camaro and Firebird models were to be an entirely new car, although its basic dimensions, including wheelbase (101.1 inches), overall length (195.6 to 197 inches), overall width (74.5 inches), and overall height (51.7 inches) would be nearly the same as the previous generation. Also as before, the cars would feature a front-engine, rear-wheel-drive configuration.

One notable change that was made to the car's architecture was its front suspension, which now included both upper and lower control arms. This configuration enabled designers to introduce a lower cowl and hood profile on the next-generation model.

"When we knew what the limitations were, the studios went through a preliminary design, which we weren't all that happy with," Jordan said. "Jerry Palmer and his guys made full-size tape drawings of the California Camaro and adapted that design to the geometry we knew we'd have in the next F-Car. Jerry's people worked independently down in the basement of our building, where nobody bothered them. I wanted to see how much of the California Camaro they could get into the production job. Eventually, we had to wrestle a little with the platform and money people, but Palmer's work had an influence on what was then moved back upstairs."

A full-scale tape drawing of the Banshee IV is shown inside the Pontiac design studio. Many of the design motifs seen here would be reintroduced a half-decade later on both the fourth-generation Camaro and Firebird models. (Photo Courtesy General Motors LLC)

The full-scale clay model of the Banshee IV begins to take shape inside the Pontiac design studio. As is common during the evolution of any new design, scale models (like the one seen here in the foreground) are often created first for preliminary design approval and later to provide sculptors a three-dimensional reference model from which to work. (Photo Courtesy General Motors LLC)

In addition to the California Camaro and the evolving Pontiac Banshee IV designs, the Advanced Studio was also developing a third Camaro design study. Designated the Camaro Tomcat, this concept model also included elements that were eventually incorporated into the production F-Car program, including the car's windshield angle and the overall character of the car's upper section.

From Clay to Drivable Concept

Working from a series of detailed sketches and scale models, the Pontiac II and the Advanced Studios began fabricating a pair of full-scale clay models of the Banshee IV. Each of these models incorporated styling elements developed between the two studios, and each used an assortment of elements previously introduced on the California Camaro and the Camaro Tomcat design study.

"We did various versions, and each time we'd take the two full-size clays out in the courtyard to compare them," Jack Folden said. "We'd say, 'Well, I like this area a little better—or that area.' And Chuck [Jordan] would point to different details that he preferred. We were constantly trying various sail-panel arrangements and configurations. It was a little like a competition between our two studios and yet a cooperative venture all at the same time."

One of the Banshee IV's more controversial design elements was the introduction of a proposed 68-degree windshield. While the design teams loved the looks of the steeply raked glass, engineers expressed concern that the windshield was "too fast" (too steeply sloped) to be functional. Specific concerns around proper airflow into the cowl vents and windshield wiper operability at driving speeds were given to

Tom Peters examines the Banshee IV model inside the Pontiac design studio. While models of this sort normally take several months to complete, designers and/or engineers may choose to refine/change the design during the clay model's ongoing development based on updated information related to chassis development, wind-tunnel testing, etc. (Photo Courtesy General Motors LLC)

To create body panels for a drivable prototype, the full-scale clay Banshee model was coated in several layers of a plaster material. Once cured, the plaster was carefully removed from the model. The negative body surfaces captured in the plaster were then used to create fiberglass body panels that were later bonded to a tubular chassis (not pictured). (Photo Courtesy General Motors LLC)

the design departments. Yet, try as they might, Folden's studio prevailed. When the production model Firebird was introduced in 1993, it included a windshield with a 68-degree rake.

Once design settled on the final exterior aesthetic for the Banshee, the project moved from clay modeling to the creation of a fully engineered and drivable concept car. A tubular chassis was fabricated with a 105-inch wheelbase (4 inches longer than either the third- or fourth-generation production Firebirds), four-wheel independent suspension, and a low center of gravity. Exterior body panels were fabricated out of fiberglass and mounted to the chassis.

The car's exterior had an aggressive, almost menacing appearance. It included a radical front end with a pair of large inlets and concealed headlamps mounted at the front of the car's prow. Everything about the car's exterior had a "slippery" aesthetic to it. There were no hard edges or straight lines breaking up its near "fluid" form. The wheel openings in each fender were carefully sculpted to push air up and around the openings,

The completed Banshee concept underwent wind-tunnel testing to evaluate its aerodynamic and downforce capabilities. As expected, the car had an extremely "slippery" profile. Even so, the car's performance limits were never identified, as the operational prototype's top speed was governed at 55 mph. (Photo Courtesy General Motors LLC)

The Pontiac Banshee IV concept was equipped with a 4.0L, double-overhead-cam, aluminum V-8 engine capable of producing 230 hp. One of the engine's most unique characteristics was its integrated block/cylinder head design, which eliminated the need for head gaskets or connecting hardware. (Photo Courtesy General Motors LLC)

The Banshee's 4.0L engine was concealed beneath a highly stylized V-shaped hood. When released, the hood opened toward the front of the car on a pivot hinge mounted along the front radiator-support assembly. When designing the hood assembly, Tom Peters incorporated the Pontiac "V" motif into his design as a not-so-subtle acknowledgement of the car's branding. (Photo Courtesy General Motors LLC)

thereby reducing drag. Even the car's dual rear wings were adjustable to allow for maximum aerodynamics during various driving conditions.

As with the body panels, all the car's glass was carefully designed to create an extremely aerodynamic surface, and each piece was integrated with the others to eliminate drag. The front glass assembly wraps up and over the top of the car, forming a hybrid windshield/glass roof assembly that effectively eliminates any forward-facing visual obstructions from inside the cockpit. The car's minimalist A-pillars were integrated into the front glass, while its stylized B-pillar/halo assembly is flush mounted with the front and rear glass panels. Even the glass on the outward-opening doors is contoured to create a nearly seamless upper assembly once the doors are closed.

Despite its incredibly low cowl height, the Pontiac Banshee IV was designed from the start to use a front-mounted engine. A 4.0L, dual-overhead-cam (DOHC) prototype V-8 engine paired to a 5-speed manual transmission was selected as the car's powerplant. Rated at 230 hp (at 5,600 rpm), the experimental engine used an integrated block-and-head configuration that eliminated the need for a head gasket. Though not originally developed for the Banshee IV, the one-of-a-kind engine proved to be a viable powerplant for Pontiac's concept car and remains its sole powerplant to this day.

A Futuristic Cockpit

While there's no denying that the Banshee IV's exterior was a radical departure from anything being produced by General Motors at that time, its fully realized interior was even more captivating. It offered its occupants a genuine look at the technologies that General Motors would begin integrating into its cars in the years and decades to come.

Designer Will Scott created an interior that has been described as "a blend of 1988 and 2008" by Pontiactransamforum.com. Yet, as advanced as it appeared (especially when first introduced), it was also intended to provide design motifs that could be adapted for future production versions of the Pontiac Firebird and Chevy Camaro. It might surprise some readers to discover just how many of the futuristic technologies introduced in the Banshee have become mainstays on many of GM's current automobiles.

One of the most notable technologies introduced in the Banshee IV was its heads-up display (HUD) system. The HUD provided the car's driver with specific vehicle information including speed, engine RPM, fuel levels, and more. This information was projected onto the Banshee's windshield directly, which enabled drivers to keep their eyes on the road.

Below where the HUD graphic was projected, a virtual image display (VID) was installed. The VID was comprised of a recessed computer screen in the upper section of the driver-side dashboard just above the steering column. This display created/projected a virtual 3-dimensional image of the car's tachometer, as well as its water, oil, and voltage gauges that the driver could quickly reference when needed. A camera mounted in the car's rear spoiler provided the driver with a panoramic view of everything happening behind the car.

Additional technologies within the car's cockpit included

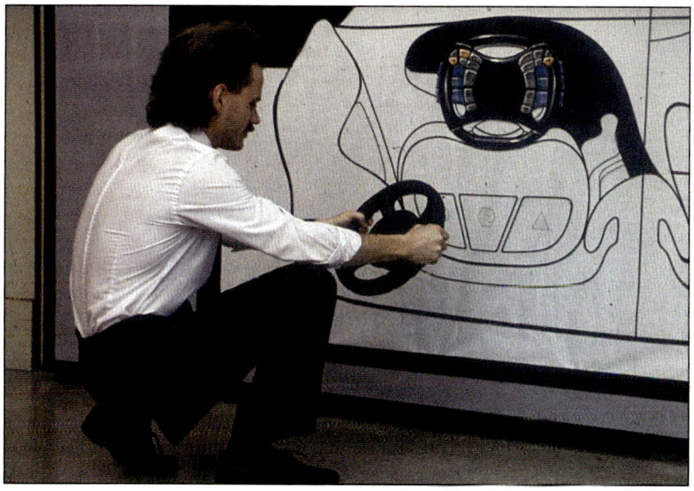

This is an interior tape drawing of the Pontiac Banshee's dashboard and forward cockpit. GM Designer Tim Grieg evaluates one of the Banshee's early steering-wheel molds against the full-scale drawing to determine additional styling changes and review control button placement. (Photo Courtesy General Motors LLC)

a g-meter, which provided the driver a readout of g-forces experienced during straight-line acceleration and when cornering/making sharp turns; a performance information center that provided real-time feedback on fuel consumption, average speed, 0–60 acceleration, and more; and a 3-dimensional electronic navigation system, or global positioning system (GPS), that provided drivers with real-time navigation and (allegedly) even identified when on-coming traffic was approaching.

Turning to the rest of the car's interior, Scott's intention was to create a space-age feel that exuded performance and style combined with practicality and ease of access. He introduced a pair of front seats that were made up of two separate sections: the lower section was pretty much a standard bucket seat with high side bolsters for reduced slip during performance driving.

Unlike most bucket seats, the backrest portion of the seats were comprised of a pair of stand-alone assemblies mounted to a stylized center arm that then mounted to the center console. By constructing the abbreviated upper sections of each seat this way, the entire upper assembly could be pivoted out of the way, allowing greater (and easier) access to the rear seats.

A pair of Pontiac's interior designers evaluate the dashboard and console component fitment/placement on a full-scale clay mock-up of the Banshee's interior. (Photo Courtesy General Motors LLC)

The car featured a cutting-edge AM/FM stereo radio with CD player. High-fidelity speakers were mounted into both the driver's and passenger's headrests, and each occupant was provided an independent volume control located in the car's center console.

In addition to these controls, the car's unique steering wheel included a second set of controls for the car's sound system, as well as additional buttons (20 in all) that controlled the car's lights, horn, radio presets, and more. While its original configuration probably

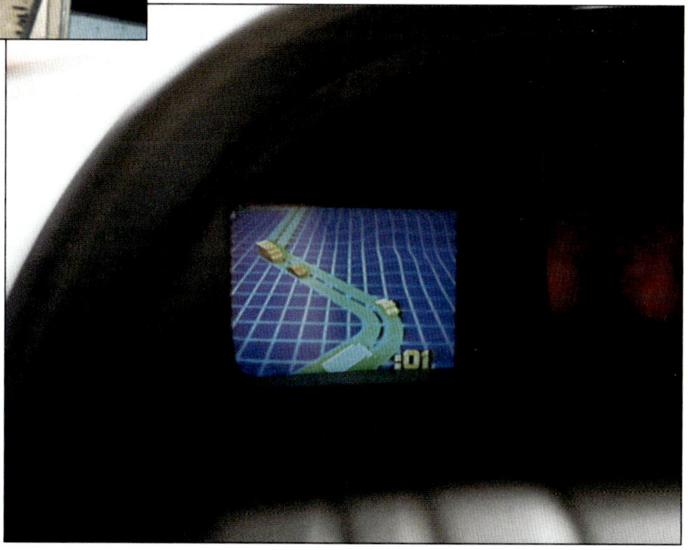

The Banshee IV concept was one of the very first cars to feature a heads-up display (HUD), a vehicle information center, rearview monitors, and an onboard global positioning system (GPS). The Etak navigational system (seen here) used a TV monitor to project a computer-generated overview of the road ahead. While it was still in development when the car was introduced at SEMA, the Banshee IV offered consumers a glimpse of what future automotive technologies would look like. (Photo Courtesy General Motors LLC)

As with the rest of the car, the Banshee IV's seats were cutting edge for their time. The driver's seat and passenger's seat were mounted on a central pivot that allowed the upper seatbacks to swing forward along the center console, making the rear seat far more accessible than in most two-door coupes. Additionally, the front seats were made up of an upper and a lower section with the contoured lower section firmly affixed to the car's floor. (Photo Courtesy General Motors LLC)

appeared daunting to anyone operating the car, a simplified, redesigned version of the Banshee IV's steering wheel was introduced on the fourth-generation Camaro and Firebird models. It contained many of the same button controls, especially those linked to the stereo system.

In addition to all the above, the Banshee also introduced a "memory recall" feature that enabled drivers to preset the position of their seat, the steering wheel, and the car's foot pedals. Each preset could be recalled by depressing a button.

The 1988 Teamwork and Technology

The Banshee IV (along with several other concept vehicles, including the Buick Lucerne, Cadillac Voyage, Chevrolet Venture, and the GMC Centaur) made its debut at GM's Teamwork and Technology—For Today and Tomorrow trade show on Tuesday, January 5, 1988. The three-day show was an invitation-only event comprised of some 14,000 dealers, customers, GM employees, suppliers, security analysts, and members of the news media.

For the first time in GM's history, the company moved one of its design studios from the Technical Center in Detroit to New York's Waldorf-Astoria hotel for GM's Teamwork and Technology show. Here, GM Design Chief Charles "Chuck" Jordan (third from left) oversees studio designers as they continue to refine a full-scale model of the SRV-1, a dramatically styled, two-passenger coupe. (Photo Courtesy General Motors LLC)

Although the show harkened back to GM's Motoramas of the 1950s, the Teamwork and Technology event had less to do with selling automobiles and far more to do with proving that General Motors still had the prowess to be a technology leader as the company entered into the 21st century. In a news article published by the *New York Times* on January 5, 1988, GM Chairman Roger B. Smith described the show as "the largest single showing of GM technology in history."

While all of the cars introduced at the show received positive feedback, the Pontiac Banshee was definitely a highlight of

The Pontiac Banshee was showcased at GM's Teamwork and Technology showcase in 1988. Hosted in the lobby of the Waldorf-Astoria hotel (where General Motors once hosted its famed Motorama events), the Teamwork and Technology showcase was the largest automobile exhibition to date. As a subtle nod to the Banshee's futuristic appearance, each of the car's presenters were dressed in *Star Trek: The Next-Generation*–inspired outfits, with the Pontiac emblem replacing the Starfleet insignia badge. (Photo Courtesy General Motors LLC)

Over the next several years, the Pontiac Banshee IV made frequent appearances in magazines, movies, and television. *Motor Trend* magazine published a three-page article about the car in its May 1989 issue. The car also made appearances in 1989's *Back to the Future II*, 1993's *Demolition Man*, and the 2001 television series *Power Rangers: Time Force*. A poorly copied mock-up of the Banshee also made an appearance as the "Knight Industries 4000" in the TV movie *Knight Rider 2000*. (Photo Courtesy General Motors LLC)

the event. Its success at GM's technology trade show motivated the company to develop a more refined version of the car as the next-generation production Firebird. Many of its styling elements would also directly influence the fourth-generation Camaro.

"That's why the Banshee IV was so important," Jack Folden said. "It put a statement out there. We could see how the public reacted and how our management responded. And that meant we were just basically testing the waters to get a direction for the new Firebird. We knew we had to do our homework to design another generation of the most expressive Pontiac of the lot."

By the time the Banshee was approved for further development, Tom Peters had been promoted to chief designer in GM's Advanced Studio Four. He was replaced by Dave Rand as the assistant design chief at Pontiac II. It was Rand, along with Craig Janos and Dave Ross, who refined the Banshee IV's styling to a point where it could be transformed into a viable production car.

Hot Rod magazine estimated the total development costs of the 1988 Pontiac Banshee concept car to be around $1.5 million. While a hefty sum, even by today's standards, the Banshee concept provided consumers with their first in-depth look at the future of Pontiac's "Driving Excitement" advertising campaign. (Photo Courtesy General Motors LLC)

Still, there's no denying the relationship between the Banshee and the fourth-generation Firebird (and Camaro models). In fact, Camaro Chief Designer John Cafaro Jr. worked closely with Folden during the development of the fourth-generation Camaro. Each visited the other's studio to exchange information and ideas. In doing so, each ensured that the Camaro and Firebird not only continued to share enough DNA to be sister cars but also that each model had an aesthetic that was unique unto itself.

"We wanted very much to make the Camaro and Firebird not look like twins," Folden said. "We didn't want to splash a big screaming eagle all over the Trans Am hood or even use chrome badges, because a car shouldn't depend on those things for identity. . . . The designers called for making the new car's shape (its stance, the posture) say Firebird, and they did this with more authority than applying symbols."

Interestingly, the Pontiac Banshee IV started appearing elsewhere, either in its entirety or through its design influence on other cars. It inspired a front-end fascia redesign of the late-model, third-generation Firebirds and Trans Ams. Both the 1991 and 1992 models received an updated front fascia that included a stylized version of the prow and nose inlets introduced on the Banshee IV concept. Both the Revell model company and Hot Wheels produced scale models of the car. Additionally, the full-size concept car appeared in the 1989 film *Back to the Future II* and 1993's *Demolition Man*.

Today the sole finished example of the Pontiac Banshee IV resides at the General Motors Heritage Center in Sterling Heights, Michigan.

There is no denying that the Pontiac Banshee successfully influenced the overall appearance of the fourth-generation Pontiac Firebird and, to a lesser extent, the fourth-generation Chevy Camaro. Its futuristic styling and low, aggressive stance still make the car look contemporary today.

CHAPTER

5 FIFTH GENERATION (2010–2015)

"THEY SAY ABSENCE MAKES THE HEART GROW FONDER, AND THAT COULDN'T HAVE BEEN MORE TRUE THAN AS DEMONSTRATED WITH THE ENTHUSIASM THAT FOLLOWED THE INTRODUCTION OF THE FIFTH-GENERATION CAMARO. AFTER AN EIGHT-YEAR ABSENCE, THE RETURN OF [THE] CAMARO WAS A THUNDERBOLT THAT REIGNITED THE PASSION OF CAMARO ENTHUSIASTS AROUND THE WORLD. IT'S A CAR DESIGN FOR THOSE WHO LIKE TO DRIVE, AND ITS ELEGANT DESIGN MAKES YOU SMILE EVERY TIME."

— TOM PETERS, CHEVROLET CAMARO EXTERIOR DESIGN DIRECTOR

The fifth-generation Camaro was one of the most highly anticipated production-car releases in the history of General Motors. SangYup Lee's design incorporated retro styling that harkened back to the first-generation model with an infusion of 21st-century technology that made it a serious contender in the modern performance-car marketplace. (Photo Courtesy General Motors LLC)

When the final fourth-generation Camaro rolled off GM's Sainte-Therese assembly line in 2002, it seemed a certainty that Chevrolet's popular pony-car brand was finished. Year over year, Camaro sales had dropped by more than two-thirds in less than a decade (from 125,244 units in 1994 to just 41,177 units in 2001). Consumer demand for sports cars had started waning well before then, but many consumers complained that the fourth-generation model lacked the character of its predecessors.

General Motors elected to allow the Camaro platform to decline. The fourth-generation Camaro's chassis had been based on outdated technologies that required expensive updates. Moreover, stricter federal safety regulations were imminent, and they would require major investment to properly update the car's architecture, an investment that GM's executives were neither able nor willing to make.

The earliest indicators that the Camaro brand was in trouble started surfacing in 1996. Traditionally, General Motors allocated funds for a mid-generation update, but there was no indication that the fourth-generation model would receive any such treatment. Worse still, when workers in the Sainte-Therese plant either resigned their position or retired, they were not being replaced.

As GM's vice president of Global Design, Ed Welburn played an integral part in the evolution of both the fifth- and sixth-generation Camaros, as well as the Cadillac Escalade and the seventh-generation Corvette Stingray. A lifelong fan of the Camaro (he owns a yellow 1969 SS featured later in this chapter), Welburn secretly solicited the development of the fifth-generation Camaro before the project was officially greenlit more than a year later. (Photo Courtesy General Motors LLC)

The final 2002 Camaro rolled off the assembly line at 9:04 a.m. on August 27, 2002.

Even long after its departure from showrooms and car lots around the world, there was no shortage of people demanding the Camaro's return. Chevrolet received an abundance of mail and email from consumers and enthusiasts expressing their extreme dissatisfaction with GM's decision to pull the plug on the Camaro. Many of GM's designers and engineers shared the same sentiments. Not only had the Camaro served as a muse for many GM designers but it also had been the reason that many got into automotive design.

In the foreword of Larry Edsall's excellent book *Camaro: A Legend Reborn*, GM former Vice President of Global Design Ed Welburn expressed this same sentiment.

"During my visits across the globe to GM's Global Design Studios, one thing consistently amazes me," Welburn said. "Many of our designers have a model of the Camaro on his or her desk. It does not matter that they did not design the Camaro, what matters is they were universally inspired by it. The Camaro unifies designers worldwide. To me, it truly signifies Chevrolet's global scope and influence."

It is significant, then, that the story of the fifth-generation Camaro's genesis (its resurrection) began at a March 2004 meeting between Welburn and GM Advanced Design Studio Director Bob Boniface. Welburn had been appointed GM's vice president of design North America on October 1, 2003, and one of his first acts in that role was to hire Boniface away from Chrysler at the start of 2004. Just two months into his career, GM's newest design director found himself in a British pub with Welburn having a conversation about potential design projects for the Advanced Design Studios.

Boniface's answer was straight to the point: he wanted to design a new Camaro.

A long-time aficionado of the Camaro himself, Welburn acknowledged Boniface's request but with the strict understanding that any work on a new F-Body platform needed to happen quietly, especially given that General Motors had formally terminated the program two years earlier and closed the plant where the Camaro and Firebird had been built. Any work on a new Camaro platform had to remain carefully hidden away within the confines of the Advanced Studio until such time, if ever, that a fully realized design was ready to be presented to management.

Boniface was elated with Welburn's answer. After returning stateside a few days later, he headed to the design studios in Warren, Michigan. There, he met with Design Manager Brian Smith and shared the exciting news with him. He also cautioned Smith of Welburn's directive that all work on a new Camaro had to be done in secret.

The pair started designing a new Camaro concept in their spare time, meeting during lunch or after hours to exchange ideas. Despite managing a busy project schedule throughout the summer of 2004, Smith created several design sketches of a potential fifth-generation Camaro. From these, the pair constructed three-eighths-scale clay "half" models (a model that depicted one hemisphere of the car along its centerline). The model was then mounted against a mirror backdrop, allowing the half model's reflection to "complete" the car.

During his tenure as GM's director of Advanced Design, Bob Boniface secretly developed the earliest styling concepts for a fifth-generation Camaro. Although his initial designs for a new Camaro borrowed heavily from the second-generation model, his Advanced Studio defined the profile, wheel base, overall dimensions, and aspects of the exterior aesthetic that was later introduced in the 2010 production model. (Photo Courtesy General Motors LLC)

Smith and Boniface based their designs on the aesthetics of the second-generation Camaro, but its proportions were built around GM's new rear-wheel-drive Zeta architecture. Developed by GM's Australian subsidiary company, Holden, the Zeta platform had been intended to become a "global RWD architecture."

Unfortunately, the severe financial challenges being experienced by General Motors at that time raised concerns about the company's ability to sustain the Zeta program. In October 2004, around the same time that Smith and Boniface were finishing work on their scale models, General Motors announced that it was canceling further development of the Zeta platform for future development projects in North America.

Frustrated and upset by the news, Boniface moved his Camaro concept models to a storeroom shelf in the back of the design studios. Not long after, Boniface received a phone call from Mike Abelson, the executive director of GM's Advanced Engineering. Abelson wanted to know if Boniface had any ideas on how they might keep the Zeta program alive. Despite Welburn's warnings to keep the project secret, Boniface told Abelson about the Camaro sketches and the models they had created over the past several months.

As originally published in Edsall's book *Camaro: A Legend Reborn*, Boniface explained Abelson's reaction to this news.

"Within half an hour, he was in the studio," Boniface said. "Mike looked at the car and the package drawings. 'You know,' he said, 'this looks like it would hold some water. Why don't we kick off an internal study on a Camaro or a Chevy coupe?'"

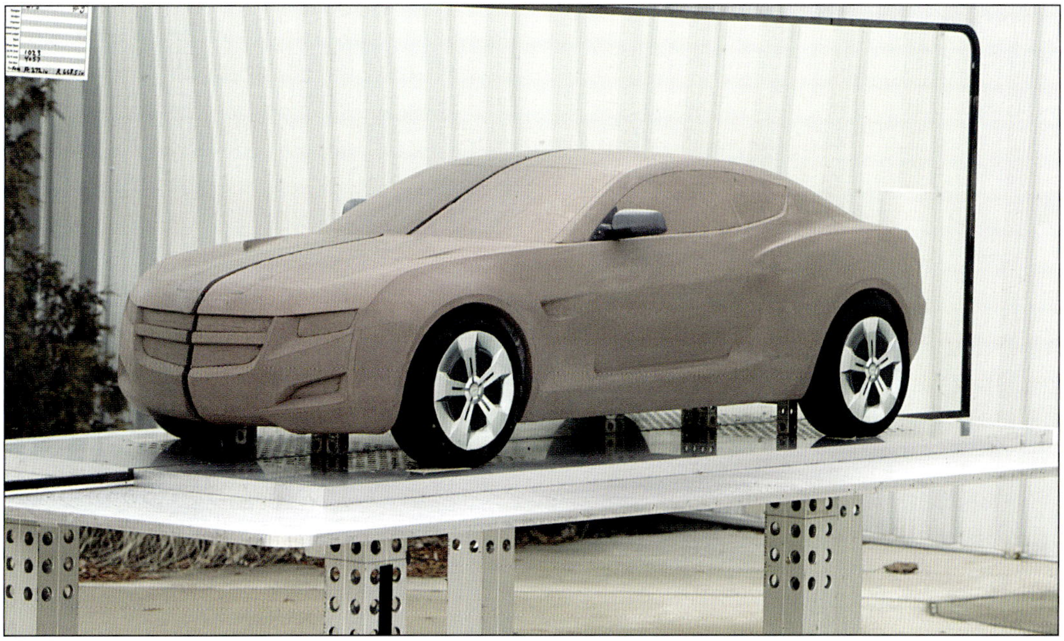

This third-scale clay model was one of Bob Boniface's early conceptual designs for a new, fifth-generation Camaro. Where his original model (not pictured) was inspired by the second-generation Camaro, this later example evolved from Ed Welburn's direction to create a design based on the first-generation model. (Photo Courtesy General Motors LLC)

Boniface's design evolved through a succession of one-third and full-scale models. While his designs captured the general profile and overall proportions that GM's managerial hierarchy (especially Welburn) were looking for, it lacked the character and charisma that makes a Camaro, well, a Camaro. (Photo Courtesy General Motors LLC)

History Repeats Itself

While Chevrolet was conducting its evaluation of the Zeta-based Camaro, Ford had started manufacturing an entirely new Mustang for the 2005 model year that would set the world (and the future of the pony-car market) on fire. Originally introduced at the North American International Auto Show in January 2004, the new Mustang was a combination of the first-generation model's styling with 21st-century comforts and technology. Its stylized fusion of old and new paralleled the concept that Boniface had envisioned for the Camaro, but Ford had done it first.

The new Mustang received high praise from the press and became the must-have sports car for 2005, which was an easy achievement given that neither General Motors nor Chrysler had anything comparable to offer would-be consumers. A total of 160,975 units were sold its freshman year.

The new Mustang proved unequivocally that there was still a viable market for a performance-based pony car. Moreover, it demonstrated that a car that featured classic automotive styling cues from generations past was attractive to consumers. The challenge that General Motors faced was that from management's perspective, the Camaro program was dead (Boniface and Smith developed their preliminary concept in secret) and the company lacked an American-built sports car that could compete with the Mustang.

GM's answer was to rebrand its Australian-built Holden Monaro as a 2004 Pontiac GTO. The Monaro featured a 5.7L front engine, rear-wheel-drive powertrain that produced a robust 349 hp and delivered a 0–60 mph time of just 5.3 seconds. It performed well and it handled well. Its two biggest problems were that 1) it had been engineered as a right-hand-drive only car, and 2) it lacked the aggressive styling that consumers expected to see from a sports car.

Pressed for time and limited on available funding, General Motors invested most of its allocated budget adapting the Monaro platform to a left-hand-drive configuration for sale in North America. For looks, the car received a split grille front fascia and a set of "GTO" badges. Faux air scoops weren't available until the 2005 model year.

The fifth-generation Ford Mustang played a significant role in the return of the Camaro in 2010. The 2005 Mustang sold 160,975 units in its first year of production, which provided General Motors with the motivation to relaunch the Camaro platform despite cancelling the program just three years earlier. (Photo Courtesy Joe Kolecki)

The Pontiac GTO was a left-hand-drive variant of the Holden Monaro. While Pontiac's rebranded version of the car provided consumers with a promising driving experience (0–60 in 5.5 seconds and a 14-second quarter mile), it lacked the muscular exterior architecture that consumers expected from the once-iconic GTO moniker. (Photo Courtesy General Motors LLC)

As history has proved, neither the GTO's robust horsepower nor its improved handling were enough to entice consumers to buy it. The car may have performed like a sports car, but it didn't look like anything resembling Pontiac's iconic muscle car. Pontiac sold just 15,740 units in 2004, and a total of 40,757 units during its three-year production run.

Meanwhile, the Mustang continued to dominate the marketplace, selling more than 326,000 units between 2005 and 2006.

Second Is Good, but First Is Better

When Bob Boniface showed Ed Welburn the scale model that he, Brian Smith, and select members of the Advanced Design Studio had spent the past several months developing, Welburn reminded the team that it was the original, first-generation Camaro that was recognized as the true American icon. That meeting, which took place in late 2004, established the tone from which the fifth-generation Camaro's design would evolve.

Ed Welburn believed that the fifth-generation Camaro should pay homage to the first-generation model. To help inspire the designers in Boniface's Advanced Studio, examples of the original Camaro were brought in for the team to observe, study, and drive. While the outward aesthetic of the fifth-generation Camaro stands alone as its own unique design statement, there's no question that the original Camaro helped define its exterior architecture. (Photo Courtesy General Motors LLC)

Ed Welburn (standing left), GM Vice Chairman Bob Lutz (center, in the gray suit), and Bob Boniface evaluate an early full-scale clay model of Boniface's fifth-generation Camaro concept proposal in May 2005. While Boniface's design communicated the general shape and overall proportions of the next-generation Camaro, it was decided that the car's exterior aesthetic needed to make a more dramatic statement. (Photo Courtesy General Motors LLC)

Already focused on developing concept cars for both Buick and Cadillac, Boniface didn't return to the Camaro concept until April 2005. As before, he turned to Smith for design assistance as well as Gary Ruiz, whom Boniface had previously recruited away from Chrysler when he decided to join General Motors. Together, the three men began laying out the profile of a first-generation-inspired Camaro on an existing, full-size clay model of the Pontiac GTO.

In *Camaro: A Legend Reborn* by Larry Edsall, Boniface described their design process.

"We taped out the side view of a Gen-One-looking car on it, we took a bunch of wheelbase out of it, and we cut the back off and we even scribed '427' on the door," Boniface said. "While we were doing that, I kicked the team off on doing a Gen-One-inspired (but a modern interpretation of a Gen-One-inspired) design theme."

Early iterations of the full-size clay model met with some resistance from leadership. Although Boniface's design captured the essential stance and profile of its predecessors, many (including Welburn) felt that the new concept lacked the signature aesthetic that each of the earlier generations of Camaro possessed.

Welburn and GM Vice Chairman Bob Lutz monitored the progress being made and offered suggestions to Boniface's team. Boniface, meanwhile, developed a series of quick sketches during his personal time to help guide the design team as the model continued to evolve. These sketches, which defined the car's unique Coke-bottle shape and its distinctively proportioned front grille and headlamp assembly, led the design team to build a concept car that was a little too synonymous with the first-generation model.

Tom Peters Joins the Fray

General Motors hosted its annual "Gang of Five" meeting in April 2005. The Gang of Five at that time was comprised of Welburn, GM Vice Chairman and Head of Global Development Bob Lutz, Group Vice President for Global Engineering Jim Queen, Vice President for Global Program Management Jonathan Lauckner, and Vice President for Research and Development and Strategic Planning Lawrence Burns. This group

A 35-year veteran of General Motors, Tom Peters is the man responsible for giving us many of Chevrolet's most popular, modern automotive designs. He was responsible for designing the fifth- and sixth-generation Camaros, the sixth- and seventh-generation Corvettes, the Cadillac XLR, the Corvette Indy Show Car, the fourth-generation Pontiac Banshee, and the 2014 Chevy Silverado. As with so many of his designs, Peters's work on the Camaro incorporated styling elements inspired by modern-day military aircraft, including the F/A-18 Hornet and the F-22 Raptor. (Photo Courtesy General Motors LLC)

met to discuss which concept vehicles General Motors would be creating for the following year's auto show circuit.

Unlike years past, where the team would assemble and focus its attention on developing concept cars that promoted new design schemes or the latest technological advances being made by the company, this Gang of Five meeting was focused on introducing products that harkened back to a brighter age in the company's history. Increasingly poor sales, rising employee healthcare costs, and higher marketing and advertising spending had cost the company billions of dollars, resulting in some of the worst quarterly losses experienced by the company in more than a decade. If General Motors was going to introduce any concept cars for the coming year's auto show circuit, the car(s) had to underscore GM's long, rich automotive heritage.

GM Chief Executive Rick Wagoner was soon added to the team. Wagoner had been given the unenviable task of trying to curtail the financial losses being experienced by the company. Like the others, he recognized the importance of creating positive brand recognition. He realized that the concept cars presented on the auto show circuit could vastly sway public opinion, which, in turn, could make a huge difference in the future profitability of the company.

Most of the recommendations being made involved creating concept cars that were based on production vehicles already in development. Nothing presented spoke to GM's heritage until Ed Welburn suggested building a new Camaro concept car.

Suggesting a new Camaro was risky. The previous model had struggled to remain relevant (and profitable) for a significant part of its production run. Moreover, it had been assumed by most of the executives present at the Gang of Five meeting that there were no plans for a new Camaro, let alone to advance a design to the point where it was ready to be showcased on the international auto show circuit. The process of designing and building a concept car normally took 40 weeks to complete.

Still, Welburn recognized that General Motors needed to make a dramatic statement. The Camaro would offer that. Boniface had already established the car's overall shape, size, and proportion, but it still lacked the energy and the vitality that was synonymous with the Camaro. Even after providing Boniface with considerable input and feedback on his design, Welburn still wanted more.

At that point, Welburn decided to introduce a second design team to the Camaro project. In keeping with some of the richest design traditions in the history of the company, that team worked out of the basement of GM's main design center inside the famous Studio X created by Bill Mitchell a half century earlier. During the week before the July 4th holiday, Welburn appointed veteran GM Designer Tom Peters to lead the second team. He gave Peters until the end of summer to come up with a viable design.

Peters's team included Steve Kim, Vlad Kapitonov, and SangYup Lee. Both Kim and Lee had grown up in South Korea, and Kapitonov had been born in the Ural Mountains of Russia. Although all three had come to the United States to study automotive design before joining General Motors, none of them understood the significance of the Camaro brand or appreciated how its rich history had positively impacted the American automotive landscape. This meant that each could bring their own fresh perspective to the design.

Aircraft-Inspired Design

Peters wanted to incorporate several unique elements into his Camaro's design. First, the car needed "distilled elements that are pure Camaro." In essence, he wanted the design to incorporate contemporary interpretations of popular design elements previously introduced on earlier Camaros. Second,

This is an early sketch of the fifth-generation Camaro by SangYup Lee. As is evident from the styling elements depicted in this image, Lee's drawing provided the foundation for the final exterior of the fifth-generation Camaro. (Photo Courtesy General Motors LLC)

Peters wanted it to harken back to its heritage as a racing and performance car. Finally, the design had to incorporate, at least symbolically, elements of design from the latest military aircraft, especially the F22 Raptor.

While each of these design elements provided direction to his trio of designers, Peters's overriding directive was simple: "I want you guys to come up with the meanest street-fighting dog you can sketch."

His team set to work at once. Over the long holiday weekend, each designer worked feverishly to get his interpretation of the Camaro down on paper. There was no time to waste. While the trio sketched, Peters worked to identify a team of

One of SangYup Lee's early color renderings of the fifth-generation Camaro concept car is shown. Although many of the body lines on this computer rendering are softer than those introduced on the final design, there is no mistaking the car's signature look. (Photo Courtesy General Motors LLC)

The front quarter view of Lee's color rendering depicts many of the styling motifs that emerged on the production model. Of particular interest is the front fascia with its pocketed headlamp assemblies. While its overall aesthetic is similar to the production model, the rounded headlamp pockets were eliminated, and the lower grille was enlarged to allow for increased airflow into and through the radiator. (Photo Courtesy General Motors LLC)

This rendering by Lee depicts a more fully realized version of the fifth-generation Camaro. The most notable difference between it and subsequent iterations of the car was that this rendering included small air extractors cut into the front fenders reminiscent of those found on the 1978 (and later) second-generation Camaro. (Photo Courtesy General Motors LLC)

sculptors who could translate their designs into a full-size clay model. He knew that they were already at a disadvantage to Boniface and the Advanced Design Studio team because all of them had been working on a pair of full-size clay models for nearly six months already. If Peters's team hoped to catch up, they needed to bypass several design steps to get a model assembled in time for presentation.

Upon their return from the long holiday weekend, the Advanced Studio team shared one of its full-scale clay armatures with Peters's fledgling team in the courtyard outside of GM's design studios. While the armature (the substructure/wireframe of a clay model) lacked exterior surface design detail, it provided Peters's team with the car's general proportions and a sense of scale. Now armed with this important information, the team prepared to set to work.

Once the styling buck is fully assembled, a team of sculptors applies layers of clay to the assembly and begins the weeks- (to months-) long process of shaping the clay into an accurate representation of the proposed automotive design. Although most designers do not actively work with the clay, they normally remain present throughout the sculpting process to ensure that the accuracy of their design(s) is captured in the final sculpt. (Photo Courtesy General Motors LLC)

Inside Studio X

Since its inception by Bill Mitchell in 1958, the history and mystique surrounding GM's "secret" Studio X has made it one of the most revered spaces within GM Design. Buried deep within the basement at GM Design Center in Warren, Michigan, Studio X was the studio where Bill Mitchell created some of the most iconic Corvette concept cars ever imagined, including the immensely popular Mako Shark and Manta Ray. It was where Tom Peters designed his revolutionary Corvette Indy in the early 1980s. It was also where Peters and his team returned nearly two decades later (at Ed Welburn's insistence) to develop the fifth-generation Camaro concept car.

This is a full-scale styling buck for the GMX521 fifth-generation Camaro concept. Assemblies of this sort, which normally include a wood and metal substructure fitted with a foam/resin upper section sculpted to the general shape of the would-be concept car, provide the skeletal structure needed when fabricating full-size clay models for design review and approval. (Photo Courtesy General Motors LLC)

The car that evolved within the crowded space of Studio X maintained many of the same overall proportions originally introduced by the Advanced Studio's model. However, Peters believed that the fifth-generation Camaro should be a contemporary, aggressively styled Camaro that should be targeted at a younger generation of consumers. He felt the design should draw some of its design inspiration from the first-generation model but should also maintain a unique identity from its 1969 Camaro counterpart.

"If you like the '69 Camaro, you can go and buy one." Peters said. "But this is the 21st century. We need[ed] to take full advantage of our technological advances. The design [had] to telegraph all of this."

A full-size clay model was assembled inside Studio X by a team of talented sculptors, including 30-year GM veteran Greg Stelmack. To maximize the team's productivity, Peters had Steve Kim lead the design/development on one half of the model while SangYup Lee focused his efforts on developing the opposing side. Kapitonov, meanwhile, focused his efforts on creating the car's front- and rear-end motifs. Each section of the car's exterior aesthetics evolved independently from the others, allowing each designer to showcase his individual vision.

As the model evolved, Peters frequently had it moved out into the studio courtyard so that his team could observe the car in more natural light. Ed Welburn was invited to attend one of these viewing sessions so he could review and offer feedback

SangYup Lee

SangYup Lee is an American-based, Korean-born industrial designer. Celebrated as the most famous automobile designer from Korea and one of the most accomplished automotive designers in the world, Lee is perhaps best known in the United States for his work on the fifth-generation Camaro and seventh-generation Corvette Stingray concepts.

Lee studied sculpture at Hongik University in Korea. In 1995, he came to the United States to study transportation design at the ArtCenter in Pasadena, California. Upon graduating from the ArtCenter College of Design, Lee traveled to Europe to begin his career at Pininfarina and Porsche Design Center.

In 1999, Lee returned stateside to accept a design position at General Motors. During his 10-year tenure with General Motors, Lee became involved in the sixth-generation Corvette production program. He also contributed to several key automotive concept projects including the 50th-Anniversary Stingray concept, the 2004 Buick Velite concept (at GM's Bertone Studio in Italy), and the Cadillac Sixteen concept.

Lee's most celebrated design accomplishment while at General Motors was his fifth-generation Camaro concept car. Lee not only designed the concept car but also oversaw its development from sketch to clay concept and fully operable prototype. His instantly recognizable concept was assembled in GM's Holden Studio (in Australia) and made its global debut as the Autobot Bumblebee in Michael Bay's 2007 blockbuster hit *Transformers*.

Lee resigned from General Motors in 2010 and joined the Volkswagen/Audi Advanced Studio in California as the chief exterior designer. In that role, Lee was tasked with leading the newly merged Volkswagen and Audi design staffs. During his tenure at the Santa Monica studio, he also oversaw concept and production programs for Volkswagen, Audi, Skoda, Porsche, Lamborghini, and Bentley.

SangYup Lee is considered one of the most talented modern-day automobile designers in the world. His early work on the Camaro and Corvette programs helped launch his career and gain recognition around the globe. Since leaving General Motors, Lee has worked for Bentley, Volkswagen/Audi, and Porsche. Today, Lee serves as the chief of design for the Hyundai Motor Company. (Photo Courtesy General Motors LLC)

In 2012, Lee moved to England and joined Bentley Motors Limited as the head of Exterior and Advanced Design. Under the direction of Bentley Chief Designer Luc Donckerwolke, a Peruvian-born Belgian, Lee led the company's exterior and Advanced Design teams in the creation of the Bentley EXP10 Speed6 concept as well as the production model Bentayga, the company's first ultra-luxury SUV.

Donckerwolke left Bentley in June 2015 to become the global head of Hyundai design as well as the head of the new Prestige Design Division. Less than a year later, 46-year-old Lee followed suit, and

A young SangYup Lee works inside of GM's design studios. Lee's contributions to the Camaro, Cadillac, and Corvette programs helped him establish a strong reputation within the international automobile design community. (Photo Courtesy General Motors LLC)

SangYup Lee *continued*

SangYup Lee, along with Tom Peters (left), evaluate proposed refinements to some of the fascia and front-fender body lines on the full-size clay model of the fifth-generation Camaro. The dark tape lines placed on the clay surfaces allow the designers to evaluate changes to the body architecture without the costly and time-consuming process of re-forming the clay assembly. (Photo Courtesy General Motors LLC)

was appointed vice president of Hyundai and Genesis design. Together, the pair started a campaign within the design studios to advance the Hyundai brand as a world-class luxury automobile.

During a 2016 interview with Reuters.com, Lee shared a bit of the philosophy behind his unique (and incredibly successful) approach to automotive design.

"For decades, luxury brands, such as Bentley, Aston Martin, and Maserati, have been about possession," Lee said. "In the future, as disruptive technologies kick in, luxury is going to be about experience. People are going to look for a special experience rather than something special to own."

Lee became the head of Hyundai's Global Design Center in 2018. In January 2021, he received the coveted Grand Prize of Design at the 36th Edition of the Festival Automobile International (FAI) for his work on Hyundai's EV concept, the 2020 Prophecy. FAI is a well-respected institution in the world of automotive design. The Grand Prize of Design is awarded to a designer or company for its global strategy of innovation or pursuit of beauty.

The GMX521 Camaro concept full-scale clay model included two separate designs. The driver's side was sculpted to the design specification of Steve Kim. Kim's vision included a dramatic, triangular-shaped door opening along/below the sill plate. It also included a slightly more prominent rear end and a larger fascia, although the latter cannot be clearly seen from this angle. (Photo Courtesy General Motors LLC)

The passenger's side of the GMX521 model showcased SangYup Lee's design. Seen here in the courtyard of the GM design studios, this half of the clay model shares a close resemblance to its 2010 production counterpart, except for minor design elements, such as the door mirrors, which were enlarged to meet safety requirements. (Photo Courtesy General Motors LLC)

on the evolving styling elements being developed by Peters's designers. It was during Welburn's visit to the Design Center that it was decided the team should use Lee's styling motifs for the entire car and several of Kim's elements should be integrated into the overall design.

The team worked feverishly to transform its evolving clay model into a showpiece that would compete with Boniface's concept model. They worked day and night to blend the two halves into a single, cohesive design that used the best elements from both halves to create a powerful, contemporary statement that was unmistakably Camaro.

Moment of Truth

The first time that both (Peters's and Boniface's) models were presented together in the courtyard of the design studios, Ed Welburn commemorated the occasion by driving his 1969 Camaro to the reveal. While both models evoked a strong emotional response, Welburn felt that the car developed by Peter's team inside of Studio X best exuded the spirit of the Camaro.

In the book *Camaro: A Legend Reborn* by Larry Edsall, Welburn explained the emotionally charged struggle that he experienced while selecting the winning Camaro concept.

"It was not an easy decision. It really wasn't," Welburn said. "It was one of the most difficult decisions I [had] to make in my job. You [had] two teams that put

The full-scale fifth-generation Camaro concept was one of two models on display in GM's design studios courtyard that afternoon. The other was the model developed by Tom Peters's team (not pictured). While Boniface's direct interpretation of the first-generation Camaro had styling elements that found their way into the fifth-generation's final design, it was the car developed by Peters's team in Studio X that ruled the day. (Photo Courtesy General Motors LLC)

The GMX521 Camaro concept clay model parked next to GM Vice President of Global Design Ed Welburn's yellow 1969 Camaro SS coupe. Welburn drove his Camaro to the event, which included both Peters's Camaro concept (seen here) and Boniface's full-scale model (not pictured). Everyone present agreed that Lee's design perfectly captured the spirit of the first-generation model while simultaneously exuding a contemporary muscle-car stance. (Photo Courtesy General Motors LLC)

so much of themselves into it, working day and night and night and day developing these designs."

Despite experiencing angst at Welburn's decision, Boniface conceded that the decision was the correct one. While Peters's car evolved into the production model that emerged from GM's manufacturing plants a few years later, Boniface's model also influenced the final look of the 2010 Camaro.

"To fight every one of those battles and to keep it a Camaro, that was a really, really difficult thing to do," Boniface said. "We really had to fight for this car. It was an uphill battle the whole time, but it worked."

Designing the Interior

The evolution of the fifth-generation Camaro's interior was led by second-generation GM Designer Jeff Perkins. The son of 39-year GM Designer John Perkins (who had, ironically, supervised Ed Welburn during his early years at GM Design), the younger Perkins had recently

This is a computer-aided rendering of the Camaro concept's futuristic interior. Much like the car's exterior, Welburn wanted the Camaro's cockpit to pay respect to the past while also showcasing the latest technologies being developed by General Motors at that time. (Photo Courtesy General Motors LLC)

Every aspect of the Camaro's design underwent a series of redesigns, reviews, and approvals. This assortment of images offers a glimpse into the complex process of defining the look of a car's interior. Every assembly, from the seats and center console to the dashboard, gauges, and steering wheel to the placement of the seatbelts, receive this same level of attention and detail. (Photo Courtesy General Motors LLC)

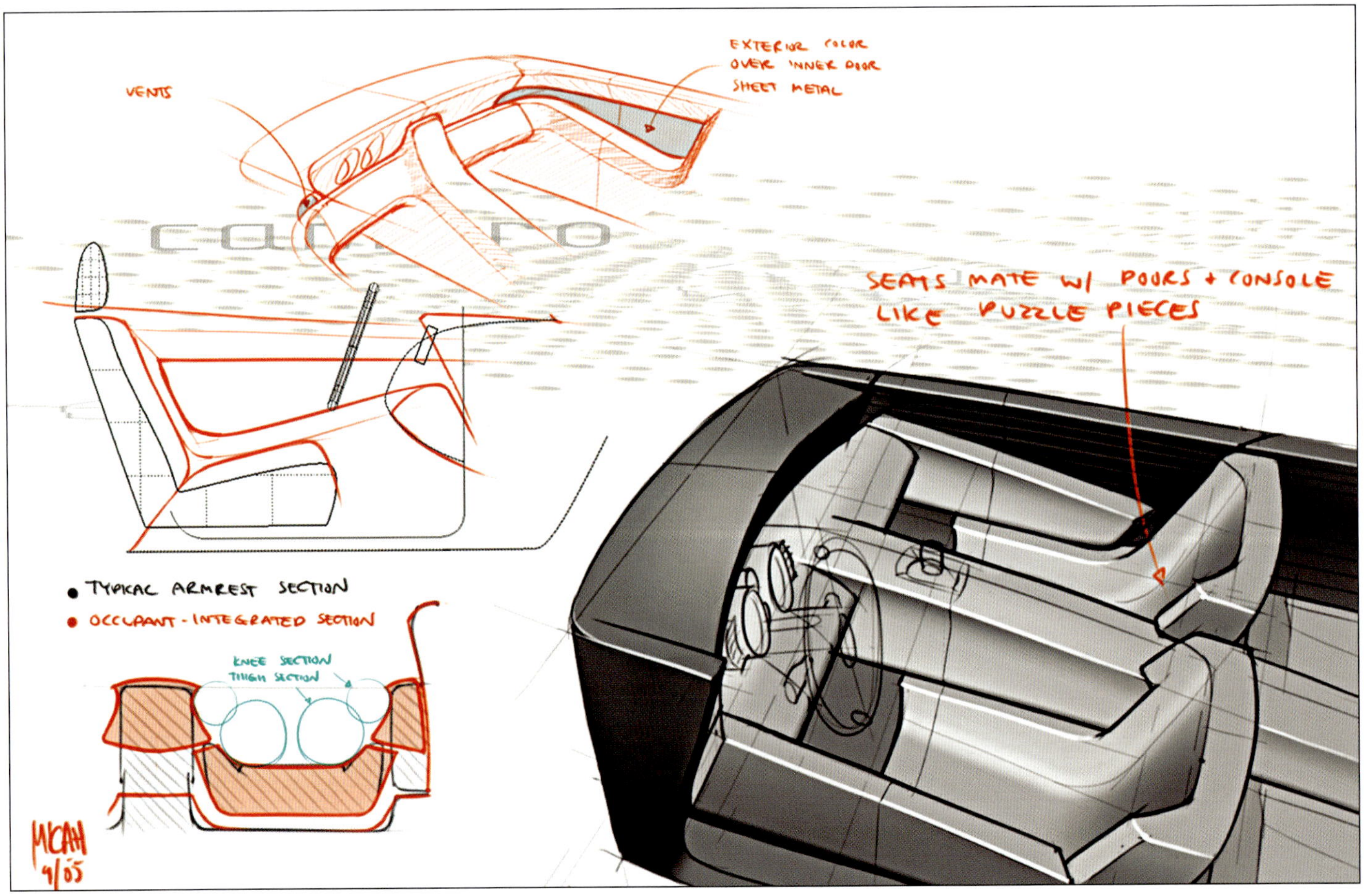

Once the interior design is approved, a full-size clay model of the car's cockpit is assembled. This enables designers to interact with the interior and make real-time adjustments and changes to ensure optimal fitment for every component. (Photo Courtesy General Motors LLC)

Once the final interior design is approved, fabricators begin assembling mock-ups of the interior using a variety of materials. Each mock-up is then submitted for subsequent approvals. These include signoffs on the material selected to how well individual components work together with each other to create an overall interior aesthetic. (Photo Courtesy General Motors LLC)

been promoted to director of performance car interiors and was now being tasked by Welburn with leading the development of the Camaro's interior as his first assignment in his new role.

Development of the car's interior began in 2005, around the same time that Boniface had started developing his initial proposal of the Camaro's exterior. Nearly a dozen GM designers from studios across the United States (and England) submitted interior design proposals to Perkins's department. These included Perkins's own design team that included Christos Roustemis (originally from Greece), Julien Montousse (France), and Micah Jones (who had been born and raised in Milwaukee, Wisconsin). From the start, it was thought that a culturally diverse group of designers would bring many fresh perspectives to the look of the new Camaro's interior.

In *Camaro: A Legend Reborn* by Larry Edsall, Perkins said, "With the diversity of designers within the studio, as well as those on the West Coast and in the United Kingdom, we had a pretty wide range of nationalities sketching on the car. It was refreshing. It was good to get that fresh perspective."

The fact that many of the designers from overseas who contributed to the Camaro's interior lacked familiarity with the brand also afforded the team with fresh perspectives on established design motifs. Because many of them had never seen a first-generation Camaro before, they worked from old photographs and identified design cues that they believed best translated into the current designs they were working on.

As the design drawings poured in, Perkins focused his efforts on identifying design elements within each that

Ed Welburn sits in the cockpit of a preproduction Camaro. Camaro designers Tom Peters and Bob Boniface can be seen through the car's windshield. (Photo Courtesy General Motors LLC)

reflected Welburn's directive to make the new car "like the first-generation Camaro." As with the first-generation model, Perkins believed that the fifth-generation's interior should be clean, simple, and straightforward. At the same time, he also believed the interior needed to balance heritage with contemporary styling. One of his design goals was to develop an interior that simultaneously attracted the established Camaro enthusiasts as well as a new generation of young consumers who might be unaware of the Camaro's decades-long automotive legacy.

In the end, it was Micah Jones's design, along with elements from Julian Montousse, that best aligned with the interior aesthetic that Perkins had been looking for. The pair partnered together to incorporate their individual ideas into a single cohesive design. While the overall theme of the cockpit had been developed by Jones, the instrument-panel and gauge-cluster elements had been developed by Montousse.

The design featured a simple, horizontal dashboard with a pair of gauge clusters (speedometer and odometer) mounted in front of the driver's field of view. The concept behind the design was simplicity, which afforded the driver minimal distractions, thereby allowing them to focus on their driving experience. The other gauges (oil, battery, etc.) were packaged together and placed just ahead of the shifter in the car's center console.

While much of the interior styling harkened back to the past, there were also elements incorporated into its design that gave the cockpit an otherworldly, futuristic feeling. One of the most notable of these was the car's unique ambient lighting system. In addition to its dashboard gauges and console-mounted instrument cluster, which illuminated whenever the car was unlocked or operated at night, a narrow band of that same iridescent lighting accentuated the length of the dashboard and interior door panels, bathing the driver and passenger in a soft glow of light during vehicle operation.

"(The result) is contemporary and new; the piece has more to do with the iPod than with the '69 Camaro," Perkins said. "We want you to see the car from the outside and love [it] but to get into the interior and go, 'Wow.'"

A team of fabricators work to assemble a fully operable fifth-generation Camaro concept car ahead of its reveal at the Detroit Auto Show in January 2006. (Photo Courtesy General Motors LLC)

SangYup Lee inspects the bodywork on the fifth-generation Camaro concept model. Like Lee, many designers prefer to remain involved with the development of the automobiles, even after the design is signed off and the vehicle moves toward prototyping or production. (Photo Courtesy General Motors LLC)

The Fifth-Generation Camaro Concept: Codename CZ6

Even after Welburn had approved the full-scale clay Camaro concept, Peters's team still had a significant amount of work that needed to be completed to transform the clay into a fully operable concept car. In addition to making both halves of the car mirror images of the other, there were still design cues from the Advanced Studios model that had to be integrated into the final design. Moreover, the limitations of the workspace within Studio X meant that the model needed to be moved into the regular design studios before the additional refinements could be completed. Once done, the team set about refining the design, each time gathering feedback from GM executives as they worked to dial-in every detail.

Once the clay model was completed, it was used to create

At long last, the fifth-generation Camaro concept is revealed at the Detroit Auto Show on January 9, 2006. Bob Lutz (white hair, center), Ed Welburn, Tom Peters, Bob Boniface, and SangYup Lee were all present for the momentous occasion. The silver Camaro concept received an overwhelming response from the press and patrons alike. It was the single largest highlight of that year's show. (Photo Courtesy General Motors LLC)

a mold for the body panels. Two body shells were produced from these molds. The first was used for additional design studies, which included everything from minor tweaks to the body line to determining what paint color would be used on the show car. The second was mounted to a rolling chassis, fitted with a complete interior, and used to develop the look of the engine bay.

While these advances continued to drive the Camaro concept program forward, the car's development team still faced a significant issue. Before the Camaro could be unveiled, a fully operable, drivable concept car needed to be assembled. The challenge here was that most of GM's divisions had shifted their focus to the development of front-wheel-drive platforms. It was true that General Motors still had the "Sigma" platform that it had developed for the Cadillac CTS sedan, as well as its newly developed rear-wheel-drive sports car platform that the company had developed for the Corvette. Unfortunately, both options would make the Camaro cost prohibitive in the marketplace.

The answer, it turned out, was that Chevrolet had to leverage its Holden's Zeta platform—the same platform the company had planned to shut down at the start of the Camaro's renaissance. Despite the suspension of its North American development division in early 2005, GM Vice Chairman Bob Lutz tasked Chevrolet's engineering team with mating the Camaro's body to the Holden's chassis architecture. The migration between the two platforms proved to be challenging, but in the end, the team was successful.

A second fifth-generation Camaro concept car, this one finished in Precision Red, was also assembled and shipped to the West Coast for its reveal in Los Angeles. (Photo Courtesy General Motors LLC)

With just days left before the 2006 North American International Auto Show in Detroit, Michigan, a debate arose between Tom Peters and other members of the Camaro team as to what paint color the concept Camaro was to wear. Peters believed the Camaro should be painted silver. Others argued that it should be painted red, which was an iconic color for any sports car. In the end, a compromise was met that satisfied both parties. The Detroit car would be painted silver and a second car (this one intended for display in Los Angeles) would be finished in Precision Red.

Bob Lutz, along with Ed Welburn (driving his 1969 SS Camaro), led a parade of famous Camaros down Woodward Avenue in the heart of Detroit before arriving at Cobo Hall for the fifth-generation's momentous unveiling. "We wanted it to be a statement of General Motors design prowess," said Lutz, who can be seen here sitting in the driver seat of the Camaro concept. (Photo Courtesy General Motors LLC)

The fifth-generation Chevy Camaro concept made its debut at the North American International Auto Show on Monday, January 9, 2006. The event was filled with more pomp and circumstance than any other event at the show that year. The Saginaw (Michigan) High School Trojans drum corps created a soundtrack for the event, while television, sports, and automotive celebrities filled the show hall, which had been dressed to look like a combination of Main Street U.S.A. and the winner's circle at the Daytona International Speedway. With a hall packed full of excited Camaro enthusiasts, media, GM employees and executives, Chevrolet kicked off the Camaro's unveiling with a parade of classic Camaros from years past. Drawing up the rear was the brand-new Camaro concept, powered by a 400-hp LS2 V-8 engine.

> "THE MOMENT THE CAR CAME INTO VIEW, THE HALL EXPLODED IN APPLAUSE THE LIKES OF WHICH HAD NOT BEEN SEEN AT A CAR LAUNCH IN MANY, MANY YEARS"

The moment the car came into view, the hall exploded in applause the likes of which had not been seen at a car launch in many, many years. Grown men, many of them enthusiasts who had implored General Motors to resurrect the Camaro, stood looking on with tears in their eyes. Famed GM auto show manager and "Fbodfather" Scott Settlemire attended the launch. His words perfectly described the crowd's reaction to the car.

"I didn't have a handkerchief, and I knew I was going to need one," Settlemire said. "I wanted to watch people's faces, so I turned around, and there's all these grown men sobbing. I've been doing this 31 years, and I've never seen this."

2011 COPO Camaro Race Car Concept

The 2011 Camaro COPO concept was a factory-built drag car developed by Chevrolet to compete with the likes of the Ford Mustang Cobra Jet and the Dodge Challenger 512 Drag Pak. Unlike its production counterparts, including the Z28 and the ZL1 packages, the COPO concept was developed without any superficial frills, such as air conditioning or even a spare tire. Instead, Chevrolet equipped the COPO concept with all the gear to make it National Hot Rod Association (NHRA) compliant. It received a roll cage, massive Hoosier racing slicks mounted to lightweight race wheels, and a specially developed GM Performance Parts LSX crate engine paired with a Whipple supercharger.

The Camaro COPO concept was developed by General Motors to be a factory-built drag racing car. It was constructed as a direct competitor to the Dodge Challenger 512 Drag Pak and the Ford Mustang Cobra Jet. (Photo Courtesy General Motors LLC)

This detailed rendering of the 2011 COPO Camaro concept was by GM Designer Jason Bliss. (Photo Courtesy General Motors LLC)

A Closer Look at the 2011 COPO Concept

Chevrolet produced the Camaro COPO concept car as a potential competitor in the NHRA Stock Eliminator drag-racing competition series. When first introduced in 2011, the car included two engine options: 1) a naturally aspirated 7.0L 427 ci engine (and homage to the original 1969 COPO Camaro) and 2) a smaller 5.3L 327-ci engine paired to a 2.9L twin-screw supercharger.

Regardless of which powerplant was selected, the COPO concept had a Powerglide 2-speed automatic transmission, although provisions were also made for 3-speed automatic and 5-speed manual transmissions. Out back, the car included a Strange Engineering S-9 solid rear axle with an aluminum third member, a 35-spline spool, 35-spline axles, and a 4.10:1 gearset.

The 2011 COPO Camaro concept also came equipped with a solid live rear axle; an NHRA-certified, full chromium-molybdenum alloy (chrome moly) roll cage; a high-rise, cowl-induction, fiberglass hood; and unassisted racing brakes with a standard line-lock system. It also had drag-tuned adjustable suspension at all four corners with

The SEMA Show COPO Camaro concept (seen here) was powered by a supercharged 327-ci engine. However, the COPO Camaro was designed to accommodate multiple engine options, including a 7.0L, 427-ci, naturally aspirated engine and a 5.3L, 327-ci supercharged engine. (Photo Courtesy General Motors LLC)

A Brief History of the COPO Camaro

The origins of the COPO Camaro began with three individuals who manipulated Chevrolet's vehicle ordering system to create custom cars that would likely never have existed otherwise. The individuals in question were Vince Piggins, the man credited with creating the Camaro Z28; Fred Gibb, a former drag racer, Illinois Chevrolet dealer, and the "father" of the ZL1 Camaro; and Dick Harrell, also known as "Mr. Chevrolet," a drag racing legend who rose to prominence in the 1960s and 1970s for his success on the drag strip and for his ability to performance tune and fabricate custom parts for his cars to make them faster.

The ordering system they used was known as the Central Office Production Order (COPO) system. Simply put, COPO was a method used by dealers "in the know" to order unique combinations of options not specifically listed on vehicle order forms.

Piggins used the COPO system to develop high-performance parts and systems without labeling them as such. In so doing, his parts passed through Chevrolet's ordering system undetected and eventually found their way to dealerships who knew Piggins's unique system.

Gibb, on the other hand, discovered that he could use the COPO system to fabricate and order complete production cars. In 1968, he successfully ordered 50 COPO Novas fitted with an L78 engine (a 396-ci big-block originally intended for use in Chevrolet's full-size sedans) paired with GM's Turbo Hydra-Matic (TH) 400 automatic transmission. Gibb was convinced the Nova SS would dominate the Stock and Super Stock automatic transmission drag-racing classes. Class requirements stated a minimum of 50 examples of the car had to be built, so Gibb placed his order with the understanding that all 50 cars would be delivered to, and sold at, his dealership, Fred Gibb Chevrolet in LaHarpe, Illinois.

In 1969, Gibb developed COPO option 9560, which equipped a production Camaro with a 427-ci big-block engine known as the ZL1. This all-aluminum engine was originally developed for NASCAR and weighed approximately 100 pounds less than the 396-ci big-block that served as the production Camaro's largest powerplant that year.

In addition to being lighter, the ZL1 engine produced significantly more horsepower than the Camaro's L78 396 (430 hp versus 375 hp). It was also speculated that the engine produced closer to 550 hp when equipped with fitted track-tuned headers.

A total of just 69 of the 1969 COPO Camaros (COPO 9560) were ordered by those same "in the know" dealers that year, making the car an instant standout among its less-powerful counterparts.

Dick Harrell helped propagate the success and popularity of the COPO Camaro program by using GM's COPO process to assemble a series of five unique 1969 Camaros. Collaborating with Bill Allen Chevrolet in Kansas City, Missouri, Harrell created his own unique COPO 9561 specification, which called for the installation of GM's robust L72 iron-block, 427-ci big-block engine; CX-code TH400 3-speed transmission; a 12-bolt rear end; a ZL2 cowl-induction hood; a heavy-duty, four-core radiator; F41 performance suspension; and power front disc brakes. Today, these cars are known as the 1969 Dick Harrell COPO Camaros.

In 1969, a total of 69 COPO Camaros (COPO option package 9650) were ordered by former Chevrolet dealer Fred Gibb. Gibb ordered these cars so that he could use some of them to compete in Stock Eliminator drag racing. As for the rest, he sold 13 to his own customers and sold or traded an additional 37 units to other dealerships. This, in turn, motivated other dealerships to use the COPO ordering system to custom order their own Camaros for resale. (Photo Courtesy David Newhardt/Mecum Auctions)

The cockpit of the 2011 COPO Camaro concept was updated to include a variety of race-specific equipment, including a 10,000-rpm tachometer, a dash-mounted shift light, a Hurst shifter, an NHRA-approved roll cage, relocated secondary gauges, and more. The rest of the factory interior remained, giving the interior a factory feel with an outwardly sophisticated-yet-edgy aesthetic. (Photo Courtesy General Motors LLC)

Strange Engineering adjustable struts out front and Strange Engineering shocks in the rear; a Custom Aeromotive fuel system with a fuel cell and integrated high-pressure fuel pump; and certified safety equipment.

The car's interior is essentially the same as the other stock Camaro models but with some notable exceptions and deletions. The car featured racing-style front seats and lacked rear seats entirely. As mentioned previously, the car was devoid of air conditioning, and it also lacked any power-steering assist. The car came equipped with a full complement of gauges, although these were placed where the central air vent had been previously. Additionally, a large tachometer with a shift light was mounted to the driver-side A-pillar.

Thunder at SEMA

Chevrolet introduced its new COPO Camaro concept on October 31, 2011 (one day before the official start of the 2011 SEMA Show), with all the fanfare of a red-carpet event. A large, sealed, wooden shipping crate with GM part number 20129562 stenciled on its exterior surfaces was positioned outside the Las Vegas Convention Center.

As the unveiling prepared to commence, GM executives began handing out hearing protection to those in attendance, which was made up mostly of the press and SEMA employees/volunteers. Moments later, with the crate's door swung aside, the 2011 Camaro COPO roared to life and slowly drove out of the crate. The massive roar of its unmuffled V-8 engine shook the entire crowd and much of the surrounding area.

The car that emerged was painted bright white with blue trim/accents. A stylized blue swoosh graphic on the car's rear fenders included a gold Chevy bowtie and the COPO logo in white lettering. The car rode on chromed racing wheels wrapped in 29x9-inch rear radical racing slicks and 4.5x28.15-inch front tires.

Like many show cars before it, Chevrolet built the 2011 COPO Camaro to gauge consumer interest. Unlike other concept vehicles, Chevrolet's intent with the COPO Camaro was to put the car solely in the hands of qualified racers. This meant that the car would have an extremely low production volume, so it was important to all involved with the COPO Camaro's creation to see how well the car was accepted by the general public.

After observing the overwhelmingly positive and enthusiastic reactions it received throughout the three-day SEMA

The 2011 COPO Camaro concept was unveiled at the SEMA Show on November 1, 2011. Packed in a massive shipping box with Chevrolet part number 20129562 stamped on its side, the COPO Camaro was unboxed, rolled out, and greeted with thunderous applause. (Photo Courtesy General Motors LLC)

Consumer response to the COPO Camaro concept at the 2011 SEMA Show was so overwhelmingly positive that General Motors decided to build a production version of the car. In 2012, a total of just 69 examples were manufactured: 67 coupes and 2 convertibles. Each sold for $89,000 when new. (Photo Courtesy General Motors LLC)

Show in Las Vegas, it seemed almost certain that General Motors was going to move forward with a production version of the car.

The Super Stock Engine

In December 2011, Chevrolet announced that it had created a new, supercharged engine for its COPO Camaro concept. It was a 5.3L Chevrolet Performance LSX racing engine equipped with a 4.0L twin-screw supercharger mounted atop its all-aluminum block. The engine was specifically developed to produce the power necessary for the COPO Camaro to compete in the NHRA Super Stock competition, where quarter-mile times are expected to be in the 9-second range (or faster). Formally designated the "Super Stock" engine, it was the third powerplant specifically developed by Chevrolet Performance for use in the COPO Camaro concept.

General Motors announced that the COPO Camaro would be available to consumers with three different engine packages: a naturally aspirated 427-ci (7.0L) or one of two supercharged 327-ci (5.3L) engines, including the one shown here. (Photo Courtesy General Motors LLC)

As part of GM's official press release for this engine, Jim Campbell, GM's U.S. vice president of performance vehicles and motorsports, made the following statement about the Super Stock engine.

"As we continue to refine our COPO Camaro concept, we are exploring all avenues to make it competitive, and Super Stock is the logical next step," he said. "The three-engine strategy would allow us to offer competition-ready powertrains across the board for Stock Eliminator and Super Stock."

From Concept to Production

In March 2012, Chevrolet announced that it would build a production version of the COPO Camaro concept car. Each car was specifically designed to compete in the NHRA's Stock Eliminator and Super Stock classes. To commemorate the original 69 COPO 9560 Camaros ordered by Gibb Chevrolet in 1969, General Motors elected to build just 69 examples of the new COPO Camaro for the 2012 model year. Each car was sold for an estimated $89,000, and the owners of each car were hand-selected by General Motors before production even began.

Each production version of the COPO Camaro came equipped with a solid rear axle, one of three engines: a naturally aspirated 7.0L V-8 and two supercharged 5.3L V-8 engines. Regardless of the powerplant, each car was also equipped with a Powerglide automatic transmission that was specially bolstered for drag racing. A total of five color options were offered, including Flat Black, Summit White, Victory Red, Silver Ice Metallic, and Ashen Gray Metallic. The race-spec interiors were stripped of all non-essential hardware, leaving only a pair of bucket seats, a competition shifter, stock- and race-specific instrumentation, and a chromoly steel roll cage assembly.

Keeping with tradition, Chevrolet built 69 additional COPO Camaros between 2013 and 2020, which included a significant redesign for the sixth-generation model that was introduced in 2016. The sixth-generation COPO Camaro included greater structural rigidity, less weight, a revamped interior, and an entirely reimagined exterior consistent with the styling of the other sixth-generation Camaros.

The 2016 COPO Camaro Courtney Force Concept

To commemorate its introduction as a sixth-generation model, the 2016 COPO Camaro Courtney Force concept was unveiled at the 2015 SEMA Show. Like its predecessors, the car was built to compete in the NHRA Stock Eliminator drag-racing series. The car's livery was developed as a collaboration between NHRA Funny Car Driver Courtney Force and Chevrolet. It featured a custom Red Hot exterior paint color with customized red and black "Courtney Force" signature graphics and red-accented grille trim. It also came equipped with wheelie bars, a parachute, and massive Goodyear racing tires.

The car's interior was equipped with a chrome-moly roll cage, lightweight racing bucket seats personalized with an embroidered COPO logo, Courtney Force's signature five-point safety harnesses, and a floor-mounted shifter. As with the earlier models, the sixth-generation COPO Camaro also included specific instrument panel–mounted analog racing gauges and a center stack–mounted racing switch panel. Also as before, the cockpit featured many of the same components/styling cues as the interior of its street-legal counterparts.

The success of Chevrolet's COPO Camaro program ensured its continued production after the launch of the sixth-generation Camaro. Chevrolet introduced the 2016 COPO Camaro Courtney Force concept at the 2015 SEMA Show. (Photo Courtesy General Motors LLC)

Beneath its high-rise carbon-fiber hood, the Courtney Force concept housed an LSX-based, 5.7L, 350-ci racing engine equipped with a Whipple 2.9L supercharger. The engine was paired to a race-built, TH400 3-speed automatic transmission. At its unveiling, Chevrolet announced that two additional engines would also be offered with the sixth-generation COPO package. These included a naturally aspirated, LS-based 427-ci engine and a naturally aspirated, LT1-based 6.2L engine.

The 2016 COPO Camaro Courtney Force concept livery was developed as a collaboration between Force and Chevrolet. After its introduction at SEMA, it was auctioned off at Barrett-Jackson in Scottsdale, Arizona, for $300,000. All the money received from the sale was donated by Chevrolet to the United Way. (Photo Courtesy General Motors LLC)

Purchasing a COPO Camaro and Uncertain Times

Throughout its seven-year production run, each COPO Camaro (other than its inaugural year) was distributed via a lottery system made up of interested buyers. This initially included the 2020 COPO Camaros. But in March of that year, the coronavirus pandemic caused massive lockdowns, quarantines, and temporarily brought many industries to a grinding halt. Prospective buyers of the COPO Camaro followed suit, leaving many of the 69 planned 2020 COPO Camaros unaccounted for. As life slowly returned to normal, Chevrolet abandoned the traditional lottery system and offered the remaining cars to consumers on a "first come, first served" basis.

Although Chevrolet did not offer a 2021 model, an announcement was made in July of that year that Chevrolet would offer the COPO Camaro as a 2022 model with a newly available 572-ci engine. The COPO 572 featured a cast-iron block with four-bolt main caps, aluminum heads, a forged-steel crankshaft, forged-steel connecting rods, and forged-aluminum pistons. The 2022 model was also offered with a pair of LSX -based small-block engines: a supercharged 350-ci V-8 rated at 580 hp and a naturally aspirated 427-ci engine rated at 470 hp. All variants of the newest COPO Camaro came equipped with an ATI Racing Products TH400 3-speed automatic transmission.

The Future of the COPO Camaro: The 2019 eCOPO Camaro Concept

On October 30, 2018, Chevrolet introduced another COPO Camaro at SEMA that was unlike any example that had come before it. Although it had been built to compete in the same drag-racing events as its predecessors, the eCOPO Camaro concept featured an all-electric powerplant comprised of an 800-volt battery pack and two longitudinally aligned BorgWarner HVH 250-150 electric motors bolted directly to the bellhousing of a race-prepared TH400 automatic transmission. Rated at an impressive 700-plus hp and an estimated 600 ft-lbs of torque, GM's official estimates put the eCOPO concept's quarter-mile times in the high-9-second range with trap speeds exceeding 140 mph.

“An all-electric powerplant comprised of an 800-volt battery pack and two longitudinally aligned BorgWarner HVH 250-150 electric motors bolted directly to the bellhousing.”

In an article published by *Autoweek* in October 2018, Russ O'Blenes, GM's director of performance variants, parts, and motorsports shared the following statement about the eCOPO Camaro.

"The eCOPO concept is all about where we go in the future with electrification in the high-performance space," he said. "The original COPO Camaro program was all about pushing the envelope, and this concept is an exploration with the very same spirit."

The eCOPO Camaro concept made its world debut at SEMA 2018. During its reveal, Chevrolet announced that it built the car to commemorate the 50th anniversary of the first COPO Camaro as well as to showcase GM's vision for electric-powered drag racing. (Photo Courtesy General Motors LLC)

Chevrolet partnered with Hancock and Lane Racing, the company that built an 8.0-second, all-electric Firebird drag racer known as *Shock and Awe*, to create the 2019 eCOPO Camaro concept. Using the same body and chassis as the 2019 COPO Camaro production model, the eCOPO concept was the first to showcase GM's new 800-volt battery and electrical system. (Photo Courtesy General Motors LLC)

Equipped with its quick-charging, 800-volt battery pack, a pair of BorgWarner HVH 250-150 motor assemblies, and its race-prepped Turbo 400 automatic transmission, the eCOPO Camaro concept produces more than 700 hp and 600 ft-lbs (estimated) of torque. The car can complete a blistering fast quarter mile of just 9.51 seconds at a speed exceeding 140 mph. (Photo Courtesy General Motors LLC)

The 2019 eCOPO Camaro concept was developed as a partnership between General Motors and Hancock and Lane Racing, a successful NHRA drag racing team best known for its record-holding, 8-second electric drag car known as *Shock and Awe*. General Motors not only chose to partner with Hancock and Lane because of its past successes in electric drag racing but also because of its long-standing relationship with an individual named Patrick McCue.

In addition to being the man chiefly responsible for engineering and developing *Shock and Awe*, McCue led an automotive technology program at Bothell High School in Seattle, Washington. Working together with Hancock and Lane Racing, McCue was able to invite more than a dozen of his students to participate in the development and assembly of the eCOPO Camaro concept car.

Since its introduction at the 2018 SEMA Show, General Motors has not released much additional information related to if or when the eCOPO Camaro will become a production model. Given the recent federal legislature that calls for a dramatic increase in the production of electric vehicles by 2030, it will be interesting to see what comes of programs like the COPO Camaro. Only time will tell.

CHAPTER

6 FIFTH GENERATION CONTINUED: THE SEMA CONCEPTS

"We have had the incredible opportunity to meet literally thousands of Gen 5 Camaro owners who provided direct feedback on what they loved about their car and what they wanted for the next-gen Camaro. As a result, the 2016 Camaro builds on what made the current Camaro such a success with more power, more agile handling, and more technology."
— Al Oppenheiser, Camaro Chief Engineer

As the launch of the fifth-generation Camaro approached, Chevrolet began showcasing concept Camaros (such as the 2010 Camaro LS concept seen here) at the SEMA Show in Las Vegas. Each of these concepts was developed to introduce a catalog of GM Performance aftermarket components ranging from unique decals/stripe kits and custom wheels to an assortment of unique performance upgrades, all of which could be purchased by consumers looking to transform their stock Camaro into a personalized, one-of-a-kind sports car. (Photo Courtesy General Motors LLC)

When the all-new, fifth-generation Camaro was introduced at the 2010 SEMA Show, it was named Hottest Car of the Year during the organization's inaugural SEMA awards presentation. SEMA created its awards event as an acknowledgment of the increased importance many automobile manufacturers placed on the association. The recipient of each award was determined by which vehicle received the highest number of votes from exhibitors who had attended that year's SEMA event. The 2010 Camaro had outperformed all of its key competitors, including the Dodge Challenger, Ford Mustang, Audi A4, Honda CR-Z, and others to earn the association's top honor.

In an interview posted at SEMA.org, SEMA President and CEO Chris Kersting shared the following about the organization's annual award show.

"The SEMA awards recognize the vehicles that SEMA Show exhibitors have identified as being at the forefront of emerging trends in the industry" Kersting said. "These vehicles are embraced by the industry due to their ability to help showcase and launch new aftermarket parts."

Two full years before the production Camaro would grace the exhibit halls at SEMA and win the association's top honors, Chevrolet had begun flooding the event with one-of-a-kind Camaro concepts that showcased the car's versatility as a cruiser, a street racer, and even a track-tuned performance machine. Each concept car was unique. Some showcased radical modifications to the car's exterior aesthetic while others demonstrated the potential power and performance that could be unlocked by consumers who dared to invest in GM's ever-growing assortment of OEM performance parts.

While none of these Camaros were true "concept cars" in the conventional sense, every one of the cars exhibited at SEMA both before and during the fifth-generation's production run represented conceptual packages from General Motors. Many of those packages demonstrated to consumers how they might choose to use GM's performance parts to personalize and customize their own Camaros.

What follows is an introduction to some of the most popular fifth-generation Camaro concepts that were showcased at each SEMA event between 2008 and 2012.

The 2010 Camaro Dusk Concept

The first in this series of fifth-generation Camaro concepts is the Camaro Dusk, a concept car that was inspired by the style of young and urban professionals. While it was more a stylized production model than a genuine concept car, the Camaro Dusk still introduced consumers to some of the unique custom body-kit accessories and performance-enhancing parts that General Motors offered.

Beginning with its exterior, the Camaro Dusk received several subtle-yet-notable accents and upgrades, including a race-inspired front splitter, rocker extensions, a rear diffuser, 21-inch wheels from BBS, taillamp and fog lamp bezels that

The Dusk Camaro concept made its debut at the 2009 SEMA Show in Las Vegas, Nevada. The car came finished in a Berlin Blue exterior paint with a Jet Black and Sedona accented interior. (Photo Courtesy General Motors LLC)

Per General Motors, the Camaro Dusk concept was inspired by the "style of young and urban professionals." It was specifically designed to give the Camaro an "international flair" and a "tailored look that was both stylish and sophisticated." To achieve this, the concept car featured all the latest technologies being offered by General Motors at that time, including Wi-Fi connectivity and a dynamic sound system from Boston Acoustics. (Photo Courtesy General Motors LLC)

were finished to match the wheels, and the production exhaust and Brembo brake systems from the Camaro SS. The majority of the car was painted Berlin Blue, except for the ground effects, which were finished in Jet Black.

Moving to the interior, the Camaro Dusk was wrapped in an assortment of premium materials finished in Jet Black, including the dashboard, the center console, the interior doors skins, and the carpeting. In contrast, its Sedona-colored leather seats, door armrests, and a handful of other trim pieces added to the interior's refined, international flair. An assortment of features, including premium sill plates, upgraded footwell lighting, and Sedona-colored stitching helped to further heighten the extravagance of the Camaro Dusk's interior.

To complement the visual aesthetic of the Camaro Dusk's interior, General Motors also elected to include a variety of "advanced technologies" (for its time) as part of its packaging. The 2010 Camaro Dusk was one of the first Chevrolet models to include onboard Wi-Fi connectivity. It also came bundled with a Boston Acoustics sound system and a convenient smart phone cradle.

Shortly after its introduction at SEMA, General Motors released the following press statement about the Camaro Dusk.

"This is a car with an international flair, bringing the Camaro to a place it hasn't traditionally been," the press release said. "It is a very tailored look that is stylish and sophisticated but with a distinct American accent."

The 2010 Camaro Jay Leno Concept

The evolution of the Jay Leno Camaro concept began with a series of meetings hosted at GM's design studios between the Camaro's development team and television personality Jay Leno. During their discussions, Leno expressed his desire to build a Camaro that offered better eco-performance through the use of lightweight components. He believed that the future of hot rodding would include the use of smaller, economical powerplants compared to the traditional V-8, and he wanted to build a Camaro with

When Jay Leno was approached by General Motors about building this concept Camaro, he said that the car should be a "modern interpretation of yesteryear's Z28." Instead of a fuel-guzzling V-8 beneath its hood, the Jay Leno Camaro concept has a twin-turbocharged 3.6L V-6 engine that is capable of producing 420 hp. (Photo Courtesy General Motors LLC)

In addition to producing nearly the same horsepower as its larger, 6.2L V-8 counterpart, the Jay Leno Camaro concept twin-turbo 6-cylinder engine is also lighter, making the car nimbler and more responsive. It also gets nearly the same gas mileage (18 city/29 highway in an automatic, 17/29 in a manual) as both the base and RS models. (Photo Courtesy General Motors LLC)

a clean aesthetic that could provide massive horsepower while maintaining fuel efficiency. That said, he also wanted to ensure the car performed well, especially when being driven hard on the open road.

As is true of many of the concept Camaros showcased at the 2009 SEMA Show, the Jay Leno Camaro concept started life as a production model. In this case, it was a base Camaro coupe equipped with a 3.6L V-6 engine rated at 304 hp. To bolster engine output, Chevrolet added a pair of Turbonetics T-3 turbochargers and a custom air-to-air intercooler that increased engine output to approximately 425 hp, which was nearly identical to the output of the Camaro SS's 6.2L engine. The benefit of the setup on the Leno concept was that the car produced the same fuel economy as it had prior to receiving any upgrades (as long as the turbochargers were not producing any boost).

To accommodate the twin-turbocharger upgrade, the Leno Camaro concept was also equipped with a larger-capacity, Be-Kool radiator and a custom exhaust system. It was also fitted with a Centerforce-supplied clutch and pressure plate to ensure positive engagement of the 6-speed manual transmission during shifting. A Brembo, six-piston brake package was installed, as was a Pedders coilover lowering kit. In fact, the car's entire powertrain was reviewed to deliver maximum performance during any driving condition—on the street or at the racetrack.

At Leno's request, the exterior of the Camaro lacked any significant bolt-on modifications, thereby maintaining its clean aesthetic. Even so, it was one of the most radically styled Camaro concepts at the 2009 SEMA Show. The car featured a one-off front fascia with custom fog lamps and front brake cooling ducts, as well as a fully custom, air extractor–style hood. It was also equipped with unique upper and lower grille assemblies and a distinctive ground-effects package (that included a rear diffuser). Even the stamped rear fender vent ducts, which are normally nothing more than a decorative

"At Leno's request, the exterior of the Camaro lacked any significant bolt-on modifications, thereby maintaining its clean aesthetic."

throwback exterior aesthetic on most production Camaros, were transformed into operating ducts that provided cooling air to the rear brakes.

The car was a huge hit at the 2009 SEMA Show and has remained one of the most-popular fifth-generation Camaro concept cars to date, so much so that the sixth-generation Camaro's reimagined front fascia incorporated design cues reminiscent of the one introduced on the Leno concept.

The 2010 Camaro Chroma Concept

Like the Camaro Dusk before it, the Camaro Chroma is less a concept car than a stylized production model.

The 2010 Camaro Chroma was developed to demonstrate how a production Camaro, using nothing more than accessories sold at most Chevrolet dealerships across the United States, could be transformed into a one-of-a-kind street machine that looked like it came straight from a high-end tuner shop. In fact, when introduced at SEMA in 2008, General Motors informed consumers that both the RS and SS versions of the Camaro could be transformed into an exact replica of the Chroma concept.

The Chroma concept began life as a stock SS Camaro finished in Summit White paint. From there, it was fitted with a silver-stripe package, 21-inch wheels, a "Blade" rear spoiler, ground effects painted Summit White, and rear fender vent graphics. Red Brembo brake calipers were also installed that added a splash of color on the Camaro's neutral-colored exterior.

The Chroma Camaro concept used existing, dealer-installed performance parts, including a high-flow intake and exhaust, short-tube headers, and a Hurst short-throw shifter. Aside from its white exterior paint, 21-inch wheels, new "Blade" rear spoiler, and silver stripe package, the only other distinguishable difference (from an aesthetics standpoint) is that the Chroma concept was fitted with a Victory Red engine cover. (Photo Courtesy General Motors LLC)

The 2010 Camaro Chroma's interior included several minor but notable red highlights, including red footwell and cupholder lamps; red accent lighting along the driver-side dashboard and door panels; red accent stitching on the center-console cover, driver's seat, passenger's seat, shifter knob and boot, steering wheel, and door armrests; and red piping around each of the car's front floor mats. (Photo Courtesy General Motors LLC)

One of the Camaro Chroma concept's most striking interior features was its introduction of two-tone leather seats and accent trim throughout the cockpit. The color choices gave the car a contemporary, cutting-edge aesthetic, which is exactly what GM's designers were going for. (Photo Courtesy General Motors LLC)

Although the Camaro Chroma concept began life as a 2010 Camaro SS with a stock 6.2L, LS3 V-8 engine, it received a number of small power and performance gains with the addition of a performance intake, a Hurst short-throw shifter, shorty headers, and a performance exhaust system. (Photo Courtesy General Motors LLC)

"With its silver graphics on the Summit White paint, this car has a tailored, tone-on-tone appearance that is simultaneously racy and subdued," said Todd Parker, GM Accessory Studio's design manager during the introduction of the Camaro Chroma. "It is a sophisticated-looking car that is easily duplicated by any customer because all of the parts are available to build it."

Unlike the Jay Leno concept, which used aftermarket turbochargers to boost engine output, the Chroma retained its stock LS3 engine but received an assortment of factory-supplied GM performance parts, including a performance intake, shorty headers, and a performance exhaust system. A Victory Red engine cover was also installed atop the intake manifolds and injector rails to improve the overall aesthetic of the engine compartment.

The interior of the Camaro Chroma concept received only minor modifications, including red accent stitching on the two-tone seats and shifter boot, custom floor mats and door trim, and an assortment of silver accessory inserts for the dashboard and door panels. As with the exterior, the intent of this concept was to showcase the variety of Chevy accessories available to transform any Camaro to whatever extent its owner desired.

"What's great about the Camaro Chroma is it speaks to the almost unlimited possibilities that the accessories offer," Parker said. "You can build your Camaro mild or wild—but build it your way."

The 2010 Camaro LS7 Concept

At first glance, the 2010 LS7 Camaro concept was indiscernible from just about every other production Camaro on display at the 2008 SEMA Show. Unlike Jay Leno's Camaro concept car, which had featured several stylized exterior enhancements, the exterior of the LS7 had virtually no perceptible differences except for these two things: 1) a matte black hood and taillight surround and 2) special "LS7" badging on the front fenders and rear decklid.

As with its exterior, the LS7 Camaro's interior received minimal upgrades. The car featured a unique red-on-black trim, with the interior door skins and the center band of the car's dashboard wrapped in red plastic. Likewise, the gauge clusters incorporated a unique red-with-white numbering. Everything else, from the seats to the center console, was finished in flat black, although the seats were accentuated with white stitching. Each of the front floor mats also included a red embroidered LS7 logo.

The true differentiators between the 2010 LS7 Camaro concept and its production counterparts were all the bits that could be found beneath the surface.

The LS7 concept featured an LS7 V-8 crate engine (GM part number 17802397) in place of the factory LS3 that was normally installed in most Camaros from that era. The engine, which featured a replacement, high-performance camshaft from GM Performance Parts, produced a staggering 550 hp.

The Camaro LS concept was developed by GM Design to showcase the fifth-generation Camaro's capabilities as a weekend bracket drag car. The car comes equipped with an LS7 crate engine fitted with a high-performance camshaft, GM Performance Parts headers and intake system, and a modified wet-sump oiling system. (Photo Courtesy General Motors LLC)

The LS7 concept was developed as an homage to the COPO Camaros made famous by Chevy dealer Fred Gibb in the late 1960s. Unlike those early racers, the LS7 Camaro was designed to be equally comfortable at the drag strip or on the open road. (Photo Courtesy General Motors LLC)

In addition to its fortified camshaft, the LS7 engine was also equipped with a wet-sump oiling system, a Brembo four-wheel-disc brake package, custom 20-inch wheels, a driveshaft safety loop, a sports exhaust system that included upgraded headers, and a bolstered air-intake system. Both the headers and air intake were newly developed performance components at the time of the car's introduction, but both would be offered to consumers through GM's Performance Parts division the following year.

As is true with many of the Camaro concept cars introduced by General Motors in 2010 (and later), the LS7 Camaro concept was developed to showcase the performance potential that could be unlocked by consumers who chose to purchase licensed, bolt-on hardware through GM's Performance Parts program.

2010 GS Racecar Concept

The 2010 Camaro GS Racecar concept was created to pay tribute to the legendary Trans-Am Road Racing Series and one of its most prominent racers, Mark Donohue. Donohue had won both the 1968 and 1969 SCCA Trans-Am series championships in his distinctive blue-and-yellow Penske Sunoco #6 Camaros. Donohue's string of wins helped the Camaro gain credibility with consumers and racers alike.

Nearly 40 years later, North Carolina–based Riley Technologies sought to pay homage to Donohue's original Camaro by building a concept race car based on GM's latest Camaro platform. Working in conjunction with Designer Tom Peters and GM's High-Performance Vehicle Operations division, Riley Technologies built a heritage-inspired race car from the

Inspired by the original Trans-Am Road Racing Series blue-and-yellow Camaro of Roger Penske and driven by Mark Donohue, the fifth-generation GS Racecar concept was developed by General Motors and North Carolina–based Riley Technologies as an early prototype for the Grand-Am Koni Challenge GS racing class. (Photo Courtesy General Motors LLC)

The GS Racecar concept uses the car's standard LS3 V-8 engine, although it is affixed to the chassis with solid engine mounts and mated to a close-ratio Tremec 6060 6-speed manual transmission. Additionally, the engine features a 3-inch exhaust system with aftermarket mufflers. (Photo Courtesy General Motors LLC)

When the GS Racecar concept was introduced at the 2008 SEMA Show, it was announced that Riley Technologies would begin manufacturing additional examples for the 2009 Grand-Am season. The original concept car was later sold at Mecum Auctions in August 2013. Although the car was expected to earn between $110,000 and $200,000, it sold for just $60,000. (Photo Courtesy General Motors LLC)

fifth-generation Camaro platform that was less concept car than it was a fully realized prototype of a future Grand-Am Koni Challenge GS race car.

The 2010 Camaro GS concept had a reinforced chassis and drivetrain built to conform to the specifications required of race cars certified for the Trans-Am series. It was powered by a production LS3 V-8 engine (attached to the frame with solid engine mounts) and a Tremec 6060 6-speed manual transmission with close-ratio gearing. The car also included a 3-inch exhaust system with Coast Fab mufflers, an upgraded engine oil cooler, a C&R racing aluminum radiator, and transmission and differential coolers.

Its exterior featured a seam-welded production Camaro body with a carbon-fiber hood, trunk lid, doors, and fenders. Like Donohue's original 1969 Camaro race car, the 2010 GS Camaro was finished in a deep blue paint scheme with yellow graphics and yellow racing wheels. It was even fitted with matching #6 graphics on the driver's door and passenger's door.

As with any SCCA-sanctioned race car, the interior of the Camaro GS featured the usual accoutrement of safety features, including a roll cage, a race-specific driver seat with a Sparco multipoint harness, a fire extinguisher, and more. Despite these radical departures from the production model, it is apparent that the car's interior was heavily modified from a donor car, indicating that the GS started life as an early preproduction Camaro from Chevrolet.

When the 2010 Camaro GS Racecar concept was unveiled at the 2008 SEMA Show, it appeared as if it had come straight from the racetrack. It lacked the clean lines of its other Camaro concept counterparts and showed a variety of dirt, bumps, and blemishes across its exterior. In truth, the car had spent many hours running wide open at a local test track as the Riley engineering team worked to finish dialing in its chassis and powertrain. While on display at SEMA, it was announced that Riley Technologies would begin manufacturing the Camaro GS Racecar for the 2009 Grand-Am season.

The 2010 Camaro Dale Earnhardt Jr. Concept

Former NASCAR driver Dale Earnhardt Jr. has always had an affinity for the Chevy Camaro. He's owned several in his lifetime, including a pro touring–style 1972 Camaro powered by an LS crate engine. When Chevrolet announced that it would be introducing a new model for the 2010 model year, Earnhardt wanted to be one of the first to own one.

Earnhardt's passion for the brand, along with his personal vision for his signature Camaro, was communicated

One of the most notable distinctions about the Camaro Dale Earnhardt Jr. concept (besides the fact that it's tied to Dale Earnhardt Jr.) is that Chevrolet was able to modify the car's 6.2L engine to run on E85. The bump in octane allowed Chevy's engineers to squeeze a bit more horsepower out of the engine, which seems only fitting for a Camaro concept named after one of NASCAR's most famous drivers. (Photo Courtesy General Motors LLC)

The exterior of the Dale Earnhardt Jr. concept is a fitting homage to the Earnhardt family and Hendrick Motorsports. The car features livery colors synonymous with cars raced by members of the Earnhardt family, and it is badged with the "JR Motorsports" insignia, a company started by Dale Jr. and his sister Kelly Earnhardt Miller. (Photo Courtesy General Motors LLC)

to GM's design team. Taking his desires to have a performance-based-yet-luxurious, two-tone Camaro to heart, the design team set about developing a special-edition Camaro concept that celebrated the driver and his incredible success in the NASCAR series.

They started with a stock Camaro SS. Before making any modifications to its exterior aesthetic, the car's 6.2L LS3 engine's compression ratio was increased to run on E85 gasoline. The engine was then calibrated to take full advantage of the flex fuel's higher octane and improved performance characteristics. The result was a small but appreciable boost in overall engine horsepower.

The Earnhardt concept received several additional mechanical modifications as well. New GM Performance Parts headers were installed directly to the block, which improved the flow of exhaust gases away from the engine. A 6-speed manual transmission equipped with a Hurst short-throw shifter transferred engine power to the rear wheels, while a four-wheel Brembo brake package improved stopping power. Finally, a suspension lowering kit was installed, allowing the Camaro to hug its 21-inch, five-spoke wheels and Pirelli P-Zero ZR-rated performance tires.

Aesthetically, the Earnhardt concept's exterior remained mostly unchanged from the donor car, except for the addition of several custom Chevy accessories. These included a unique grille, ground effects, a rear diffuser, an exhaust system, and an early Camaro-style dovetail rear spoiler. The car was also given a custom dark-gray-over-white paint scheme with a single orange stripe dividing the two paint colors along the car's beltline.

To complement the paint scheme, the interior of the wheel spokes were similarly painted dark gray, and an orange stripe was added around the wheel's rim. The front and rear calipers were also painted orange. Finally, a pair of black "JR" decals with orange graphics were added to each of the front fenders.

The interior received a number of notable upgrades as well. Each of the seats were trimmed in custom leather with suede inserts and stylized orange stitching. Likewise, the steering wheel, shift knob, door armrests, and the center-console lid were similarly wrapped in leather with more of the same orange accent stitching throughout.

The door-panel inserts and the instrument panel were wrapped in carbon fiber, while the remaining trim pieces came finished in painted orange plastic. Custom white-faced gauges (and auxiliary gauges), all with black lettering/numbering, finished the look of the dashboard, while black-and-orange "JR" logos adorned the otherwise all-white custom sill plates.

In addition to its performance and cosmetic upgrades, Dale Earnhardt Jr. also specified that the car should have an improved sound system. As such, the Earnhardt Camaro concept was fitted with an upgraded stereo system through Chevy Accessories, along with an improved speaker system (including amps and subwoofers) from Boston Acoustics.

The 2010 Camaro Black Concept

Where the Camaro Chroma concept proved that an (almost) all-white Camaro could be both racy and subdued, the Camaro Black concept took a similar-but-different approach. On one hand, the 2010 Camaro Black concept *is* subdued, as much as any black sports car can be. At the same time, its matte-black-finished hood, its color-matched ground effects, and its gloss-black wheels all gave the car a low-slung, stealthy stance that looks both aggressive and sinister.

As its name implies, the Camaro Black concept transformed a stock base-model Camaro into a machine that would be at home on the set of a Batman movie. As mentioned, the car received a matte-black-finished hood, black 21-inch alloy wheels, and color-matched ground effects that included a rear diffuser. In addition, it was equipped with a darker grille, tinted RS taillamps, a black SS rear spoiler, and color-matched exterior badging. To add to the car's ominous appearance, the car also received a set of red-glowing HID headlamp halo rings.

Inside, the Camaro Black featured an all-black interior, with black chrome trim accents, black leather seats with gray accent stitching, red LED instrument lighting, and red footwell ambient lighting. Dark finished accents included the shift knob, radio face, steering wheel ring, gauge trim, sill plates, and door handles. The interior also received a Chevy Accessories premium audio upgrade, which included a set of MTX speakers.

The Camaro Black concept was created with the sole intent of showing consumers just how far they could personalize the aesthetic of their cars. Everything about the Black concept (from its high-intensity headlamps with the unique red halo-ring coloring to its window tint and color-matched exterior badging) was intentionally integrated together to create a stealthy, sinister-looking street cruiser. (Photo Courtesy General Motors LLC)

Two of the more captivating elements introduced on the Camaro Black concept were its 21-inch wheels with their darkened finish and the ground effects and rear diffuser packages. Together, these elements provide a more planted look that enhances the already-aggressive stance of the fifth-generation Camaro. (Photo Courtesy General Motors LLC)

No mechanical alterations were made to the car's 3.6L, 304-hp V-6 engine, although a black Chevy Accessories engine cover was installed to further enhance the overall theme of the car.

The 2010–2011 Synergy Series Camaro Concepts

The Synergy Series Camaros were "born" at SEMA after Chevrolet introduced the first Camaro Synergy concept, a 2010 Synergy Green special-edition model, at the 2009 SEMA Show. The car, which was essentially a stock 6-cylinder Camaro finished in Synergy Green paint with black race stripes and an assortment of GM-licensed accessories, was an instant crowd favorite. Its introduction at the 2009 SEMA Show led to GM's introduction of Synergy Green as a factory paint color beginning in 2010. It also compelled Chevrolet to create the Synergy Series Camaro, a show/concept car that could be debuted each year at SEMA packaged with the latest technology offerings and accessories from General Motors.

For the 2010 SEMA Show, Chevrolet created a second Synergy Series concept and announced that the Synergy Series Camaro would be offered to consumers in the first half of 2011 as a special-edition model. The 2011 Synergy Series Camaro concept was developed with a specific emphasis on "new approaches to accessory parts and customization," according to General Motors.

Chevrolet planned to create a Camaro that offered consumers unique interior and exterior combinations not available on any other production models. Their concept included an exclusive gray interior highlighted with red accent stitching throughout.

"The Synergy Series reflects the strong response consumers have consistently had towards Camaro," said Chris Perry, Chevrolet's vice president of marketing, in a statement made at the 2010 SEMA Show. "At the same time, it provides an example of how Chevrolet is renewing its commitment to expanding accessory offerings."

For the SEMA Show, Chevrolet introduced the Synergy Series Camaro concept as a convertible model finished in a Silver Ice exterior with black Synergy stripes on the hood and rear decklid, as well as a black decal insert for the front "mail slot" (the air scoop in the front fascia). All the striping also included red-line insert accents. Complementing the bright exterior was a black leather interior finished in red accent stitching on the

The original Chevy Camaro Synergy concept introduced at SEMA in 2009 was so named because of its Synergy Green production exterior color. The concept car was developed to introduce the unique paint color, which was offered to consumers as part of a special-edition Camaro in the first half of the 2010 model year. (Photo Courtesy General Motors LLC)

In addition to its unique paint color, the Camaro Synergy concept was equipped with a variety of factory accessories, including 21-inch wheels with a black center finish and polished rims, a ground-effects kit finished in gloss black, Cyber Gray Rally hood stripes, a high-wing rear spoiler, and a performance air intake. (Photo Courtesy General Motors LLC)

seats, console, doors, steering wheel, and shifter boot.

Stylized, colored ground effects were introduced on the 2011 Synergy concept. The "body lowering" ground-effects kit included a front splitter, rocker-panel extensions, and an amped-up rear lower fascia with integrated exhaust ports. To enhance its lowered, road-hugging aesthetic, the Synergy concept was also equipped with a Pedder's suspension lowering kit (an officially licensed product of Chevrolet) and a set of 21-inch, five-spoke wheels finished in black with red-accent striping.

Unlike the original 2010 Synergy Camaro production model, which was only offered in a single color (Synergy Green) and as a base-model coupe, the 2011 Synergy production model was offered in four colors: Cyber Gray, Victory Red, Summit White, and Black. Additionally, it could be purchased by consumers as either an SS (at or above the 2SS trim level) or as an RS (at or above the 2LT trim level).

The production variant of the 2011 Synergy Camaro contained many of the same features as the concept model, including a Chevrolet Accessory grille and ground-effects package, 21-inch painted wheels with a silver finish, and a body-colored antenna. It also had the previously mentioned gray interior with red stitching (which, like the concept model, included stitching on the seats, steering wheel, door panels, console lid, shifter boot, shift knob, and headrests), Chevrolet Accessory interior trim kit in Silver Ice, floor mats with red border stitching and silver Camaro lettering, and special footwell and cupholder lighting.

Mechanically, anyone who ordered the Synergy Series Camaro with the SS package received the LS3, 6.2L engine paired to a 6-speed manual transmission, a Chevrolet Accessory Hurst shifter with red stitching, a Chevrolet Accessory red engine cover, red Brembo brake calipers (on the 2SS package only), and the same Pedders lowering kit as that introduced on the concept car.

2011 Chevrolet Camaro SSX Track Car Concept

From the moment of its unveiling in January 2006, the fifth-generation Camaro had become the topic of almost constant conversation among consumers and enthusiasts alike. Chat rooms and message boards were flooded with discussions around the car's potential performance capabilities. When Chevrolet announced that it was going to produce the Camaro beginning in 2010, those conversations only intensified. Finally, when consumers were able to get their hands on the first examples of the 2010 Camaro SS, they began transforming the cars into track-capable race cars, thanks to the ever-increasing availability of factory-built performance parts.

Recognizing the incredible demand for increased performance by Camaro owners everywhere, Chevrolet elected to develop its own closed-course track car out of a stock Camaro SS. Dubbed the Camaro SSX Track Car concept, the car provided consumers with a glimpse of the Camaro's track potential while doubling as a showcase for the latest performance parts being manufactured by General Motors.

The Camaro Synergy Series concept was one of four new Camaro concepts introduced by Chevrolet at the 2011 SEMA Show. Unlike its predecessor, which was wrapped in Synergy Green paint, the new concept came finished in Silver Ice paint with black Synergy stripes on the hood. The car pictured here was one of four Synergy production variants based on the second concept and available to consumers for the 2012 model year. (Photo Courtesy General Motors LLC)

The Camaro SSX Track Car concept was developed by General Motors to demonstrate how a production-model Camaro SS could be transformed into a closed-course track car using available performance parts. It featured a variety of carbon-fiber body panels designed to reduce weight and suspension modifications aimed at improving road-course handling and performance. (Photo Courtesy General Motors LLC)

"The SSX concept explores taking Camaro's excellent street performance and extending it into a road-course context," said Chevrolet Vice President of Marketing Chris Perry as part of a press release. "The car expresses Camaro performance while also signaling Chevrolet's new commitment to developing and offering a portfolio of performance parts for racing enthusiasts."

The Camaro SSX Track Car combined a number of available aftermarket parts with parts specifically developed as part of the new concept car's development. In addition, the SSX Camaro benefitted from the removal of materials, including its rear seat, carpeting, and sound-deadening materials, to help reduce its weight. It was developed with input from Pratt and Miller, Chevrolet's partner company for the Corvette Racing program, and Riley Technologies, which advised Chevrolet on the racing components to be used (and licensed) by the automotive manufacturer.

Outwardly, the Camaro SSX Track Car was fitted with a variety of carbon-fiber aero parts, including a front splitter, rockers, and an adjustable rear wing, as well as carbon-fiber body panels (hood, fenders, doors, and rear decklid) and an updated lower grille that included integrated front brake-cooling ducts. The entire exterior was finished in an Icy White Metallic paint, which was specifically chosen because of how well it contrasted with the carbon aero parts. Each door was also fitted with unique "SSX" graphics. Lastly, the car was equipped with unique, track-specific, 20-inch wheels and tires.

In addition to the rear seat and carpeting deletions, the interior of the SSX Camaro received several track-specific

The Camaro SSX Track Car was developed by Chevrolet in cooperation with Pratt and Miller (the company behind the Corvette Racing program) and Riley Technologies. The car uses parts developed for the Grand-Am racing series and rides on purpose-built wheels and tires designed specifically for the racetrack. (Photo Courtesy General Motors LLC)

While the exterior aesthetic is a fusion of form and function, the SSX Track Car concept's powertrain was developed to ensure the car performed as well as it looked. It featured an LS3 6.2L V-8 engine equipped with a Chevy Performance Parts camshaft, cylinder heads, and a dry-sump oil system. It also included a factory 6-speed manual transmission bolstered with a twin-disc clutch from a Corvette ZR1. (Photo Courtesy General Motors LLC)

appointments including an SCCA-approved roll cage and window net, a five-point harness for the driver's seat, racing pedals, a fire-suppression system, a unique fuel cell, an Ace suede-covered racing steering wheel and shifter, and a video-camera system installed into the car's roll cage.

Beneath its hood, the SSX received an LS3 V-8 engine enhanced with a Chevrolet Performance Parts camshaft, cylinder head, and dry-sump oil system. A production 6-speed manual transmission was fitted with a twin-disc clutch out of the sixth-generation Corvette ZR1. Its modified production suspension featured Pfadt Race Engineering–licensed components, low-restriction air induction and exhaust systems, and four-wheel disc racing brakes with six-piston front calipers out front and four-piston calipers in the rear. All four wheels also received cross-drilled rotors for quicker cooling and reduced brake fade.

Although Chevrolet never built the Camaro SSX as a production model, it did offer consumers the option to purchase the same parts used in its creation through the GM Performance Parts (GMPP) catalog. The announcement was made in November 2010 at an invitation-only GMPP event that General Motors hosted at Spring Mountain racetrack in Nevada.

The announcement, which came in conjunction with the SSX's premiere at the 2010 SEMA Show, stated that all the components used in the creation of both the Camaro SSX and the Z06X Corvette were going to be offered through GMPP to anyone who wished to transform their Camaro (or Corvette) into the concept cars on display at SEMA.

The 2011 Camaro Hot Wheels Concept

Arguably one of the coolest Camaro concepts to make an appearance at the 2011 SEMA Show, the 2011 Camaro Hot Wheels concept fulfilled the fantasies of every child (and adult) who ever dreamed that their 1:64-scale toy could be transformed into a real, full-size car. This concept car, which was developed as a partnership between Chevrolet and Hot Wheels, did just that.

The Camaro Hot Wheels concept car was inspired by the

The 2011 Camaro Hot Wheels concept was Chevrolet's answer to every child's wish to have a real, full-size version of his or her beloved 1:64 scale toy car. The car debuted at the 2011 SEMA Show, the same year that the show hosted the aftermarket industry's premier display of automotive toys. (Photo Courtesy General Motors LLC)

Hot Wheels "Custom Camaro," which was a 1:64-scale 1968 Camaro finished in lime green Spectraflame paint. The model was one of the original 16 Hot Wheels cars introduced by Mattel on May 18, 1968. The Custom Camaro model, along with the other model cars in that series, helped catapult the Hot Wheels brand to prominence. In turn, its toy cars and trucks helped inspire generations of car enthusiasts (including Camaro), many of whom collected the small, scale-model toy cars as they worked to afford the real thing.

Forty-three years later, when Chevrolet suggested building a full-size Hot Wheels Camaro concept car, the response received from Hot Wheels studios was immediate.

"The Camaro has been a mainstay in the Hot Wheels lineup since 1968," said GM Design Director Phil Zak. "Several generations of car enthusiasts grew up playing with Hot Wheels Camaros, while dreaming of driving the real thing, so this was a once-in-a-lifetime opportunity to make that dream a reality."

Development of the 2011 Camaro Hot Wheels concept was a collaborative effort between the two studios from the start. Although the designers at the Chevrolet studio (Michigan) and the Hot Wheels Studio (California) were separated by thousands of miles and a couple of time zones, each group worked diligently to capture their individual ideas of what a life-size Hot Wheels Camaro should look like. Then, they traded notes with one another until both studios had agreed upon a design motif for the car.

The Camaro Hot Wheels concept was inspired by the Hot Wheels Custom Camaro, the enormously popular Spectraflame 1:64-scale Camaro that was released as part of the original 16-car Hot Wheels set in 1968. (Photo Courtesy General Motors LLC)

The reflective paint finish featured on the 2011 Hot Wheels concept was created using Gold Touch Inc.'s Cosmichrome product. The paint was applied in multiple layers: a primer coat, a liquid-metal solution (to give the surface a mirror-smooth finish), a silver-chrome base coat, and several layers of green tint. (Photo Courtesy General Motors LLC)

"The Hot Wheels and Camaro brands have been paired together since their inception," said Felix Holst, vice president of design for the Mattel Wheels Division. "As part of the brand's historic Sweet 16, the Camaro was the first Hot Wheels car ever produced. The Spectraflame paint and red-line tires of those first Hot Wheels cars have been the dreams of guys for generations, and it was thrilling to inject these elements into a Camaro for real."

Although the 2011 Hot Wheels Camaro concept was unmistakably a fifth-generation SS Camaro, it contained several unique styling elements that paid tribute to the original "Custom Camaro" toy. For starters, the car was dressed in flat-black graphics, had 20-inch red-line wheels, and was painted in a spectacular metallic lime-green paint. While the graphics and the wheels had been simple to replicate, the unique paint introduced on the Hot Wheels concept was

The interior of the Camaro Hot Wheels concept received several custom updates as well. These updates included custom red stitching throughout, Hot Wheels sill plates, Hot Wheels cut-and-sew embroidered logos in the front seat-backs (as seen here), unique Chevrolet Accessories pedal kits, and custom footwell and cupholder lighting packages. (Photo Courtesy General Motors LLC)

Not to be outdone by the competition, the Camaro Hot Wheels concept display included a massive, full-scale, 50-foot-long section of the classic Hot Wheels orange track. Spectators could almost visualize the concept car racing through the 270-degree looping turn before coming to rest on the SEMA showroom floor. (Photo Courtesy General Motors LLC)

not. In essence, Chevrolet had to invent a new way to paint the car.

To achieve the highly reflective finish seen on the Hot Wheels Camaro concept, the design team had to use Cosmichrome, a unique paint product by Gold Touch Inc. First, a primer was applied to the car's pristinely cleaned exterior. Any imperfections, such as dust, debris, etc., created blemishes in the primer, thereby ruining the mirror-like effect. Second, a liquid-metal solution was sprayed onto the primer to create a mirror-smooth, silver-chrome base coat. Finally, the green tint was applied in several layers until the proper color effect was achieved.

"It may sound pretty straightforward, but no one had ever tried using this process to paint a whole car," Zak said. "The bodywork and paint team experimented with several processes before spraying the first body panel. There were so many variables that contributed to getting the finish perfect, from the drying time to the air pressure of the spray guns (none of which was known before this project), and the team absolutely nailed it perfectly."

In addition to the paint and graphics packages previously listed, the exterior of the 2011 Camaro Hot Wheels concept was also fitted with stain-black ground effects (comprised of a splitter, rocker panels, and rear fascia side extensions), a ZL1 grille with Hot Wheels badging, ghosted Hot Wheels logos on the quarter panels, Hot Wheels badging on the decklid, Euro-style taillamps with new inner smoked lenses, Euro-style rear fascia with new diffuser and exhaust bezels, a ZL1 rear spoiler, black aluminum "CAMARO" fender badges with milled faces, and black aluminum hood inserts with milled hood vent extractors.

Inside, the Camaro Hot Wheels concept was fitted with black leather-wrapped seats and door inserts with Torch Red accents and cut-and-sew flames, Hot Wheels sill plates, Hot Wheels cut-and-sew embroidered logos in the front seat-backs, a Chevrolet Accessories pedal kit, and a Chevrolet Accessories footwell and cup holder lighting kit with red lights.

Although the car retained its stock LS3 6.2L V-8 engine and Tremec TR6060 6-speed manual transmission, a number of mechanical upgrades were included elsewhere, including a pair of six-piston Brembo brake calipers and two-piece rotors out front, as well as four-piston Brembo brake calipers for the rear. It was also equipped with a Pedders suspension lowering kit, a Chevrolet Accessories strut tower brace, black aluminum cover, and complete exhaust system.

The 2012 Red Zone Camaro Concept

Introduced on a 2011 Camaro convertible (a new offering for the fifth-generation's sophomore year), the Red Zone concept used a collection of carefully selected accessories and a heritage-inspired exterior stripe kit to create a unique design statement that was a blend of "contemporary styling with a classic flair," according to General Motors.

Starting with its exterior, the Red Zone concept featured a Crystal Claret Red tint coat (a paint color that would be offered to consumers for the 2012 model year) combined with a black convertible tonneau cover. A silver heritage-stripe graphic, an accessory inspired by the accent stripe that adorned the nose of the first-generation SS models, framed the top half of the car's front fascia. Instead of entirely wrapping around the fascia, the heritage stripe kit included a Z-shaped transition along the leading edge of each front fender that then receded back to a point (and looked a lot like a lightning bolt) on each side of the car.

The Red Zone Camaro's suspension was lowered at all four corners via an aftermarket suspension lowering kit manufactured by Pedders (an officially licensed product of Chevrolet). Though not visible under normal circumstances, a polished strut tower brace was added beneath the hood. Custom 21x8.5-inch silver/polished-face, five-spoked wheels finished the look of the car's exterior. Paired with the silver stripe kit, the custom wheel package provided the car with enough bold, bright accents to instantly capture the attention of anyone who saw it.

The 2012 Camaro Red Zone concept was developed by Chevrolet to showcase how custom accessories could enhance the Camaro convertible's styling. It was also used to introduce GM's new heritage-inspired vinyl stripe decal, which provided consumers with a contemporary graphic that also harkened back to the classic striping on the first-generation Camaros. (Photo Courtesy General Motors LLC)

In a 2011 press release from General Motors, Designer Adam Berry shared the following about his Red Zone concept. "This is a Camaro for those who want great looks and a performance personality," he said. "It's a simple yet dramatic statement that is uniquely Camaro." (Photo Courtesy General Motors LLC)

Inside, the Red Zone Camaro's interior was lined in titanium-colored leather with Silver Ice accents on the doors and instrument panels. A unique, soft black instrument panel insert was also introduced, giving the car's cockpit a classic-but-contemporary feel. A convertible windscreen from Chevrolet Accessories was installed behind the driver's seat and passenger's seat while a pair of unique floor mats, each showcasing an embroidered version of the car's signature "CAMARO" logos, completed the look of the interior.

Although the Red Zone Camaro concept was little more than a dressed-up production-model Camaro, it provided would-be consumers with a vision of how their personal vehicles could be personalized using products produced and/or licensed by Chevrolet.

Per the Red Zone concept Camaro's designer Adam Barry, "This is a Camaro for those who want great looks and a performance personality. It's a simple yet dramatic statement that is uniquely Camaro."

> "THIS IS A CAMARO FOR THOSE WHO WANT GREAT LOOKS AND A PERFORMANCE PERSONALITY. IT'S A SIMPLE YET DRAMATIC STATEMENT THAT IS UNIQUELY CAMARO."

The 2012 Camaro 1LE Concept

The 2012 Camaro 1LE concept marked the return of Chevrolet's famed performance package.

Originally introduced in 1988 to make the third-generation Z28 and IROC-Z Camaros more competitive at road racing events, the original 1LE package equipped said Camaros with bigger brakes, an aluminum driveshaft, a larger gas tank, and larger hollow sway bars. It also deleted the factory air conditioning.

Although a very limited number of third-generation Camaros were ever equipped with the package during the remainder of the car's production run, its popularity among serious Camaro enthusiasts was sufficient enough that Chevrolet continued offering it as an option on the fourth-generation model. When the 1LE package was unveiled on the new

Following in the tradition of its third- and fourth-generation road-racing performance package counterparts, the fifth-generation 1LE concept was designed to be an "all-out race car package" capable of holding its own on any road course. (Photo Courtesy General Motors LLC)

The Camaro 1LE concept borrowed components from both the SS and ZL1 production models. It featured the same Goodyear Eagle F1 Supercar G asymmetrical tires, active exhaust, shifter, and flat-bottom steering wheel (trimmed in suede-microfiber) as the ZL1 Camaro. It also came equipped with Brembo's massive six-piston calipers (front) and four-piston calipers (rear), sport suspension with magnetic ride control, and lightweight 20x10-inch (front) and 20x11-inch (rear) racing wheels. (Photo Courtesy General Motors LLC)

Beneath its hood, the 1LE concept was equipped with the same 426-hp LS3 V-8 engine found in the SS production model, although the 1LE's engine was fitted with a red engine cover from Chevrolet Accessories. The engine was paired to a TR6060 6-speed manual, close-ratio transmission. (Photo Courtesy General Motors LLC)

The production version of the 1LE Camaro Coupe went on sale in the fall of 2012 as a 2013-model-year offering. The 1LE Camaros had a starting price of $37,035, which was more than $20,000 less than its ZL1 counterpart. Admittedly, the 1LE lacked the supercharged engine (and corresponding horsepower), but for its price point, it was an affordable upgrade to the SS model. (Photo Courtesy General Motors LLC)

1993 Z28 Camaro, it transformed an already-capable sports car into a machine that could hold its own against the likes of Ford's GT350 Mustang and the Corvette Grand Sport.

For 2012, Chevrolet elected to reimagine the 1LE option and introduce it as a concept at the 2011 SEMA Show in Las Vegas. Unlike its Red Zone and Synergy Series counterparts, this concept Camaro was built to offer consumers a glimpse at the capability of a competition-ready Camaro. The car was developed with technologies borrowed from both the Camaro SS and ZL1 models (the latter of which was still in development as a 2012 production vehicle).

Outwardly, the 2012 1LE concept Camaro came finished in Victory Red paint with a flat-black hood and hash-mark extensions on each of its front fenders. The satin-black mirrors, rocker panels, front splitter, and rear spoiler help round out the car's exterior aesthetic while simultaneously helping to produce additional downforce and/or air movement around the car. Lightweight 20x10-inch (front) and 20x11-inch (rear) racing wheels, also finished in satin black and wrapped in Goodyear Eagle F1 Supercar G asymmetrical tires (the same tires were introduced on the ZL1 the following year) helped maximize the car's grip on the road, even during extreme driving conditions.

The 1LE concept car's interior was essentially unchanged from the production model, except for a few new features and a unique color palette. The car's seats came wrapped in black leather with light stone stitching while the dashboard and door panels received graphite-silver inserts. The most notable additions to the 1LE's cockpit were the introduction of a flat-bottom steering wheel and an all-new short-throw shifter, both of which were borrowed from the ZL1 model. A unique Chevrolet Accessories pedal kit was also installed, although it was intended more for show than substance.

While both the interior and exterior suggested that the 1LE was more than just another pretty face, it was the components that couldn't be seen that separated this Camaro from the competition. Although equipped with the same 6.2L engine as the SS model, the 1LE received a 6-speed manual, close-ratio transmission; dual exhaust outlets with ZL1-style active exhaust and diffuser; Brembo six-piston front calipers with two-piece front rotors; four-piston rear calipers; sport suspension with Magnetic Ride Control; electric power steering; a shock tower brace; and, just to dress up the engine a bit, a Chevrolet Accessories red engine cover.

The 2012 Camaro ZL1 Carbon Concept

While the 1LE Camaro concept reintroduced a performance package to a stock Camaro, the ZL1 Carbon concept took the already-impressive ZL1 Camaro and made it even more formidable. In much the same way that Chevrolet dressed up the Carbon Edition Z06 Corvette, the 2012 Carbon concept received several signature upgrades to its exterior, interior, and chassis/powertrain.

The exterior of the ZL1 Carbon concept came finished in an as-yet-unreleased Ashen Grey paint scheme (though

The 2012 Camaro ZL1 Carbon concept was less a concept car and more a brilliant marketing ploy by General Motors to commemorate the arrival of the 2012 ZL1 Camaro marque. The car was virtually identical to its other production ZL1 counterparts, save for the addition of exposed carbon fiber to its hood extractor, rear spoiler, and interior. (Photo Courtesy General Motors LLC)

One of the most notable elements on the ZL1 Carbon concept was the car's carbon-fiber "mohawk" hood insert. The sinister-looking insert, which included a set of four air ducts to help cool the car's superchargers, created an aggressively stylized focal point on the car's massive hood. (Photo Courtesy General Motors LLC)

Some of the most notable refinements to the ZL1 Carbon concept were found inside the car. Jet Black leather adorned many of the interior surfaces, including the seats, which also included suede microfiber inserts and Torch Red stitching. The interior door panels and the instrument panel were also fitted with carbon-fiber inserts. (Photo Courtesy General Motors LLC)

A carbon-fiber spoiler fitted with a stainless-steel wicker bill was installed on the rear decklid of the ZL1 Carbon concept. Like its other carbon-fiber elements, the spoiler enhanced the car's aesthetic while simultaneously improving downforce. Simply stated, the Camaro ZL1 Carbon concept followed the popular GM mantra that form follows function. (Photo Courtesy General Motors LLC)

this same color would be introduced for all iterations of the 2012 Camaro). It also featured an exposed-weave carbon-fiber "Mohawk" hood insert, a carbon-fiber rear spoiler with a stainless-steel wicker bill, and lightweight 20x10-inch wheels out front and 20x11-inch wheels in back, all finished in satin black with machined faces.

On the interior, the car's seats were wrapped in Jet Black leather with suede microfiber seat inserts and Torch Red stitching throughout. A suede-trimmed, flat-bottom steering wheel and ZL1 short-throw shifter were also included to provide the driver with an exciting yet luxurious driving experience. In addition to its suede accents, the shifter knob also included carbon fiber–trimmed accents. The instrument panel, the driver's door, and the passenger's door were all appointed with custom carbon-fiber inserts as well.

Adding some much-needed stopping power to offset the ZL1 Carbon Camaro's robust 580-hp powerplant, this immensely powerful concept car was fitted with Brembo six-piston calipers and two-piece composite rotors at each of its front wheels along with four-piston calipers in the rear. Additionally, the car was also equipped with magnetic ride control, dual exhaust outlets with active exhaust, and a diffuser.

During its reveal at the 2011 SEMA Show, Tony Roma, the ZL1's program engineering manager, said the following about the immensely powerful Carbon Fiber concept.

"This concept's dramatic appearance matches the extreme performance capabilities of the Camaro ZL1," Roma said. "Even if its styling doesn't intimidate you, its performance on the track will."

kind to celebrate the Custom Camaro diecast toy introduced by Mattel in 1968. Unlike its predecessor, which was essentially a stylized version of the fifth-generation Camaro, this model was built as a stylized interpretation of the original Hot Wheels toy car. Developed by Chevrolet Performance, the designers "interpreted the original toy in a way that conveys its spirit in a realistic form," according to General Motors.

"A literal interpretation of the toy car would have been too cartoony—it just wouldn't look right on a full-size car," said Chevrolet Design Manager Dave Ross. "The stance and wheels of the concept vehicle are different, as well as some of the proportions the toy has, but the body lines and styling cues are all the same."

At first glance, the car looked remarkably like a 1967 Camaro. Upon closer examination, there were many subtle (and some not-so-subtle) changes made to its exterior body architecture. The front grille included a revised mesh design, an updated Chevrolet bowtie emblem, and "Hot Wheels" badging near the driver-side headlamp assembly. Similar "Hot Wheels" badges were also installed on the car's fenders and trunk lid. The exterior door handles were shaved and replaced with a remote keyless entry system that allowed the doors to be opened from the outside. The entire exterior was painted Kinetic Blue, a brand-new color that was developed for the 2013 Hot Wheels Camaro production model.

In addition, there were three significant design elements introduced on this Hot Wheels Camaro concept that differentiated it from its 1967 counterpart. First, the car was fitted with a custom hood that matched the design introduced on the

2012 1967 Hot Wheels Concept

It's with a bit of irony that the final concept car introduced in this book is one that pays tribute to the very first Camaro model ever built. While the 1967 Camaro Hot Wheels concept may be less a homage to Chevrolet's original pony car than it is a full-scale re-creation of the Hot Wheels company's original 1:64-scale model Custom Camaro, the 1967 Hot Wheels concept still bears an undeniable resemblance to the first-generation model. As such, it brings this exploration of Camaro concept cars full circle as we essentially finish where we began.

This full-scale Hot Wheels concept Camaro is the second of its

The 1967 Camaro Hot Wheels concept was developed by Chevrolet Performance to pay tribute to the original Hot Wheels model. This full-scale re-creation featured a custom hood, shaved door handles, stainless-steel side-exit "zoomie" exhaust pipes, and 18-inch alloy wheels with red-line accents. (Photo Courtesy General Motors LLC)

A 430-hp LS3 E-Rod Connect and Cruise V-8 crate engine powers the 1967 Camaro Hot Wheels concept. The custom engine is paired with a 4L65-E 4-speed automatic transmission. When Chevrolet introduced the powerplant at that year's SEMA Show, it shared that the E-Rod Connect and Cruise powerplant met and exceeded emissions requirements across the continental United States, including California. (Photo Courtesy General Motors LLC)

original Custom Camaro toy. Second, stainless-steel side-exhaust assemblies (zoomie headers, which were another Hot Wheels throwback) were installed below the front fender just behind the front wheels.

Finally, a set of custom 18-inch aluminum wheels (18x9 up front and 18x11 in the rear) with red-line accents were fabricated for the car. While the rim was not unique to the concept car, the red-line finish harkened back to the wheels found on most Hot Wheels cars from that era.

The interior of the 1967 Camaro Hot Wheels concept was a fusion of old and new. While the dashboard, doors skins, center console, steering wheel, and pedals were all throwbacks to the original Camaro, the instrument cluster and console gauges contained contemporary hardware reminiscent of those used in the fifth-generation Camaro. Likewise, the front bucket seats were the same as those used in the 2012 Camaro, albeit with shortened head restraints more befitting the original model.

Each seat was trimmed in white leather with blue accent stitching, while the steering-wheel rim was wrapped in white leather. Much of the remaining interior surfaces (including the dashboard, center console, door skins, and inner quarter panels) were wrapped in silver vinyl. The headliner and sunshades were covered in silver fabric, and the floorboards were covered in silver carpeting.

Beneath its custom hood, the car featured an all-new, emissions-compliant LS3 E-Rod Connect and Cruise crate powertrain comprised of a 430-hp LS3 engine paired to a 4L65-E 4-speed automatic transmission. Its drivetrain and suspension were comprised of contemporary hardware as well, including a hydroformed front subframe with tubular control arms and adjustable coilover shocks, a four-link rear suspension with adjustable coilovers, rack-and-pinion steering, and heavy-duty disc brakes with six-piston calipers at all four corners.

The 1967 Camaro Hot Wheels concept made its debut at the 2012 SEMA Show in Las Vegas. It was parked beside a prototype of the 2012 Hot Wheels production model on a platform designed to look like a full-scale version of the orange Hot Wheels track pieces that kids (both young and old) have played with for generations. The pair of Camaros was one of the star attractions of that year's show.

In addition to the 1967 Camaro Hot Wheels concept, Chevrolet also introduced the 2013 Hot Wheels Camaro at the 2012 SEMA Show. Marketed as a special-edition Camaro in 2013, the Hot Wheels Camaro sold just over 1,500 units during its single-year production run. (Photo Courtesy General Motors LLC)

EPILOGUE

SIXTH GENERATION AND BEYOND (2016+)

"THE CAMARO WENT TO THE GYM AND CAME OUT WITH A LITHE, MORE ATHLETIC PHYSIQUE FOR THE SIXTH GENERATION. IT'S A MORE EXPRESSIVE EVOLUTION OF THE CAMARO'S ICONIC CHARACTER—AND ONE THAT COMPLEMENTS ITS LEANER SIZE AND SHARPER REFLEXES."
— ED WELBURN, VICE PRESIDENT OF GM GLOBAL DESIGN

The sixth-generation Camaro took everything good about the previous generation's design and made it better. While it is true that the sixth-generation Camaro is an almost entirely new car, there's no denying that everything about it, from its exterior aesthetic and its dramatically improved interior to its updated 6- and 8-cylinder powerplants, was a reimagining of what came before. (Photo Courtesy General Motors LLC)

To say the sixth-generation Camaro is merely an evolution of the fifth-generation model would be doing a huge disservice to the men and women who contributed to its creation. The sixth-generation model took a huge leap forward in terms of its dynamic performance, track-capable handling, immersive technologies, and exterior and interior design motifs.

It was built on the smaller Alpha architecture, which was GM's newest rear-wheel-drive platform (originally created for the Cadillac CTS and ATS sedans). Its exterior was developed around a design vocabulary of lean "mascularity," taking what was good about the fifth-generation Camaro's identity and literally making it leaner and meaner. Its interior was given a bolder-yet-more-refined form language, and was packaged with a variety of advanced technologies ranging from dramatically enhanced interior lighting and entertainment packages to extensive driver performance data and feedback via a display screen mounted between the car's speedometer and tachometer. Even the powerplants offered with the sixth-generation Camaro were new to the brand. These included the 455-hp 6.2L LT1 V-8, the 335-hp 3.6L LGX V-6, and a 275-hp turbocharged 2.0L 4-cylinder.

Like the fifth-generation model before it, GM Design Chief Ed Welburn invited designers from GM studios around the globe to submit proposals for the sixth-generation Camaro. Ultimately, the winning proposal was created by Hwasup Lee from the Warren Performance Studio. Lee previously served as the lead exterior designer of the seventh-generation Corvette Stingray. After reviewing his sketch proposals, along with those received from other studios, Lee's design was selected. He was chosen to lead the sixth-generation's exterior design team as well.

From the start, Lee's objective had been to "build on

First introduced in 2012, the GM Alpha platform became the underpinning for GM's small and mid-size vehicles. The Alpha platform increased the Camaro's structural rigidity by 28 percent and lightened the chassis by more than 200 pounds from the fifth-generation model. (Photo Courtesy General Motors LLC)

Hwasup Lee was the lead exterior designer of the sixth-generation Camaro. A graduate of the ArtCenter College of Design, Lee has worked his entire career (to date) at General Motors and has been one of the lead designers for many of Chevrolet's top marques, including the fifth-generation/sixth-generation Camaros and the C7 and C8 Corvette Stingrays. (Photo Courtesy General Motors LLC)

Tom Peters is often celebrated for his major contributions to the Camaro and Corvette programs. He is also considered one of the world's best automobile designers. In his career at General Motors, he has served as chief of design for the sixth-generation Corvette and the seventh-generation Stingray. He also served as the director of design for the eight-generation mid-engine Stingray. Additionally, he has lent his design talents to the Camaro (fifth generation and sixth generation), Silverado, the Pontiac Aztek, the Cadillac XLR, and several key concepts, including the Pontiac Banshee IV (see Chapter 4), the Cadillac Sixteen, and the Buick Velite. (Photo Courtesy General Motors LLC)

Kirk Bennion served as the sixth-generation Camaro's exterior design manager. Before joining General Motors, Bennion studied automotive design at the Cleveland Institute of Art. In his role as exterior design manager, Bennion has also been involved with many of GM's most iconic automobiles, including the seventh- and eighth-generation Corvette Stingrays. (Photo Courtesy General Motors LLC)

Compared to the rest of the sixth-generation Camaro's principal design team, Design Manager of Performance Car Interiors Ryan Vaughn is a relative newcomer. Even so, his resume is nothing short of spectacular. Vaughn's early success included designing the interior of the seventh-generation Corvette. He has since served as the director of interior design on the sixth-generation Camaro and the eighth-generation Corvette Stingray. (Photo Courtesy General Motors LLC)

A camouflaged sixth-generation Camaro test mule/prototype is shown parked at one of GM's proving grounds. The "Find New Roads" marketing campaign played a significant part in the new Camaro's launch. (Photo Courtesy General Motors LLC)

the success" of the fifth-generation car, thereby retaining the established Camaro identity while building a car that was "more expressive, more sculptural, and more function-driven," according to *Camaro: 2016* by Larry Edsall.

In addition to Lee, the sixth-generation Camaro's design evolution was led by Tom Peters, head of Chevrolet Performance design; Kirk Bennion, head of GM Performance Car exterior styling; and Ryan Vaughn, Camaro's interior design manager. Like Lee, the trio had previously partnered on the seventh-generation Corvette, and each brought elements from that earlier design program forward into the sixth-generation Camaro platform. According to Peters, the Corvette had shown them ways to design certain features, including proportions, sculptural quality, and dramatic sectioning.

While the relationship between the seventh-generation Corvette and the sixth-generation Camaro is undeniable, each evolved from a very different proportion: true sports car versus true muscle car, respectively. Each remains a distinct and instantly recognizable staple of its own brand. Still, each has been hailed as being the most iconic contemporary example of its kind, which is a testament to the talented individuals who figuratively breathed life into these cars.

Still, it is important to note that while the sixth-generation Camaro appeared to borrow elements from the fifth-generation Camaro (and the seventh-generation Corvette), the only carryover parts shared among any of these cars were the SS badge and the Chevrolet bowtie emblems previously used on the fifth-generation Camaro's rear decklid.

Additionally, Tom Peters explained that "the [Camaro's] proportions are so unique and different [from Corvette]. There were some things we could translate through a Camaro filter but nothing direct."

A Different Kind of Launch

As we have established throughout this book, General Motors traditionally introduced its newest automobiles by showcasing them at specific auto shows across the United States. While the sixth-generation Camaro certainly participated in these (including its formal unveiling on May 16, 2015, during a huge celebration at Belle Isle Park in Detroit), Chevrolet also decided to showcase the new Camaro by engaging in a less conventional but ultimately more rewarding venture. It invited members of the automotive press to drive several examples of its new sixth-generation Camaro across the continental United States.

General Motors called the program "Find New Roads." Its premise was to allow reporters, many of them automotive journalists, an opportunity to become familiar with the newest Camaro by allowing them to drive it along various legs of the nationwide tour.

In addition, Chevrolet's marketing department encouraged local Camaro clubs across the United States to join the caravan as the tour stopped at unique and/or historic locations that promoted "ingenuity" and "innovation." These two key words had defined the development of the sixth-generation

On May 17, 2015, GM Executive Vice President of Product Development Mark Reuss revealed the sixth-generation Camaro to a packed house of enthusiasts at Belle Isle Park on the outskirts of Detroit. The last car to roll out onto the stage (seen here) was finished in Red Hot paint, a new color for the sixth-generation model. (Photo Courtesy General Motors LLC)

The ceremonial unveiling of the sixth-generation Camaro at Belle Isle Park provided fans and media alike with their first real look at the new car. During this initial reveal, three Camaro coupes were driven onto the stage and down the catwalk: one in Hyper Blue Metallic (pictured here), one in Nightfall Gray Metallic, and one in Red Hot. (Photo Courtesy General Motors LLC)

Camaro. The team wanted to make sure that current Camaro owners also had an opportunity to get up close and personal with the new car.

A total of 150 reporters were invited and approximately two dozen new Camaros were slated to participate in the "Find New Roads" Camaro relay event. The initial block of reporters assembled in Detroit for the launch of the tour and selected car keys at random from a black bag. Next, each reporter found the car that matched their selected key. Once that had been accomplished, the reporters climbed into their cars and journeyed out. Half the team headed west and the rest headed east.

Each reporter was assigned a specific destination city. Upon arrival, they were instructed to connect with the next group of reporters at a prearranged meeting place and turn over the car. Before the event got underway, the promotional team in charge of the unique relay event issued the following recommendation: each reporter was strongly encouraged to avoid following a specified route. Instead, they were instructed to simply find new roads—but with just one caveat. Each reporter had just 36 hours to reach their specified rendezvous point.

A black 2016 SS Coupe cruises down an interstate in Utah. This Camaro, and several others like it, were all part of GM's "Find New Roads" campaign, wherein a group of automotive journalists randomly selected the keys to a new Camaro and then spent the next 36 hours driving it to a predetermined destination. Once there, they handed their car off to another reporter who would repeat the pattern until, collectively, the collection of Camaros had been driven across all 48 continental United States. (Photo Courtesy A.J. Mueller)

The "Find New Roads" program started in Detroit with approximately 24 Camaros (a mixture of RS and SS models) and an equal number of reporters. From there, half the team of drivers headed east while the other half headed west. They had only one instruction: to literally "find new roads." The success of this program changed the way Chevrolet revealed its products from that time forward. (Photo Courtesy General Motors LLC)

Although this unique promotional event caused some angst within GM's managerial hierarchy, they need not have worried. The success of the Find New Roads launch program led General Motors to begin showcasing all of its latest models, including other iterations of the sixth-generation Camaro, the 2020 mid-engine Corvette Stingray, and the 2023 Corvette Z06, at numerous automotive venues across the United States. From major race events (such as the Rolex 24 and the Daytona 500) and sanctioned events (such as the annual Corvette Bash at the National Corvette Museum) to small, more intimate introductions at its dealerships across the United States, Chevrolet embraced the notion of showcasing its cars anywhere consumers could get up close and personal to its latest offerings.

Sixth-Generation Concepts

As with the fifth-generation Camaro, Chevrolet introduced an assortment of sixth-generation concept cars at SEMA events during the early years of the car's production run. As before, each of these Camaros was designed to showcase specific GM-licensed components developed by the automotive manufacturer. These parts could then be purchased by Camaro owners to enhance the look or performance of their own cars.

The 2014 Chevrolet Camaro Bumblebee concept is shown parked in the courtyard of GM's design studio with the now-famous Eero Saarinen Design Dome in the background. While it was likely built to evaluate a Camaro built of the Alpha platform, this car rose to prominence as the character Bumblebee in the movie *Transformers: Age of Extinction.* (Photo Courtesy General Motors LLC)

Chevrolet introduced the Camaro Red Line concept specifically to showcase a range of new accessories that the automaker planned to market to consumers the following year. It was one of several Chevrolet Red Line concept vehicles introduced at the 2015 SEMA Show. (Photo Courtesy General Motors LLC)

All of the Red Line concepts, including the Camaro (seen here), as well as the Chevy Trax, Malibu, Colorado, and Silverado 1500 models came finished in Enhanced Silver Metallic paint with a custom Charcoal roof panel and Satin Graphite trim with red accents. (Photo Courtesy General Motors LLC)

Chevrolet introduced the following concept cars at the 2015 SEMA Show:

Camaro Concept Cars Introduced at the 2015 SEMA Show	
Name	Details
Camaro Chevrolet Performance Concept	This was a Summit White SS coupe with unique red accents; lowered suspension; Brembo brakes; billet-cut, 20-inch forged-aluminum wheels; and performance upgrades
Camaro Hyper Concept	This was a V-6-powered LT coupe finished in Hyper Blue paint with white rally stripes, heritage-style fender badges, and polished 20-inch forged-aluminum wheels.
Black Accent SS Concept	This was an SS coupe fitted with black ground effects; darkened taillamps; satin-black rally stripes; black bowtie emblems; black 20-inch, five-split-spoke, low-gloss black wheels; and a black fuel door cover. The car also featured a lowered suspension, Brembo front brakes with red calipers, a performance air intake, and a red-accented engine cover.
Camaro Black Concept	This was a blacked-out SS coupe finished in Mosaic Black Metallic paint with darkened trim, tinted glass, lowered suspension, and 20-inch black wheels.
Camaro Red Line Series Concept	This was a V-6-powered coupe finished in enhanced Silver Ice Metallic paint with custom fender hash marks, Satin Graphite accents, 20-inch wheels with painted Performance Red accents, mirror caps, grille surround and accents, and Jet Black leather interior with Satin Graphite interior trim.
Camaro Red Accent Concept	This was an SS convertible finished in Switchblade Silver Metallic paint. It was accented with red accessory trim and an Adrenaline Red leather-trimmed interior. It included a lower grille with red inserts, red hash-mark fender graphics, black bowtie emblems, and 20-inch five-spoke Gloss Black wheels with a Red Outline Stripe. Under the hood is a red-accented engine cover.
Camaro Krypton Concept	This was finished in unique Black-over-Electroluminescent Krypton Green paint. It featured illuminated Chevrolet bowties that cascaded down the body sides at the activation of a switch inside the cockpit. Chevrolet also introduced a handful of additional concept Camaros after the sixth-generation's inaugural production year. While many of these offerings had waned from full concept-car designs to production models fitted with concept components (such as stripe kits, custom ground effects, etc.), there were still some notable examples that made appearances during the 2016 and 2017 auto show seasons, both domestically at SEMA and abroad at the Geneva International Auto Show.
2017 Camaro SS Slammer Concept	This was a customized sixth-generation Camaro riding on 22-inch front and 24-inch rear chrome wheels. The Camaro's body was modified to accommodate the larger wheel/tire combinations, with included 245/30R22 tires up front and 275/25R24 tires in the rear. The entire car was finished in Dazzling Black paint and rode on air-adjustable suspension.
2017 Camaro Turbo Autox Concept	This was a 2.0L turbocharged coupe equipped with a performance suspension, brake system, air intake, and exhaust system. It featured the Chevrolet Performance lowering kit, 20-inch aluminum wheels, and performance front brakes with six-piston calipers and two-piece slotted rotors. The turbocharger can produce up to 20 pounds of boost. The car came finished in Shock Yellow paint with Pearl Nickel hood stripes and Carbon Flash Metallic accents on the hood vents, rockers and rear diffuser.
The 2017 Camaro Track Concept	This was an SS Camaro equipped with additional engine, transmission, and differential coolers, an upgraded FE4 Magnetic Ride Control suspension system that rides 1.18 inches (30 mm) lower than normal Camaro SS models, a limited-slip differential, Brembo six-piston front brakes, an enhanced aero package, 20-inch Gloss Black aluminum wheels wrapped in Goodyear Eagle F1 Supercar tires, and a performance-oriented chassis with magnetic dampers, springs, and stabilizer bars. The Camaro Track concept had Satin Green paint with a Gloss Black hood and roof stripes.

The 2016 Camaro Krypton concept was also unveiled at the 2015 SEMA Show. Like the Red Line concepts, it offered little in terms of new technology except for one unique feature: its electroluminescent paint job. The paint work, which was performed by Lumilor Labs for a staggering $80,000, lights up when a low electrical current is applied to it. The result is a Camaro that glows a bioluminescent green in the dark of night. (Photo Courtesy General Motors LLC)

In addition to its unique electroluminescent paint, the Krypton Camaro concept was equipped with 20-inch wheels, high-intensity discharge (HID) headlamps custom trimmed in green, darkened taillamps, unique upper and lower grilles, and a rear spoiler. (Photo Courtesy General Motors LLC)

An Uncertain Future

In 2018, General Motors underwent major restructuring to return the company to profitability. This restructuring required the company to make an estimated $3 billion in budget cuts and other changes to help it reestablish significant positive cash flow by 2021. As part of these cuts, it was announced that the seventh-generation Camaro program, as well as several key engine programs, including the 6.6L LT3 engine that had been proposed for the stillborn sixth-generation Camaro Z28, would be indefinitely canceled.

Since that time, General Motors has remained silent about the future of its beloved pony-car brand beyond its current generation. The continued popularity of the Ford Mustang and Dodge Challenger platforms combined with the critical commercial success of the mid-engine Corvette Stingray appear to have adversely impacted the Camaro's sales numbers. While the sixth-generation model sold 72,705 units during its freshman year, its year-over-year sales numbers showed a rapid and consistent decline with just 21,893 units sold in 2021.

Rumors have circulated across several reliable automotive news and media sources that indicate that Chevrolet may be looking at following the direction taken by Ford with its Mustang Mach-E SUV. Namely, it would transform the Camaro brand into something other than the traditional two-door sports coupe that has graced our roadways for the past half century. Some of the latest rumors suggest that a high-performance EV sedan and/or an SUV might be on the horizon.

While not a concept car, the 50th Anniversary Edition Camaro is significant in that it commemorates a major milestone in the history of the Camaro brand. To help celebrate Camaro turning 50, GM's designers created unique "FIFTY" badging for the car. Additionally, each anniversary car was finished in Nightfall Gray Metallic paint with satin chrome accents and orange brake calipers. The interiors were trimmed in black leather with orange accent stitching. (Photo Courtesy General Motors LLC)

Sadly, it seems increasingly certain that Chevrolet intends to discontinue the Camaro after the 2024 model year. General Motors has announced its discontinuation of the Alpha platform, and internet rumors speak of a high-performance EV sedan replacing the traditional two-door Camaro. While General Motors has not released an official statement yet, the sheer volume of information available online strongly supports these rumors. It is also rumored that Chevrolet will produce a final farewell Camaro called the 2024 Heritage Edition model beginning in late 2023. (Photo Courtesy General Motors LLC)

According to an article written by Jonathan Lopez at GM Authority, the current sixth-generation Camaro is slated to see its final sendoff in late 2023 with the introduction of a special collector's farewell edition for the 2024 model year. Although Chevrolet has not announced the retirement of the Camaro yet (at least at the time this book was submitted for publication), it seems likely that this special-edition Camaro, which many are already calling the 2024 Heritage Edition, will be limited to updated exterior and interior components, especially given the aforementioned cancellation of GM's performance engine programs.

On August 17, 2022, Dodge unveiled the Charger Daytona SRT Banshee concept to a crowd of devoted Mopar enthusiasts and owners. The concept car featured an exterior that shares more than a passing resemblance with the second-generation Charger. Slated for production as early as the 2024 model year, this latest EV from Dodge suggests that there is still a viable market for muscle cars, even if the muscle comes from a massive bank of batteries instead of an internal-combustion Hemi engine.

Given the specific market targeted by Dodge's announcement combined with the utter lack of information from Chevrolet on the Camaro's future, it leaves many to ponder whether or not General Motors might be planning something similar for its beloved muscle car. Only time will tell.

A Lasting Legacy

Despite its seemingly uncertain future, there is little doubt that examples of the Chevy Camaro will continue to fill our highways and backroads long after that dreaded day when the final production model rolls off the assembly line at GM's Lansing Grand River Assembly Plant. Every generation of Chevrolet's iconic muscle car has its own dedicated fanbase that works tirelessly to keep their Camaros looking and running like new. In so doing, they help preserve the history and the heritage of their beloved cars. Even if production of the Camaro is discontinued after the 2024 model year, it seems certain that Chevrolet employees and enthusiasts alike will continue to celebrate its rich legacy.

On June 28, 2016, 50 years (to the day) after the Camaro name was publicly revealed, Chevrolet unveiled its plans to commemorate the Camaro's 50th anniversary with a series of celebratory events that included tours of the Lansing Grand

Camaro owners are some of the most dedicated enthusiasts in the automotive world. Here, a lineup of first-, third-, fourth-, and fifth-generation Camaros assemble to commemorate the launch of the sixth-generation model. (Photo Courtesy A.J. Mueller)

A local Camaro club congregates at a cars-and-coffee cruise-in event. Although General Motors may stop producing new Camaros after the 2024 model year, the rich heritage that has been created by Camaro enthusiasts around the globe will live on for decades. It will be up to us, the enthusiasts and the owners, to keep the Camaro legacy alive.

River plant (where the sixth-generation Camaros are built), a unique Camaro and Coffee car show in Detroit, and a special Camaro heritage display at the 2016 Woodward Dream Cruise (the world's largest single-day automotive enthusiast event).

While the cynics might argue that these events were little more than a carefully crafted marketing campaign put on by Chevrolet to promote the sixth-generation Camaro, the success of these events were wholly dependent on the participation of Camaro owners and enthusiasts from around the globe. Each of these events was a huge success. Thousands of attendees showed up for the plant tours and the Camaros and Coffee show, and more than 1.5 million spectators and more than 40,000 cars (including thousands of Camaros) showed up for the Woodward Dream Cruise event.

In a GM press release for the event, Steve Majoros, marketing director of Chevrolet Cars and Crossovers, made a statement that perfectly expresses the rich heritage that comes with Camaro ownership.

"Over the past half-century, the Camaro has fostered enthusiasm, camaraderie, and memories like few other vehicles," Majoros said. "It's a passion Chevrolet takes seriously, and the activities this summer are a way of giving back to those who have made the Camaro an icon."

But even more significant than Majoros's comments was the sentiment shared by Cory Lawson of Hutchinson, Kansas.

"It's a dream come true," Lawson said. "I got to share something that is going to be ongoing with my son for the rest of my life."

Lawson, along with son Logan, are the owners of the original VIN #001 1967 Camaro, and both were onsite (along with their car) for the 2016 Woodward event. Documented as part of a Chevrolet video press release that summarized the weekend festivities, Lawson's comments speak to the very heart of the Camaro ownership experience.

In the time since I started writing about cars professionally, I have had the great fortune of meeting countless Camaro owners at cruise-ins, car shows, and assorted track events. We've spent hours discussing our combined passion for this amazing brand. Many still own the first Camaro they ever purchased, and some examples date back more than 50 years. Others have purchased multiple examples of Chevy's beloved pony car over the course of their lifetime, and each car has become a cherished part of their collection. Still others (and these are my favorite) have a Camaro that was handed down to them, often from an elderly parent or a deceased loved one. The stories shared by this third group are often the most special because of

My son Kendyll and I are shown attending a local car show. To me, this image strikes at the very heart of what owning a Camaro (his) or a Corvette (mine) is all about. It's about sharing the heritage of these iconic sports cars with the next generation so that they might learn to appreciate the incredible legacy that was started when the earliest examples of these cars rolled off the production line and changed our American roadways forever.

what their Camaro represents: a lasting reminder of the special relationship that was once shared by its current and former owners.

I have personally owned two Camaros: a 1984 Berlinetta and a 1989 RS Coupe (as well as a 1995 Pontiac Firebird coupe). Even though it has been nearly 30 years since I've owned these cars, I still remember each fondly. These cars were a major part of my late adolescence and early adulthood, and each afforded me with experiences and memories that I will treasure for the rest of my days.

More recently, my son purchased his first Camaro, a white 2010 RS coupe, and soon traded it for his second, a black 2012 SS coupe (go figure, he needed more horsepower). While I have since moved on to Corvette ownership, he and I routinely show our cars at the local Cars & Coffee cruise-ins here in Tennessee, and we drive them across the country to various car shows and race events in Georgia, Florida, Ohio, etc. While those shared experiences are something I will always treasure, they also illustrate the concept that made the Camaro brand a success for so many years.

Just as the 1967 Camaro was originally marketed when new, the used Camaro market continues to represent a fun yet reasonably priced driving experience to young consumers seeking high performance from a car they can afford to own. While this may not hold true with some of the most modern sixth-generation models, there exists an abundance of older Camaros in today's automotive marketplace that continue to offer practical performance for just about any budget. Comparatively speaking, even the newest Camaro ZL1 is a bargain compared to most similarly equipped European sports cars.

So, if the rumors *are* true, and General Motors does discontinue the Camaro after the 2024 model year, then it will become our responsibility (the fathers and sons, mothers and daughters, the owners and enthusiasts alike) to ensure that the Camaro in all of its forms remains an indelible part of the automotive landscape. If we are successful, then it is my personal belief that the Camaro's heritage will continue to resonate with people of all ages (both in the United States and around the world) for decades to come.

000-000

Additional books that may interest you...

See OVER 700 auto books at www.CarTechBooks.com!

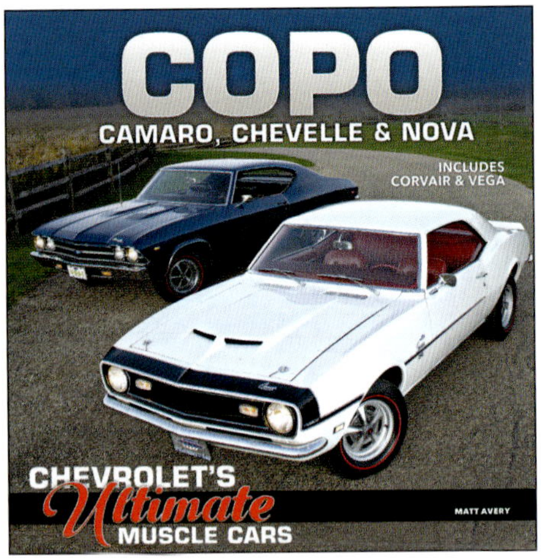

COPO CAMARO, CHEVELLE & NOVA: Chevrolet's Ultimate Muscle Cars *by Matt Avery*
Chevy muscle car aficionado and author Matt Avery retraces the history of the COPO program and the creation of these premier muscle cars. He has scoured archives and tracked down owners and personnel involved in the program to deliver a comprehensive story and complete guide to the COPO cars. 10 x 10", 204 pgs, 400 photos, Hdbd. ISBN 9781613253915 Part # CT620

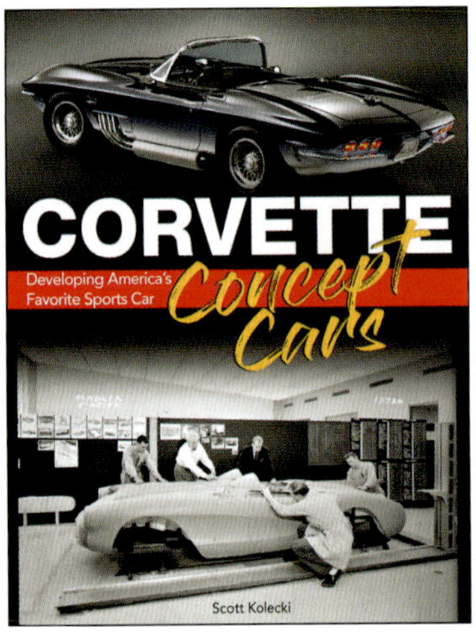

CORVETTE CONCEPT CARS: Developing America's Favorite Sports Car
by Scott Kolecki
Dive into the origins of the Chevrolet Corvette and the countless designers, engineers, drivers, and dreamers responsible for its creation. It also explores the personal histories of Corvette's greatest visionaries. 8.5 x 11", 176 pgs, 427 photos, Sftbd. ISBN 9781613257135 Part # CT686

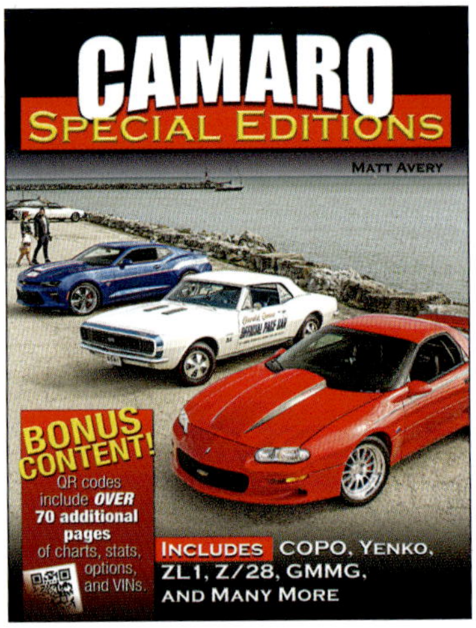

CAMARO SPECIAL EDITIONS
by Matt Avery
In *Camaro Special Editions* author and expert Matt Avery spotlights the most significant special editions, closely exploring the pinnacles and highpoints of the model's lineage. 8.5 x 11", 224 pgs, 400 photos, Sftbd. ISBN 9781613254912 Part # CT658

Check out our website:

CarTechBooks.com

✓ Find our newest books before anyone else

✓ Get weekly tech tips from our experts

✓ Featuring a new deal each week!

CHEVY DRAG RACING 1955–1980: A Celebration of Bowtie's Success at the Drag Strip *by Doug Boyce*
Accomplished racing author Doug Boyce takes a celebratory look at Chevy's years of drag racing success, with a focus on the first 25 years (1955 through 1980). 8.5 x 11", 176 pgs, 313 photos, Sftbd. ISBN 9781613254998 Part # CT659

www.cartechbooks.com or 1-800-551-4754